INTO THE
RISING
SUN

In Their Own Words,
World War II's Pacific Veterans
Reveal the Heart of Combat

PATRICK K. O'DONNELL

THE FREE PRESS
NEW YORK • LONDON • TORONTO • SYDNEY • SINGAPORE

This book is dedicated to the World War II generation,

whose personal sacrifices made possible the freedom we enjoy today.

THE FREE PRESS
A Division of Simon & Schuster, Inc.
1230 Avenue of the Americas
New York, NY 10020

First Free Press trade paperback edition 2003

The Free Press and colophon are trademarks of Simon & Schuster Inc.

Designed by Kevin Hanek   Set in Electra

Manufactured in the United States of America

1 3 5 7 9 10 8 6 4 2

The Library of Congress has cataloged the hardcover edition as follows:

O'Donnell, Patrick K.,
Into the rising sun : in their own words, World War II's Pacific veterans
reveal the heart of combat / Patrick K. O'Donnell
p. cm.

Includes bibliographical references and index.

1. United States. Army—Parachute troops—History—20th century. 2. United States. Marine Corps—History—20th century. 3. World War, 1939-1945—Personal narratives, American. 4. World War, 1939-1945—Campaigns--Pacific Area. 5. World War, 1939-1945—
Commando operations—United States. 6. World War, 1939-1945—Regimental
histories—United States. 7. Oral history. 8. United States—Armed Forces—Biography.

D811.A2 I58 2002
940.54/8173 21   2001059779

ISBN 0-7432-1480-3
0-7432-1481-1 (Pbk)

For information regarding special discounts for bulk purchases please contact Simon &
Schuster Special Sales at 1-800-456-6798 or business@simonandschuster.com

Contents

Introduction

"WE WERE ON TRUCKS heading to the ships to enter the war. There was a lot of singing—the men were jubilant. This is before the combat and none of us really knew what to expect. I knew most of the men in my company and the next time I saw many of these men, they were dead. I was on burial detail. We had a huge open grave maybe twenty feet long and we laid them in there side by side in their ponchos.

"I have a hard time talking about how I felt about that day. Even talking to you I can feel a rush. Those feelings sleep inside you."[1]

Over 250,000 Americans were killed during World War II. It's a chilling statistic. Those who perished remain undisturbed and largely forgotten except by the occasional visitors to military cemeteries and the tourists who notice local monuments. For nearly sixty years, most survivors have chosen to remain silent about their past, almost as unnoticeable to society as their dead brothers.

Memories of the war sleep inside those who were there. They are the ones who can best look beyond the numbers and recognize the fallen as human beings, with personalities and stories of their own. It's these living veterans who can best take us back to their war. This book provides a window into that hidden war by letting hundreds of veterans speak. These men relive the valor, fear, love, and myriad of emotions that only those on the front lines of the Pacific war understand. It was an unsanitized war that remains as raw and shocking as an open wound. For many of these citizen soldiers and Marines, the wounds have never healed.

This book tells that hidden story through the voices of America's elite infantry troops in the Pacific: paratroopers, Marine Raiders, Marauders, and Rangers. Their decisive actions cover nearly every major campaign in the war in the Pacific. They were in the eye of the storm and can rightfully claim to be among the war's finest troops. America's elite infantry played a key role in everything from making a last-stand defense at Bloody Ridge that saved Guadalcanal, to seizing key ground in New Guinea and the Philippines, to spearheading the offensive into Burma, to assaulting Iwo Jima and even raising the flag on Mount Suribachi, to turning the tide on Okinawa. The men recorded here, individually and collectively, have an amazing story to tell.

The genesis of *Into the Rising Sun* began ten years ago when I began a personal journey of my own, interviewing the veterans of World War II. I've interviewed over a thousand veterans and, whenever possible, their former adversaries. Here, I have selected some of the best unedited accounts of the Pacific war, the term I use to refer to the entire Asia-Pacific war. Each tells a piece of a larger campaign or battle. The unedited accounts, interwoven with minimal narrative, tell complete battle stories from the ground up. Overall strategy, hindsight analysis, and background detail were purposely kept in the background so the men's voices could be heard.

In retrospect, it is surprising to me that so many veterans were forthcoming. Perhaps they talked out of a sense of duty to their friends who did not return. It was often difficult for them. A common sentiment was best stated this way: "I've never really talked about this to anyone. The only reason that I am now is if someone doesn't relate it the way it actually was instead of the Hollywood version, it's going to be lost."

One veteran remembered walking through an airport during the Gulf War and seeing about a dozen people huddled around a television watching CNN as an American cruise missile slammed into an Iraqi bunker. To his dismay, everybody started cheering and clapping. Later he shook his head and said, "Don't people realize that there are human beings in there? That's why I'm telling you my story."

I focused on the elite infantry of the war originally out of a personal interest and the fact that some of my relatives fought in these units. I did not have a particular goal in mind at the start; I just gathered their stories. In 1995, I created www.thedropzone.org, the first on-line oral history project, which greatly facilitated the gathering of what are now known as e-histories. Volunteers maintain the project; funding was not accepted for these efforts.

In 1998, several veterans asked me to record their experiences in a book. I originally planned to include the campaigns in both Europe and the Pacific but quickly found that was not possible. Europe and the Pacific were two entirely different wars within World War II and have to be treated separately. *Beyond Valor*, the first book that resulted, is a history of combat in Europe.

The war in the Pacific does not parallel the war in Europe or even the Russo-German war on the Eastern Front. Many factors contributed to making it perhaps the most savage and brutal theater in World War II. Terrain, climate, and disease pushed both sides to the limits of their endurance. Casualties were horrendous. But it was the intensity with which both sides prosecuted the war that made it unique. No quarter was given on either side: as one author put it, the Pacific was "a war without mercy."

The ground combat in the Pacific came close to a war of annihilation. Dark undercurrents, such as racism, fueled a visceral hatred of each side for the other. The Japanese saw surrender as dishonorable and typically fought to the last man when other soldiers under similar circumstances would have capitulated. Death was considered part of their duty. As the war progressed, this cult of death was manifested in the form of kamikaze planes, rockets, boats, and even human-guided torpedoes.

After the Bataan Death March and Guadalcanal, the Japanese reinforced their reputation for cruelty. Incidents in which captured Marines were tortured or wounded Japanese pretended to surrender only to have an armed grenade waiting for anyone providing help reinforced a belief held by Allied soldiers and Marines that the Japanese were a dangerous and fanatical enemy—making Allied troops reluctant to take prisoners. America's top leadership also made clear the duty of all Americans under arms—best expressed in a well-known sign that hung in Admiral William Halsey's headquarters: "Kill Japs, kill more Japs. You will help kill the yellow bastards if you do your job well." All of these factors created a perpetual cycle of violence that both sides embraced.

Nobody interviewed for this book "gave" me their story. I did not get a flood of war stories in the mail. I went out and personally interviewed each of these men in their homes, at scores of veteran reunions, and sometimes by e-mail. Most were at first reticent. But everybody in the book was referred by his peers, and in most cases the recommendations independently came from as many as four or five other veterans.

The veterans who relayed their stories were ordinary men who did their duty, and many went far beyond it. This book is packed with recollections of men who received the Navy Cross, Distinguished Service Cross, Silver Star, and other medals of battlefield valor. It's fair to say that most of these men are heroes among heroes. But these awards carry no joy. As Olin Gray put it, "When somebody gets decorated, it's because a lot of other men died. They don't hand them out because you were a good guy or whatever. If the rest of the men up there hadn't died, I would have walked out of there with nothing . . . which I would have much rather done."

The interview process was difficult on many levels. I tried to remain objective and never went to an interview with prepared questions. I knew the history of each man I talked to and the men alongside whom he fought. During the discussions, I dropped memory markers to help them recall their past. I probed and cajoled them, but mainly I listened. These were conversations rather than interviews. Many of the men I interviewed openly wept about their experiences as they revisited these battles, sometimes for the first time since the war. I could see it in their eyes as they went back in time and relived the war in front of me.

I put forth my best efforts to verify the material in this book. For example, I spent an enormous amount of time going through each of the units' official records in order to verify the accounts. Other individuals I interviewed backed up each of the stories. Nevertheless, oral history has its shortcomings. Fragile memories, self-service, and individual memories that do not jibe with the collective memory are inherent dangers. However, these same flaws are also found in the documentary record. Nevertheless, oral histories are perhaps one of the best means available to reveal the horrors and pathos from the foxhole.

On a strategic level, *Into the Rising Sun* captures the major campaigns and offensives in the Pacific war, in the inexorable advance toward Japan. We begin in this book eight months to the day after Pearl Harbor, with the decisive American battle of Midway, which marked the beginning of the Allied offensive on Guadalcanal in August 1942. There were initially two major lines of advance.[2] In the Southwest Pacific Area, General Douglas MacArthur was in command of a sizable strike force of Army and Australian units. Advancing up New Guinea, MacArthur isolated the massive Japanese air and naval base at Rabaul, located on New Britain Island. Ultimately, his forces would end up in the Philippines. Simultaneously, Admiral Robert Ghormley, who was soon replaced by Admiral William "Bull" Halsey, the naval commander in the South Pacific Area, advanced toward Rabaul up the Solomon Islands, starting on the island of Guadalcanal. Both campaigns were long and bloody, with outcomes that remained in doubt.

In November 1943, Admiral Chester W. Nimitz began offensive operations in the Central Pacific Area. This drive would pass through the Marianas, touching islands like Guam. Later, the advance would pierce the heart of Japan's inner defensive ring on islands such as Iwo Jima and Okinawa. In Asia, this book covers American ground operations in Burma, which were ultimately geared to opening land-based supply lines to China. The lines of advance and campaigns are shown on pages 6 and 7 and in the chapter maps.

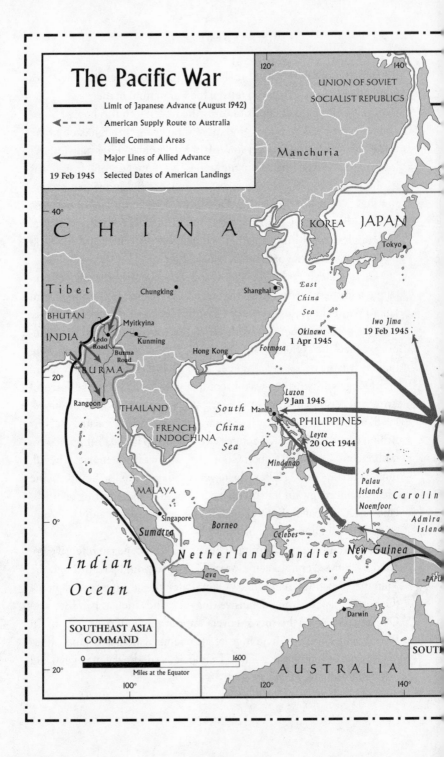

The Pacific War

- —— Limit of Japanese Advance (August 1942)
- ◄--- American Supply Route to Australia
- —— Allied Command Areas
- ◄—— Major Lines of Allied Advance
- 19 Feb 1945   Selected Dates of American Landings

120°

140°

UNION OF SOVIET
SOCIALIST REPUBLICS

Manchuria

40°

C H I N A

KOREA   JAPAN

Tokyo

Tibet

Chungking   Shanghai

East
China
Sea

Iwo Jima
19 Feb 1945

BHUTAN

Myitkyina

Okinawa
1 Apr 1945

INDIA

Ledo
Road   Kunming

Burma
Road

Hong Kong   Formosa

20°

BURMA

THAILAND

Rangoon

FRENCH
INDOCHINA

South
China
Sea

Luzon
9 Jan 1945   Manila

PHILIPPINES

Leyte
20 Oct 1944

Mindanao

MALAYA

0°

Singapore   Borneo

Palau
Islands   Carolin

Noemfoor

Admira
Island

Sumatra

Celebes

New Guinea

Indian

N e t h e r l a n d s   I n d i e s

Java

Ocean

PAPU

Darwin

SOUTHEAST ASIA
COMMAND

SOUT

20°

0   1600

A U S T R A L I A

Miles at the Equator

100°

120°

140°

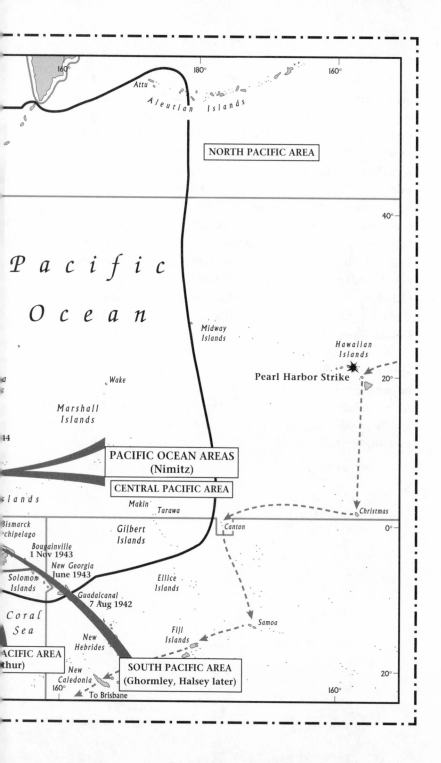

Over the past ten years of recording World War II veteran stories, I've made many friends. Sadly, it's a generation slipping away, with over 1,100 veterans passing each day. I'll never forget the long evening I spent interviewing Andy Amaty, only to find out he passed away the next day from a stroke after straining to lift a heavy suitcase into his car. Or Frank Varelli, who courageously battled cancer for several years. He ignored unbelievable pain to keep his chapter of the 82nd Airborne Division Association together and get the *Scuttlebutt* newsletter to the press or conduct a flag ceremony at Arlington National Cemetery to honor the fallen. Frank never talked about the war to anybody, choosing instead, humbly, to recommend other veterans I should interview. One Sunday in April, however, he walked me through the yellowed scrapbooks that stored a large part of his life. He revealed something he had never previously talked about: he was awarded the Silver Star in World War II and the Distinguished Flying Cross in Korea. He lived only a few months longer.

My work has been that of preservation, done in gratitude for a generation that sacrificed so much. I hope readers will ask their relatives, neighbors, and even strangers about their experiences in World War II. Ask the initial questions, and then step back and listen. You will learn something about the war, the human spirit, and maybe something about yourself.

The Elite Infantry of the Pacific

ALL OF THE GREAT ARMIES OF HISTORY had elite units: the Praetorian Guard of Rome, Napoleon's Imperial Guard, and the Civil War's Iron Brigade. As historian Geoffrey Perret stated, "In battle they were the ultimate reserve if things went wrong, and the exploiting force if things went right."[1] Nevertheless, America's elite infantry troops in the Pacific during World War II—Marine Raiders, Rangers, Mauraders, and airborne troops (paratroopers and gliderists)—were different and special compared to the elites of other eras, as well as to the regular troops of their own.

MARINE RAIDERS

The Raiders were an elite infantry unit within the Marine Corps. Prewar amphibious landings faced numerous obstacles, including a lack of adequate landing craft (before the famous Higgins boat landing craft were available in large numbers). One solution included landing an advance company of Marines on the beachhead using rubber boats from destroyer transports known as APDs. The spearhead unit would move inland, capture key positions, and guard against an enemy counterattack while the main force made the landing. In June 1941, Lieutenant Colonel Merritt Edson's 1st Battalion, 5th Marines was chosen as a spearhead unit. Shortly after the war broke out, Edson's battalion was redesignated the 1st Separate Battalion.

The real impetus for the Raiders came in the middle of January 1942 when commando enthusiasts such as Lieutenant Colonel Evans Carlson and the president's son, Captain James Roosevelt, urged the commander in chief to prod the Marine Corps to form a separate commando force. At the time, Germany and Japan were at the height of their power, and commando units offered the possibility of quickly striking a blow against the enemy, as British commandos had done along the coast of Europe.

The prodding produced the 1st and 2nd Raider Battalions. Edson's 1st Separate Battalion became the 1st Raider Battalion, and Carlson commanded the 2nd Raider Battalion with James Roosevelt as the executive officer. As the program expanded, the Raiders would receive the best men and equipment that the Marine Corps could offer.

The two battalions differed enormously. Before the war, Carlson had spent time as an observer in the Chinese Communist Army, and that experience heavily influenced the way he shaped the battalion. As the Marine Corps historian put it, "Carlson inculcated the unit with an unconventional military style that was a mixture of Chinese culture and Communist egalitarianism and New England town hall democracy. Every man would have a right to say what he thought." [2] It was best expressed in the 2nd's battle cry "*Gung Ho*," which in Chinese means "work together." Carlson stressed hand-to-hand combat, demolitions, and physical training that built mental toughness. He trained the 2nd to be employed for infiltration and guerrilla tactics.

Edson did not share Carlson's vision of using his men as guerrillas. Instead, he focused the 1st's training on more conventional light infantry tactics, along with special operations training. He later wrote, "I recommended a battalion so organized and equipped that it could easily take its place as part of a Division in a major offensive, while still being perfectly capable of carrying out special raiding operations." Edson was also more of a traditional Marine officer and did not embrace Carlson's *Gung Ho* leadership style. Nevertheless, some of the Marine Corps' best battalions, which would make their mark on Guadalcanal and throughout the war, emerged from the Raiders. Edson's combined 1st Raider and 1st Parachute Battalion held Bloody Ridge, saving Henderson Field in one of the greatest small unit actions of World War II.

As the war progressed, two more Raider battalions were created: the 3rd and 4th. In March 1943, the 1st Raider Regiment was formed out of the four Raider battalions, but the need for lightly armed raiding forces was passing. Since Guadalcanal, the Raiders had been used as line infantry, but their élan did not make up for their lack of heavy weapons against a fortified enemy position, especially in operations on New Georgia at Bairoko.

As the Allies moved up the Solomon Islands, the Raiders were often in the van. Meanwhile, the 2nd Raider Regiment was formed around the 2nd and 3rd Raider Battalions and spearheaded the landings at Bougainville, in the northern Solomons. Bougainville would prove to be the last Raider operation. The changing nature of the Pacific war reduced the need for specialty units in favor of massive amphibious assaults followed up by the destruction of Japanese strong points by heavily armed units. The need diminished for light units that could strike deep into enemy territory. This fact, combined with senior Marine officers who never accepted the idea of an elite within an elite and the need for additional manpower to fill out the new Marine divisions being formed, led to the Raiders' being disbanded. Most of the 1st Raider Regiment was redesignated the 4th Marines, which later would form the core of the 6th Marine Division, which would play a key role in the battle for Okinawa. Other Raiders were transferred to the 5th Marine Division and distinguished themselves on Iwo Jima. Small numbers of Raiders would also filter into other Corps units.

6TH RANGER BATTALION

Surprisingly, around the time the Raiders were disbanded, the Sixth Army created its own specialized elite infantry unit for raids and diversionary attacks. Resources were scarce, so the 98th Field Artillery Battalion was selected to be converted into a Ranger battalion on December

26, 1943. Continuing the tradition of volunteer Ranger units in Europe, the men of the 98th were given the option of transferring to other units or becoming Rangers. Most men stayed and were all too happy to part with the mules that carried their artillery; those who opted out were replaced by volunteers from the replacement depots. After a rigorous training program that focused on infantry skills, the men were ready by the summer of 1944.

The Rangers' first combat mission came when they were ordered to seize three islands in the Leyte Gulf prior to the main Leyte landings marking MacArthur's return to the Philippines. For the next several months, the Rangers would serve as headquarters guard and patrol rear areas, biding their time for the next mission that would come in January 1945. Shortly after the Luzon landings, the Rangers conducted their most famous raid, freeing over five hundred POWs from a camp near Cabanatuan. Afterward, the Rangers performed a variety of odd jobs, patrolling areas of bypassed Japanese, and a few long-range reconnaissance patrols, culminating with the capture of the northern Luzon town of Aparri. The 6th Ranger Battalion was an anomaly compared to the other elite infantry units of the war, suffering few combat casualties thanks to the Sixth Army's resolve to avoid misusing the unit for line infantry roles.

MERRILL'S MARAUDERS

Merrill's Marauders, officially known as Galahad or the 5307th Composite Unit (Provisional), can trace its beginnings to an eccentric British brigadier named Orde Wingate. During the spring of 1943, Wingate launched his first raid deep behind Japanese lines in Burma. His force, known as the Chindits, conducted hit-and-run attacks on Japanese bridges and communications for three months. After the success of these raids, the U.S. Joint Chiefs approved the long-delayed offensive into northern Burma, and General George Marshall even agreed to supply Wingate with a special U.S. raiding force.

The U.S. force that emerged was Galahad, and the personnel who formed the unit came from a variety of places. Men were recruited from units in the South and Southwest Pacific, the United States, and the Caribbean, and there were even some who had been misfits in their former units (some division commanders took the opportunity to get rid of unwanted men). Few details were given to the recruits other than that their mission would be hazardous, high losses were expected, and there was even a rumor that the unit would be withdrawn in three months. From the start, the skimpy details, along with the diverse makeup of the unit, led many of the Marauders to consider themselves a "bastard organization."[3]

Galahad was divided into three battalions and modeled after the Chindits, with each battalion having the ability to operate as a self-contained entity.

In October 1943, Galahad finally arrived in India and went into intense training, including small-unit tactics, demolitions, and resupply by air. They later joined Wingate's Chindits for more specialized training.

The Marauders spearheaded the Allied offensive in northern Burma, culminating in the capture of the main air and rail terminus at Myitkyina. As these men relate in their stories, the cost was enormous: disease, exhaustion, and action with the enemy nearly destroyed the entire unit. By August 1944, some of the survivors, along with replacements, had reorganized into the 475th Infantry Regiment and combined with the 124th Calvary and other support units to form another long-range group known as Mars Task Force. Mars would eventually help facilitate the linkup of a road from India through Burma to China, reopening overland supply to China. The Marsmen and remaining Marauders were finally disbanded in July. Their proud legacy lives on: every U.S. Army Ranger today wears the Marauder patch.

THE AIRBORNE

The largest elite infantry unit was the airborne. The first practical plans for employing parachute troops in combat were conceived in the waning months of World War I by U.S. aviation pioneer Brigadier General William "Billy" Mitchell. Mitchell proposed outfitting the 1st Division with a large number of machine guns and parachuting them in behind the lines on the German-held fortress city of Metz. A ground attack would be coordinated with the paratrooper assault, otherwise known as a "vertical envelopment." The war ended before Mitchell's innovative plans could be tried.

After the war, the concept of vertical envelopment was neglected in the United States. The Soviet Union, on the other hand, pushed ahead with large-scale airborne exercises in the 1930s. Germany took notice of the Soviet exercises and began building its own airborne program made up of paratroopers and infantry who would ride in gliders.

With the outbreak of war, the Germans successfully used paratroopers to seize critical objectives in Norway, the Netherlands, and Belgium, where a small group of paratroopers and glidermen seized Fort Eben Emael, which many had considered impregnable. These victories spurred the creation of the U.S. Army airborne program. A fifty-man test platoon was formed on June 25, 1940. On August 16, Lieutenant William Ryder became the first member of the test platoon to make a parachute jump. In one demonstration jump, the famous airborne word *Geronimo!* was born when Private Aubrey Eberhardt yelled it after exiting the plane.[4]

Over the next few months, parachute tactics and techniques were developed and borrowed from Germany and the Soviet Union. The fledgling Army program expanded as volunteers formed the 501st Parachute Infantry Battalion. In October 1940, the Marine Corps also embarked on its own parachute program, with the first group of Marine parachutists graduating in February 1941. The Corps' airborne program preceded at a slow pace. Two understrength battalions were in place by the end of March 1942.

A special élan, part of both the Army and Marine Corps programs, stressed that each individual had to be capable of fighting against any opposition. As the parachute program evolved, men were taught that they were the best, a lesson reinforced by rigorous training that had a high washout rate. Training in all of the elite units created mental toughness and a strong sense of camaraderie that would serve these men well in battle and in the rest of life. Beyond the rhetoric, the troops began demonstrating their worth by smashing previous Army training records.

Parachute training culminated with the individual completing five parachute jumps. The successful trooper earned the right to wear a small silver pair of jump wings designed by a young Army airborne officer, William Yarborough. Special leather jump boots and jump suits were also issued to paratroopers (the Marines and Army each had their own version). Army troopers embraced an unofficial ceremony known as the "Prop Blast," which marked the completion of airborne training. The new paratroopers drank a secret concoction and toasted their success. The recipe was then encoded into an old M-94 signal-encrypting device with "Geronimo" as the key word. (The Prop Blast is a rite of passage that still exists today.)[5]

Both the Army and Marine Corps programs remained relatively small until a pivotal German airborne operation occurred in May 1941. The Germans captured the British-held island of Crete in the largest German airborne operation ever. Losses were enormous, and Hitler was persuaded never again to launch a major airborne operation. Not privy to the magnitude of German losses, however, the U.S. command looked at Crete as a success and began building up its airborne.

The U.S. Army buildup was led by General George Marshall, who foresaw large-scale U.S. airborne operations. The Provisional Parachute Group was created, along with three new battalions. When the United States entered the war in December 1941, six new airborne regiments consisting of roughly two thousand paratroopers were authorized; most of the men were handpicked.

Divisions came next. The Army created five airborne divisions — 11th, 13th, 17th, 82nd, and 101st — plus several independent battalions and regiments, such as the 503rd, 509th, 517th, 550th, and 551st. The only airborne division in the Pacific was the 11th, which consisted of three regiments — 187th, 188th, and 511th — along with artillery and engineer support units. Initially, the 187th and 188th were glider regiments, but later they were cross-trained to be parachute qualified. (The glider program slowly took shape in 1942 but was not widely used by U.S. forces in the Pacific, largely because of the jungle terrain. Nicknamed "canvas coffins," the flimsy gliders had plywood floors and were constructed with a steel tubing frame covered with a canvas skin. The standard Waco CG-4A glider had a troop capacity of fifteen men and could carry a jeep or small artillery piece. The glider was towed by a C-47 transport plane over the landing zone, where it would release a 300-foot nylon towrope. The glider made what amounted to a crash landing.)[6]

The independent 503rd Regimental Combat Team also played a key role in the Pacific. It initially consisted of a parachute regiment and later was joined by an artillery battalion and an engineer company.

The Marine parachute program never got close to the size of its counterpart in the Army. A total of four battalions were created: the 1st, 2nd, 3rd, and 4th. The first three battalions were eventually formed into the 1st Parachute Regiment and saw combat overseas: the 4th was activated but never transferred overseas. None of the battalions would take part in a combat jump. The need for manpower forced the Corps to disband specialty units like the Marine parachutists and Raiders in early 1944. The 1st Parachute Regiment formed the core of the 5th Marine Division where many parachutists and Raiders would distinguish themselves on Iwo Jima. Several former parachutists and Raiders would participate in the flag raisings, and five Marine paratroopers would win the Medal of Honor.

CHAPTER ONE

Operation Shoestring

> *We are the Dead. Short days ago*
> *We lived, felt dawn, saw sunset glow,*
> *Loved and were loved, and now we lie,*
> *In Flanders fields.*
>
> —COLONEL JOHN MCCRAE, "IN FLANDERS FIELDS"

O N A CLOUDY AUGUST DAY IN 2001, more than one hundred veterans stood shoulder to shoulder at Arlington National Cemetery. They were there to honor thirteen fellow Marines who were finally returning home—Marines whose bodies had been left behind in a daring 1942 raid on Makin Atoll. After numerous attempts starting in 1948, Army investigators finally found the remains of the men in 1999. The ceremony brought closure to a remarkable chapter in history that had begun almost six decades earlier.

Following the decisive Allied victory at Midway in early June 1942, the Joint Chiefs of Staff, driven primarily by Admiral Ernest King, drew up ambitious plans for offensive operations in the South Pacific. At the time, most of America's combat troops were being sent to Europe; leftover resources were scarce. Practically no one, including the Japanese, anticipated America on the offensive in the Pacific until 1943.

The Joint Chiefs' plan had three major tasks: (1) seize Tulagi and adjacent islands in the Solomons, (2) capture the remainder of the Solomons and the northeast coast of New Guinea, and (3) take the huge

Guadalcanal Landings—August 7–8, 1942

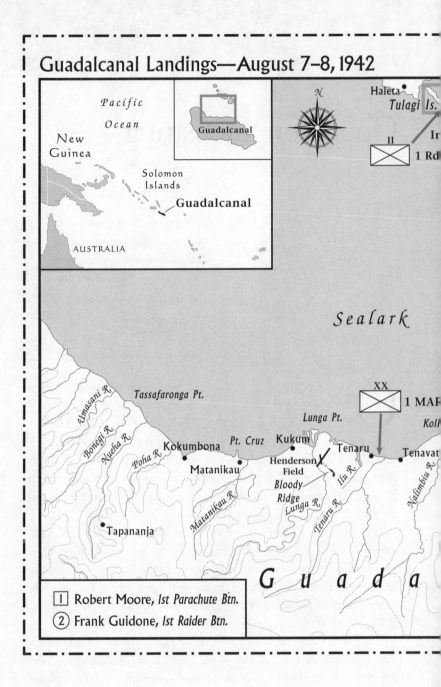

Pacific Ocean

New Guinea

Guadalcanal

Solomon Islands

Guadalcanal

AUSTRALIA

Haleta

Tulagi Is.

N

II | 1 Rd

Sealark

Tassafaronga Pt.

Lunga Pt.

XX | 1 MAR

Koli

Umasani R.

Bonegi R.

Nueha R.

Poha R.

Kokumbona

Pt. Cruz

Kukum

Tenaru

Tenavat

Matanikau

Henderson Field

Bloody Ridge

Ilu R.

Matanikau R.

Lunga R.

Tenaru R.

Nalimbiu R.

Tapananja

Guada

1 Robert Moore, *1st Parachute Btn.*

2 Frank Guidone, *1st Raider Btn.*

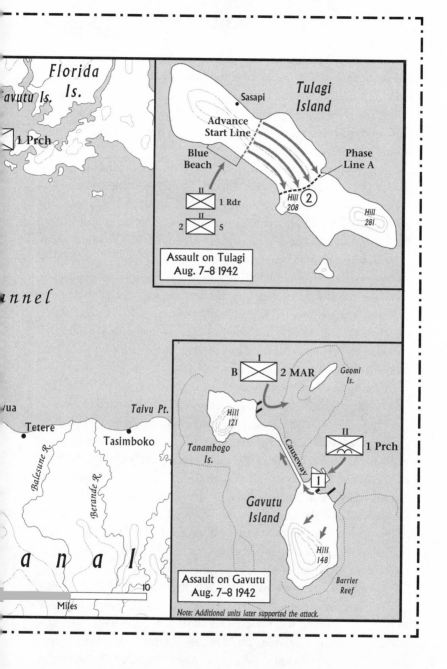

Florida Is.

avutu Is.

1 Prch

Sasapi

Tulagi Island

Advance
Start Line

Blue
Beach

Phase
Line A

Hill
208 ②

Hill
281

II
1 Rdr

II
2 5

**Assault on Tulagi
Aug. 7–8 1942**

nnel

I
B 2 MAR

Gaomi
Is.

vua

Tetere

Taivu Pt.

Hill
121

Tasimboko

Tanambogo
Is.

Causeway

II
1 Prch

1

Gavutu
Island

a n a l

10

Miles

Hill
148

Barrier
Reef

**Assault on Gavutu
Aug. 7–8 1942**

Note: Additional units later supported the attack.

Japanese anchorage and airdrome on New Britain Island known as Rabaul. Japan's actions accelerated the Joint Chiefs' plan. Aerial reconnaissance showed that the Japanese had established a seaplane base at Tulagi and were building a runway on Guadalcanal. Japanese control of the islands threatened the vital sea-lanes between the United States and Australia.[1]

Operation Watchtower was thrown together to quickly land American troops on Guadalcanal and the nearby islands of Tulagi and Gavutu. A basic premise of military planning is that if an attacker is to have any chance of success, he must possess material superiority over the defender. But for Watchtower, the Allies would be outgunned. The situation was so grim that the operation was nicknamed Shoestring. At one point, the theater commander, Admiral Robert Ghormley, became so pessimistic about the viability of the operation that he secretly gave the commander of the 1st Marine Division the authority to surrender.[2] Yet Watchtower went forward and eventually encompassed seven major naval battles and scores of air and land battles. The outcome of the campaign was very much in doubt for months.[3]

It began less than auspiciously, with the understrength 1st Marine Division, which included the elite 1st Raider and 1st Parachute Battalions.[4]

The bulk of America's invading force, totaling 11,300, landed on Guadalcanal while about 3,000 men commanded by Brigadier General William H. Rupertus were sent to grab several islands north of Guadalcanal: Tulagi, the twin islands of Gavutu-Tanambogo, and portions of Florida Island. The smaller islands of Tulagi, Gavutu, and Tanambogo were considered the operation's most difficult objectives. Accordingly, Major General Alexander A. Vandegrift assigned these targets to his best-trained units: the Raiders and Marine parachutists. They would get a bitter foretaste of the fighting that faced Americans in the Pacific.

H-hour on Tulagi was 8:00 A.M., August 7, 1942. The 1st Raider Battalion came ashore on the island's southern coast, designated Blue Beach. The landing was unopposed, and the Raiders were later supported by the 2nd Battalion, 5th Marines. Around noon, they ran into heavy resistance that continued into the night, culminating with several

Japanese banzai attacks on the Raider lines. Japanese troops fought to the death from caves and dugouts that had to be blasted with high explosives and grenades. By the next day, Colonel Merritt "Red Mike" Edson, the 1st Raider Battalion commander, declared the island secure. Raider losses were 38 killed and 55 wounded; about 350 defenders were killed, and only 3 prisoners were taken.[5]

The twin islands of Gavutu-Tanambogo lie 3,000 yards east of Tulagi. On the afternoon of August 7 (H plus four), the 1st Parachute Battalion landed on Gavutu after a brief shore bombardment. The first company met no resistance, but the succeeding waves were raked by fusillades of machine-gun and rifle fire.[6] Within minutes, 10 percent of the 397 Marine parachutists were killed or wounded. The surviving paratroopers moved inland, destroying Japanese holed up in caves and seizing the island's high ground.[7] But the island was not yet secure. Tanambogo, connected to Gavutu by a 500-yard causeway, still had to be subdued. General Rupertus sent B Company of the 2nd Marines against Tanambogo. Their initial assault was a disaster. Heavy small-arms fire smashed into B Company's Higgins boats (landing craft), and the landing was aborted. The company tried again, and this time reached the shore. An additional battalion was brought in, and the island was firmly in Marine hands on August 8. By the end of the operation, more than 20 percent of the paratroopers were killed or wounded, the highest casualty rate of all of the initial landing forces on Guadalcanal.

Ten days after the landings at Guadalcanal, A and B Companies of the 2nd Raider Battalion, led by Lieutenant Colonel Evans Carlson, would make one of the most perilous raids of the war. The raid on Makin Atoll, primarily a diversion to lure Japanese attention away from the main landings at Guadalcanal, went badly from the start. The Raiders approached Makin in two submarines, *Nautilus* and *Argonaut*. When they surfaced, the men set out for shore in rubber boats in heavy rains and a tumultuous sea. Most of the outboard motors on the boats failed, but the men nevertheless made it ashore.

Shortly after the landing, the Raiders engaged the Japanese garrison in a fierce firefight that included two banzai attacks. Raider casualties

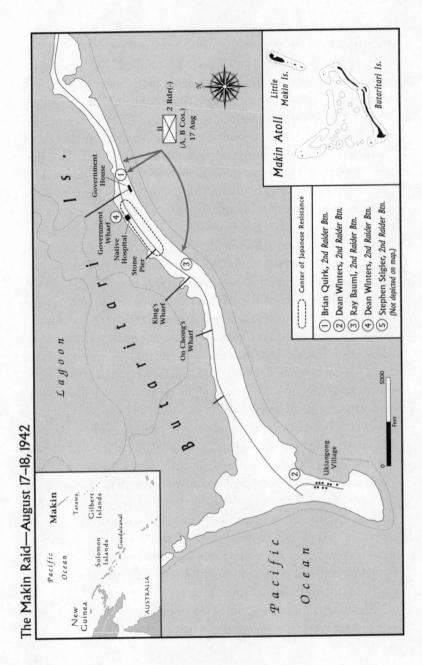

The Makin Raid—August 17-18, 1942

Makin Atoll
Little Makin Is.
Butaritari Is.

II 2 Rdr(-)
(A, B Cos.)
17 Aug

Government House

Government Wharf
Native Hospital
Stone Pier

King's Wharf

On Chong's Wharf

Ukiangong Village

Center of Japanese Resistance

① Brian Quirk, 2nd Raider Btn.
② Dean Winters, 2nd Raider Btn.
③ Ray Bauml, 2nd Raider Btn.
④ Dean Winters, 2nd Raider Btn.
⑤ Stephen Stigler, 2nd Raider Btn.
(Not depicted on map.)

Lagoon

Butaritari Is.

Pacific Ocean

Makin
Tarawa
Gilbert Islands
Guadalcanal
Solomon Islands
New Guinea
Pacific Ocean
AUSTRALIA

Feet
0   5000

began to mount, but the Americans' attack was more successful than they realized: they had unknowingly killed most of the Japanese on the island.

The Japanese attempted to reinforce Makin by air and sea. Seaplanes carrying reinforcements were destroyed by ground fire, and the submarines managed to sink the boats using indirect fire from their deck guns. But the Japanese retained control of the air. Several enemy planes strafed the Raiders. American plans did not call for holding the island, however; the Raiders were scheduled to assault Little Makin Island the next day. Carlson and his officers (including the battalion executive officer, Major James Roosevelt, the president's son) agreed to withdraw from the island rather than continue to engage the Japanese.

Withdrawing from Makin was more difficult than invading, however. Outboard motors once again failed to start, and heavy surf capsized many of the boats, keeping many of the Raiders on shore. A few boats made it to the waiting submarines, but Carlson and about 120 men were stranded, most weaponless and weakened from their battle with the sea.

The situation worsened over the next few hours. A Japanese patrol struck the Marines, wounding a sentry. Without working radios to contact the submarines or even knowing whether the subs had survived the air attacks, or if his men had reached them, and believing he was facing a reinforced Japanese force, Carlson called a council of war and decided to surrender.[8]

Before dawn, the battalion operations officer and another man delivered to a Japanese soldier a note discussing the surrender of the remaining Raiders.[9] But the Japanese commanders didn't get a chance to accept the surrender: the soldier was killed before he could deliver the note to his superiors (Japanese troops found it a few days later, and Tokyo Rose announced the note on Japanese radio).*

---

* During the war, Japanese Radio Tokyo beamed an English-language propaganda show throughout the Pacific, designed to hurt morale among Allied servicemen. The broadcasts featured the voices of about twenty women who collectively became known as "Tokyo Rose." After the war, Iva Toguri, a Japanese American, was wrongly convicted of treason for being Tokyo Rose and was sentenced to ten years in prison and fined $10,000. After serving six years, she was released. Over thirty years later, President Gerald Ford, in his last official act in office, pardoned her.

By dawn, a few hours after Carlson sent the surrender note, things started to brighten for the Raiders.[10] Several men made it through the surf to the subs. Carlson and the subs established contact by flashlight and arranged a rendezvous in the calmer waters off the island's lagoon. After lashing several boats to a native outrigger, the men paddled out into the lagoon, meeting the subs about 11:00 P.M. Only when the Raiders returned to Pearl Harbor could they get an accurate head count, listing eighteen as killed in action and twelve as missing. And only after the war did the Raiders learn what had happened to some of those men. Nine lost their way during the evacuation. After evading capture for twelve days with the help of some natives, they surrendered on August 30 and were eventually beheaded by the Japanese on Kwajalein Island.

ROBERT MOORE
1ST PARACHUTE BATTALION

Four hours behind the main landings on Guadalcanal and Tulagi, the 1st Parachute Battalion made America's first contested assault landing of the war on the tiny island of Gavutu. Robert Moore recalls the operation.

As we approached the island, we were raked by machine-gun fire — men were dropping all around me. We had to wade through water up to our necks. I finally got to the beach, and we were held down under heavy fire at the seawall there. I was a BAR [Browning automatic rifle] man, and when I pulled the trigger on my BAR, the damn thing didn't fire. My platoon leader was Warrant Officer Robert Manning, and he said, "Throw it away!" and gave me a .45 pistol and said, "Stay close!" Anyway, we were under fire all the way in. We tried to go up the hill to some kind of building. On our way up, one of our planes dropped a bomb, causing several friendly casualties.

When we finally got to the top of the hill, one kid was all upset because his buddy from the same town was killed. The buddy had just made second lieutenant and had been killed in the landing. He went up and fired into and beat several bodies to a bloody pulp with his weapon. I don't know if they were dead or not. We continued clearing out Japanese bunkers and caves.

There was only supposed to be a couple of hundred Japs on the is-land, and part of them were supposed to be construction troops. We found out later there were many more, including Japanese marines. They were six feet or so—big guys. There were hardly any survivors. We only took a few prisoners.

That night it was raining very hard. It was raining all night. You know when your hands wrinkle after you've been in the bathtub too long? That's how we were the next morning. We assembled and got everyone together. Instead of thirty-six men, we had enough men to make one squad of about twelve men. That morning, my first sergeant called me. It was in my records that I had graduated from embalming college before I went into the Marine Corps, so he elected me to go and take the dog tags off of the dead on the beach. It had never bothered me seeing dead peo-ple I hadn't known, but when you see your buddies there with their heads blown open [chokes up] . . . it's a different story.

Over thirty were dead. Many had been shot in the head. Brains were all over [sigh]. I remember Johnny Johns; he was a rigger [parachute maintenance], a real nice fellow. He was in sort of a ditch, shot in the head, brains all over the place. I'll never forget this. How can you for-get it?

After Gavutu, I was badly wounded on Guadalcanal, sent home, and discharged from the Corps. I recovered and tried to reenlist in the Corps, but I was turned down for medical reasons so I joined the Merchant Ma-rine. Our ship served in the Pacific. One of my shipmates had a neighbor that was killed on Iwo Jima. In December 1945, our ship stopped on Iwo, and I accompanied my shipmate to the cemetery. As you entered the cemetery, they had pieces of old planes—propellers, wings, rocks that had names etched into them. I noticed parachute symbols etched into these crosses and Stars of David. I started going down the roster, and it included most of the men I served with in the 1st Battalion. I was one of the very few that survived. So I found a quiet place and cried. I still cry about it.

FRANK GUIDONE
1st Raider Battalion

On August 7, the 1st Raider Battalion assaulted Tulagi. The landing was unopposed, but by noon the Raiders were heavily engaged fighting the veteran rikusentai *(Japanese elite troops) of the 3rd Kure Special Naval Landing Force. That night, the* rikusentai *struck A Company, as Frank Guidone, then a squad leader, remembers.*

We encountered light action until we got to this one ridge, which was kind of a take-off point. We spread out and formed a skirmish line on the slope of the ridge, and the order came down: "Move out." The Japanese opened up with their machine guns. It was at this time that we lost two men in our squad. They were Louie Lovin and Leonard Butts. Louie was

A chaplain prepares crosses for Marines killed on Tulagi. (U.S. Navy)

my BAR man. They both died later of their wounds. Butts died while being treated on a hospital ship and was buried at sea. The squad and I took the news of their death hard. They were family.

As we moved forward, we were on the same ground as the Japanese, but they were about two or three hundred yards ahead of us. Every once in a while, we'd see them pop up and take a shot or two. After we got down there, I couldn't advance because I had nobody on my right or left flank. The other platoons got orders to pull back, so we were on our own. Al Belfield, one of my riflemen, was wounded while we were moving ahead. He was wounded in his right upper arm and bled profusely until we applied a tourniquet. They ordered us back up to the high ground. I reported to Captain Antonelli, my company commander. He had a lieutenant escort me to a gap in our line, where I assigned members of my squad to their area of responsibility. We didn't have time to dig foxholes. We just threw our packs down and got behind them and put our rifles up on our packs and waited. Fires burning below us lighted up the skyline, giving an eerie look to the whole area.

Just after dusk, they started to attack, crawling over the ridge. You could look over the ridgeline, and you could see these forms crawling. That's when we started throwing our first grenades. We threw grenades all night. Then we heard them yelling at each other and then the moaning. It went on all night long. The closest they got to us was about twenty yards from our line.

At daybreak we heard a rooster crow. Man, that was a good sign. We knew that daylight was coming. It was gray and kept getting lighter. As I looked out toward the ridgetop, I couldn't believe what I was seeing. There were about twenty-five to thirty Japs piled up. They were slaughtered. We threw about two cases of grenades that night—easily. One Jap was still alive. He got up and started running and got picked off; he didn't get very far. Later that morning, I went back to the CP [command post] area. I knew this was for real when I noted seven or eight bodies under ponchos—they were in a row. Gifford, Jerry DiSalvia, and Sergeant Luke were among the dead, along with four or five others. This first loss of our brothers was difficult to digest, but it was just the beginning.

BRIAN QUIRK
2ND RAIDER BATTALION

A and B Companies of the 2nd Raider Battalion raided Makin Atoll in an attempt to draw Japan's attention from Guadalcanal, which the Marines had invaded ten days earlier. Brian Quirk recalls the chaos surrounding the landing.

The rain was coming down in sheets. The swells were so high that they brought the rubber boats up, and then they would drop down fifteen or twenty feet, so you had to make the jump from the submarine into the boat when it was at its zenith. Then you'd have to wait for the next guy because you couldn't jump in two at a time. I remember when it came my time to jump, and I thought, "If I miss that son of a bitch, I'm going down like a rock." Luckily, I made it into the boat. The water would go up, and when it would hit the top of the submarine, it would come down like you were under a waterfall.

We tried starting the motors, but the motors wouldn't start! Now we got two things going against us: it was slow as hell getting off and getting into a formation, and secondly our motors won't start. There was the feeling that time was running away from us. We're paddling like hell. We knew that we're going to land, but we were supposed to land at 5:00 A.M., and you could see all the boats milling around; most didn't have power. Things were pretty fucked up. If you had any intelligence at all, you knew that everybody was going the wrong way, which they couldn't help. The second thing you knew was that the sun was going to be coming up in about forty-five minutes, and if you weren't on the beach and moving out, you were in tough straits.

What Colonel Carlson did, he made the rounds of all the boats and he said, "Head to the beach and follow me!" So we furiously paddled for the beach. We landed at the beach about 5:00 A.M., and I think that was about an hour before sunup. When we hit the beach, the schedule called for specific assignments off of a landmark, so boat number 1 landed on the right, 2, 3, 4, 5, 6, 7, 8, 9, 10 . . . to the left or the other way, I can't remember. The first modification was to say, "Follow me," so in we went.

Dean Winters (right) and Walter "Tiny" Carroll (left) debark from the USS *Nautilus* for the Makin Raid on August 17, 1942. (courtesy of Dean Winters)

This was a good example of Colonel Carlson's leadership. It was part of the training that he had put his officers and noncommissioned officers and these privates through so that they could handle any adversity. That's very important, in my mind.

Eventually we made it to the beach, and all of the sudden this BAR goes off, and you say, "Jesus, they can hear that in Tokyo." So they're going to be up waiting for us, and we aren't even ready to move off the beach yet. We put our boats under the trees and camouflaged them and all that, and now we're laying down there waiting to get the order to move out. That was a very apprehensive time of trepidation because you said, "Well, wait a minute, we're supposed to already be killing these guys while they're sleeping in their bunks. Now we haven't even left the beach yet and we told them we're here!"

DEAN WINTERS
2ND RAIDER BATTALION

Shortly after landing, the Raiders attacked Makin's Japanese garrison. The Japanese stubbornly defended the island, inflicting heavy casualties on the Raiders, but the biggest obstacles were the surf and the motors on the rubber boats that would not start.

We landed about 100 to 150 yards from the main landing point. We hid the boat as best we could and crossed a road, contacting B Company in the village. The Japanese were in trenches outside the village and were manning several machine-gun nests. There was a lot of small-arms fire. Tiny Carroll and I had the Boys [antitank] gun. A truck was coming down the road, so I hit the deck, braced myself, and fired, hitting the truck in the radiator. Steam poured out, and several Japs tumbled out.

I also used the gun on two seaplanes that landed in the bay. All of us were firing them. The smaller one caught fire and burned. The bigger plane was a four-engine seaplane. I remember firing about twenty rounds. It took off, and flames came up on it, and then it went down.

We were ordered to withdraw, and the Japanese hit us with a banzai attack, but we stopped them. After that, they offered very little resistance. We were called back to the makeshift field hospital. There were quite a few guys that were shot, and I saw several men dead on the ground. It's always hard to see a buddy get killed, but you don't have time to think about it. You have to do your job. But it's something you'll never forget.

In the evening when we were supposed to evacuate, we got into our boat and tried to get it out, but the surf was too high. The waves were fifteen feet or higher, and they were breaking three at a time. The boat kept tipping over backwards, and we lost everything. To keep from drowning, I took all my clothes off. The last thing we tried to do is swim out to the reef with a long rope and tow the boat with the rope. As we got near there, the guy I was with yelled, "Shark!" I never saw him again. I immediately turned around and rode the waves back in to the beach.

RAY BAUML

2ND RAIDER BATTALION

Ray Bauml was one of the lucky men who made it off Makin on the first day.

It was dark. They [the Japanese] were surrounding our perimeter. There was a lot of confusion and a discussion on how we should leave the island. We got in the rubber boats. Doc Stigler was carefully holding a wounded man [Lenz] at the prow of our boat; he had a head wound.

How I remember that scene. There were about ten of us, paddling out over the breakers, and we were tipped over three times before we got past them. We lost all of our weapons. The boat was full of water about up to our waists. It was miserable. After we passed the breakers, we were paddling and paddling. We were so exhausted paddling, yet we kept on. You can't believe when there is danger how you respond to it. The current was pulling us back, but we somehow made it to the sub.

There were about four of us holding to the side of the sub while the rest of them got Lenz up and carried him up to the conning tower and down the hatch. I was straining to hold the rubber boat, the sub was going, and you were trying to hold the rubber boat close to the sub, and all of the sudden the sub started going *uuurrrrhhhhgggggaaaa*. It's diving! And here I'm still out there in the boat! I looked up, and I'm the only guy holding the rubber boat. I heard a guy in the conning tower yell, "Get your ass up here, we're going down!" I said, "Holy shit." I never swore before I got in the Corps, and I haven't stopped since. I dove down the hatch, and somebody caught me. They were diving because a plane was approaching.

My thoughts are on Makin quite frequently. My squad had the nickname the Flying Wedge. Makin means a lot to me because I lost five men from the squad. They were killed or beheaded. I think about these guys. I remember Gaston, Larson, Nodland, and the others. But Bud Nodland really gets to me. He was only seventeen at the time and was going to be married when he got back. Over the past year, I've been in contact with his fiancée. In August I'm going to be a pallbearer when they reinter some of the men at Arlington. I'm glad they're finally coming home.

DEAN WINTERS
2ND RAIDER BATTALION

Dodging frequent air raids, Colonel Evans Carlson and the remaining men on Makin contacted the submarines at night by flashlight, signaling them to move to the calmer waters off the island's lagoon. To make the journey to the subs, the men lashed four rubber boats to a wooden outrigger canoe dubbed Lambs Ark *and paddled all night to the waiting submarines. Dean Winters relives the experience.*

I got back to the beach, and somebody was shooting at me. I crawled in these bushes, and the firing stopped. There wasn't much I could do, so I went to sleep. The next morning, I was awoken by giggling women. I got away from them and knelt down and prayed. I was over two thousand miles away from America and felt helpless. As soon as I finished praying, there was a native standing in the coconut tree, and he motioned for me to sit down. He came down out of the tree and made me understand that he was going to help me. And then he was gone.

I went and hid. I wasn't sure if he was going to turn me in or what. So he came and handed me three hand grenades and a pair of Japanese skivvy shorts and a coconut shell full of some kind of juice. I don't know what it was, but it tasted pretty good. It lit me up. I hadn't eaten or drank anything since we were on the sub. The shorts were ripped in the front and back, so I was exposed again, but I was able to attach the grenades to the waistband.

He knew that the submarine was still there, and he was going to take me out on this outrigger. We began paddling toward it, and I turned around and he wasn't in the boat. I looked up, and Jap planes were strafing us, so I dove into the water. I went clear to the bottom as far as I could get. I could see the trails as the bullets streamed underwater around me. I got out of the water and went down the beach.

I had three hand grenades, and I was two thousand miles away from friendly territory, so I decided the best thing for me to do was take two hand grenades and throw them into the Japs and use the other one on myself. I wasn't going to get captured!

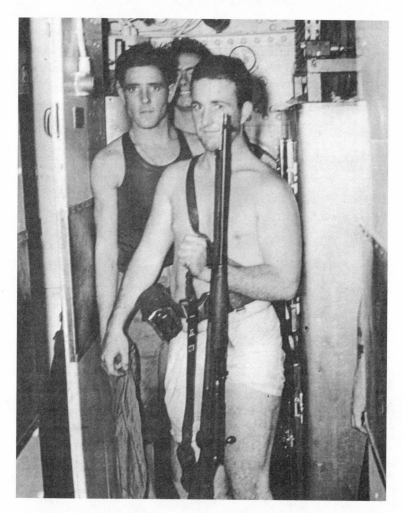

Dean Winters holding a captured Japanese rifle and wearing Japanese skivvy shorts after returning to the *Nautilus* on August 18, 1942. Many Raiders lost their uniforms and equipment on the return trip to the sub. (courtesy of Dean Winters)

I got down the beach about a mile or something. I saw some Marines, and boy I thought they were beautiful. They told me there was another group trying to leave because Carlson had sent a couple of his men to the Japanese with a note offering to surrender.

I wandered down the beach some more and found several men in a hut. My feet were bleeding and sore, so one of them told me he'd help me find a pair of shoes. We went up to where the battle had been the day before. We passed a pit, and there were about ten men [Japanese] laying with their faces down. I could see that they were breathing. One opened his eyes. I jumped on him, and [one of the other men] shot him in the head and finished off the rest. I put on their shoes. I couldn't stand them so I took them off. Then I found a rifle, and I went to look at the truck that I shot the day before. I hit it right through the motor and back through the cab out back.

All day the airplanes were coming over. They bombed the village. Our guys got in touch with the submarine and took the rubber boats around to the lagoon. We tied the boats to a wooden outrigger. I was the front man on the right side of the boat. We put our wounded on the big wooden boat. It wasn't going fast, but we paddled. It took us a long time and the wooden boat was full of water. We finally made it to the *Nautilus*. I was never so happy in my life.

STEPHEN STIGLER
2ND RAIDER BATTALION

Dr. Stephen Stigler recalls the Raiders' triumphant return to Pearl Harbor.

I spent the trip back tending to the wounded. I was very busy with the wounded. Some were in a state of shock. Fortunately, I didn't have to perform any major surgery. I'm proud of the fact that we got all of our wounded back.

It took several days, but we got back to Pearl, and this was a very emotional thing. We thought that we had sneaked out of Pearl; it was supposed to be a secret mission. When we left, we were all below decks. On the return trip, we were also below decks because we thought we were sneaking back in.

By the time we got abreast of the first ship, they were out on deck, standing at attention, saluting us. Each ship we passed saluted us. They were playing the Marine Corps Hymn and cheering. It was very emotional. I was an officer and in the conning tower, so the captain quickly got the rest of the men on deck. We were not exactly dressed to be saluted or salute back because most had lost a lot of our clothes when the surf was so heavy. Most of us had to divest ourselves of our clothing just to handle the heavy surf and swim. The Navy folks loaned us some clothes, but we were a pretty ragtag bunch.

It was my most vivid memory of the war. I was so moved they were cheering us; it felt like we had really done something meaningful and good.

CHAPTER TWO

Starvation Island: Guadalcanal

Some people wonder all their lives if they've made a difference.
The Marines don't have that problem.

— RONALD REAGAN

O N GUADALCANAL, the Marines gained a foothold after their landing on August 7, but the Japanese built up their forces. The 1st Raider Battalion and 1st Parachute Battalion were recalled from Tulagi and Gavutu and placed in reserve near Guadalcanal's Henderson Field at Lunga Point. The airfield, dubbed an "unsinkable aircraft carrier," became the focus of Japanese attacks. As long as Allied squadrons operated from the airfield, they could use airpower to protect their convoys and attack Japanese reinforcements.

The Raiders put their specialized training to the test by conducting two raids in defense of Henderson. The first occurred on Savo Island, where two Raider companies encountered no enemy soldiers. The second was on the key Japanese supply base at Tasimboko. Both the Raiders and parachutists participated, and the raid was a resounding success: several Japanese artillery pieces and a large cache of supplies were destroyed. More important, it provided an intelligence windfall that revealed the size of the Japanese force that was converging on Henderson Field.[1]

Marine Raider and Para Operations on Guadal[canal]

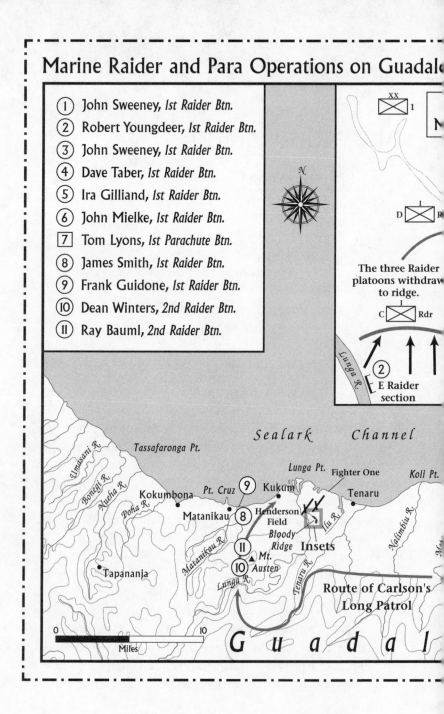

1. John Sweeney, *1st Raider Btn.*
2. Robert Youngdeer, *1st Raider Btn.*
3. John Sweeney, *1st Raider Btn.*
4. Dave Taber, *1st Raider Btn.*
5. Ira Gilliand, *1st Raider Btn.*
6. John Mielke, *1st Raider Btn.*
7. Tom Lyons, *1st Parachute Btn.*
8. James Smith, *1st Raider Btn.*
9. Frank Guidone, *1st Raider Btn.*
10. Dean Winters, *2nd Raider Btn.*
11. Ray Bauml, *2nd Raider Btn.*

The three Raider
platoons withdraw
to ridge.

C [XXX] Rdr

② E Raider
section

Sealark Channel

Tassafaronga Pt.

Umasani R.
Bonegi R.
Nueha R.
Poha R.

Lunga Pt.   Fighter One   Koli Pt.

Kokumbona   Pt. Cruz ⑨ Kukum   Tenaru

Matanikau ⑧ Henderson
              Field

Matanikau R.

⑪   Bloody
    Ridge **Insets**

① Mt.

Tapananja   ⑩ Austen

Lunga R.   *Tenaru R.*   *Nalimbiu R.*

**Route of Carlson's
Long Patrol**

0 _____ 10

Miles

Guadal[canal]

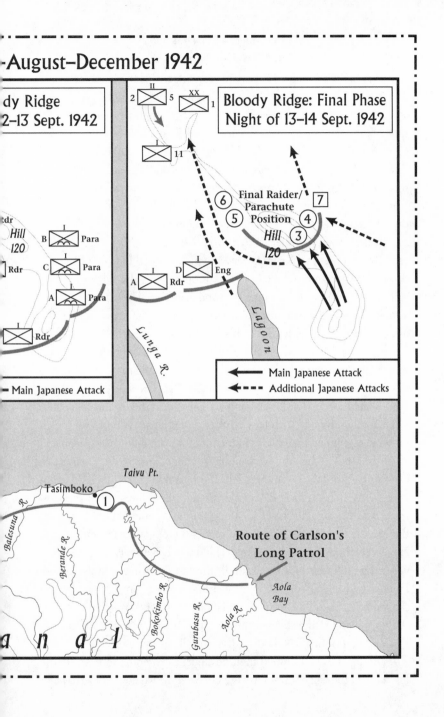

-August–December 1942

dy Ridge
2–13 Sept. 1942

Hill
120

Bloody Ridge: Final Phase
Night of 13–14 Sept. 1942

Final Raider/
Parachute
Position

Hill
120

Lunga R.

Lagoon

← Main Japanese Attack
←--- Additional Japanese Attacks

— Main Japanese Attack

Taivu Pt.

Tasimboko

Route of Carlson's
Long Patrol

Balesuna R.

Berande R.

Bokokimbo R.

Gurabusu R.

Aola R.

Aola
Bay

a   n   a   l

After the raid, Colonel Edson was convinced that the Japanese would attack Henderson from the south, which was lightly guarded. After consulting with division personnel, he moved his men (including the attached 1st Parachute Battalion) to a broken grassy north-south ridge about a mile from the airfield. The ridge was shaped like a giant centipede, with leglike spurs extending on each side. Edson's men hastily dug in and strung their limited supply of barbed wire along the ridge. The spine of the ridge provided a rough dividing line. Paratroopers were dug in on the east side, and the Raiders manned the west.

By dusk on September 12, 1942, over two thousand Japanese soldiers, led by Major General Kiyotaki Kawaguchi, lay coiled in front of Edson's 840 paratroopers and Raiders. A breakthrough along the ridge would result in the capture of the landing strip and lead to the loss of Guadalcanal, a major blow to the American war effort. As Kawaguchi prepared for the assault, he realized only one of his battalions had reached its assigned jump-off point and tried to delay the attack, but faulty communications prevented him from relaying the order.[2] After a bombardment from Japanese cruisers and destroyers, the Japanese launched piecemeal attacks that isolated several Raider platoons stationed near the lagoon side of the ridge, forcing them to withdraw.[3] By dawn, the Japanese broke off the attack and regrouped their forces in the jungles around the grassy hogback.

Edson pulled his line back along the ridge, forcing the Japanese to cross open ground. As darkness fell, the Japanese surged forward again with more men, striking B Company's right flank near the lagoon. At 10:00 P.M., Kawaguchi struck all along the ridge, buckling the center of the Marine line. About sixty Raiders from B Company, now cut off and exposed on both flanks, nevertheless held steady before Edson ordered a general withdrawal to a small knoll, the last defensive position before Henderson Field. There, about three hundred men formed a horseshoe-shaped line around the knoll to make the final stand. When a few men started moving farther toward the rear, the officers rallied them for the final stand, shouting, "Nobody moves, just die in your holes!"

The Japanese continued their advance, threatening to envelop the left flank of the ridge, but they were checked by two companies of parachutists who launched a bold counterattack. Marine artillery continued taking a toll on the attackers, and the men lobbed cases of grenades at the Japanese. At about 4:00 A.M. on September 14, Kawaguchi launched two more attacks on the ridge. Both failed. A small group of Japanese soldiers did reach the western fringe of the airfield (Henderson's Fighter One), but men in the 1st Engineer Battalion and Headquarters Company turned them back. Dawn revealed the broken bodies of seven hundred Japanese attackers, along with scores of Marines, on the hogback the Marines appropriately named Bloody Ridge. But Henderson Field remained in American hands.

More than half the men in the 1st Parachute Battalion were wounded or killed in action during their month and a half of fighting on Guadalcanal. Shortly after the battle for the ridge, the survivors departed for much-needed rest and an infusion of replacement troops. The Raiders lost 163 men on Bloody Ridge but would endure another month of combat.[4]

Not content to remain on the defensive, General Vandegrift tried to dislodge the Japanese from the west side of the Matanikau River (several miles west of Henderson) where they were building up their forces. The area had been a battleground in August, and three U.S. battalions began the Second Battle of the Matanikau with an assault in the last week of September.[5] The exhausted Raiders were joined by the 2nd Battalion, 5th Marines. They would pressure the Japanese near the mouth of the Matanikau, while the bulk of the 1st Battalion, 7th Marines made an amphibious assault farther west at Point Cruz in an attempt to cut off a potential Japanese withdrawal. The attack failed when Raiders and the 2nd Battalion, 5th Marines ran into heavy opposition from the Japanese defenses near the river and had to withdraw. While the 1st Battalion, 7th Marines was surrounded, and nearly annihilated after making its amphibious landing, most of the men were safely evacuated in a mini-Dunkirk. It was the only defeat the Marines suffered during the Guadalcanal campaign.

Intelligence reports soon suggested that the Japanese were making preparations for another offensive, and on October 7, the 5th and 7th Marine Regiments (each less one battalion) and the weakened 1st Raiders were sent to deal with the threat. This Third Battle of the Matanikau was a U.S. success: the Marines mauled a Japanese infantry regiment and disrupted their offensive by capturing assembly and artillery positions on the east bank of the Matanikau.

On October 13, the Raiders embarked by transport to New Caledonia for rest and reinforcements. The Guadalcanal campaign had taken a heavy toll on the 1st Raider Battalion. Only about five hundred men from the battalion's original strength of around nine hundred would board the transports.

On November 4, the rested 2nd Raider Battalion was sent to Guadalcanal. They landed at Aola Bay, about forty miles east of Henderson Field. The battalion's commander, Colonel Evans Carlson, was ordered to pursue about three thousand Japanese troops under the command of Colonel Shoji. Shoji's regiment had retreated to the eastern part of the island after the final failed Japanese offensive on Henderson in late October. Marine units from Henderson Field already were pursuing the retreating regiment, and Carlson's 2nd Raider Battalion was dispatched to harass it from the rear. The mission would be called the Long Patrol, as the Raiders trekked through the rain forest for a month pursing Shoji and whittling away at his unit. The battle casualty figures were lopsided: 488 Japanese soldiers killed, compared to 16 Raiders killed and 17 wounded. The figures don't tell the whole story, however: an additional 225 Raiders were plagued with malaria, dysentery, dengue fever, and other maladies.[6]

As 1943 approached, the fighting on the island entered a new phase. In early December, the 1st Marine Division left, replaced by U.S. Army units. The 2nd Raider Battalion followed on December 15, returning to Espíritu Santo. The Marine Corps authorized the formation of two new Raider battalions, the 3rd and the 4th, and the four battalions were eventually placed in two Raider regiments.[7]

The Marine elite infantry had played a key role in many of the major battles on Guadalcanal, America's first toehold in the Pacific. Yet it was just the beginning of a long journey west; sadly, it was the last that many of the men would make.

JOHN SWEENEY
1ST RAIDER BATTALION

After an uneventful raid on Savo Island in the early morning hours of September 8, the first elements of Colonel Merritt Edson's provisional parachute and Raider battalion waded ashore at Taivu Point. They quickly pushed inland and destroyed the main Japanese supply terminus at Tasimboko, gleaning a windfall of documents revealing Japanese strength and other details of the upcoming Japanese attack. Captain John Sweeney chronicles the 1st Raiders' journey from Tulagi to Tasimboko.

I went over on the *Kopara*, a flimsy cargo ship loaded with aviation gas and bombs on the deck. Naturally, we wanted to get the trip over. One of the other ships bringing in Raiders was the *Colhoun*, and it had just debarked D Company. That's when the air raid started. As the *Colhoun* was trying to get out of there, it was bombed and went down in seconds. Fortunately, we didn't have any Marines on board, but tragically there were fifty sailors that went down with her. We avoided a near disaster there.

We weren't ashore more than a couple of days when we had orders to reconnoiter Savo Island because there were indications that the Japanese were on the island. We didn't find any Japs, but we found the remnants of the disaster that hit the night of the eighth—the big naval battle off Savo Island. We lost four cruisers there and found many gravesites including the grave of one of the skippers from a cruiser, whom the natives had buried. There was wreckage of sunken ships all over. The shark activity was also very evident. Still lingering from a few days before were bodies, pieces of bodies—that sort of thing.

After we got back, Edson got wind of a buildup near Tasimboko and sold the idea of making a raid down there. We got two destroyers and two converted tuna boats we called Yippees. The flight down to Tasimboko included sparks coming out of the tuna boat smokestacks that made the convoy kind of a ridiculous thing to be going off to war because they could so easily be seen by the Japanese.

We landed just before dawn; it was early light. We moved down the coastal trail. The first thing I ran into was a lineup of soldiers' marching packs and life preservers. We learned this later: about midnight the Tokyo Express [Japan's system providing reinforcements] landed elements of an artillery regiment that was going to be with Kawaguchi. There must have been about a thousand packs. The hair went up on the backs of our necks. No weapons, no noise, until a shot went off. We found out an anxious Marine had a round in his chamber and accidentally pulled the trigger. There was no response, no bodies, but we knew they were there someplace. I swung my platoon to the left of the trail, and we began moving down the trail to Tasimboko, not knowing what was in store for us.

There was a small stream that we came to and a little embankment on the other side. I was looking to see if I could see anything, and ten or fifteen feet ahead of me was Edson, looking around with binoculars. He motioned me forward.

We got up on a grassy area, and there was a big hulk covered with palm fronds. It was an artillery piece, 75 mm gun, with piles of shells laying around. Obviously, it belonged to the people that had just landed. Our people got all excited about it, and I remember one guy, a colorful guy who wore a wide-brimmed hat and fought against Franco in the Spanish Civil War, was raising hell, shouting like a cheerleader. I looked at him and said, "What the hell are you doing? Shut up! They're out there, and we don't know where they are. Shut up!" He did.

We started to move out. Just as we were about to enter the clearing, a gun, fifty yards or so into the jungle, fired. It was the brother of the gun we just found, and fired a shell that went over our heads. We heard three or four more go over. Then they began bursting in the trees just behind us. One of the men, Corporal Carney, was killed, and Corporal Maurice Pion had his left arm hanging in shreds. A corpsman came up and used a penknife to amputate his arm. They got him evacuated, and the longer part of the story is that Pion ended up as a one-armed Marine Corps recruiter.

The second gun is firing, and some of the shells went through the CP.

It fired maybe five or six shots as we were ducking this—pretty low. They were going right over our heads. We had to get the gun out of the way, so I was hollering for a machine gunner or a BAR man, but my runner [messenger] Klejnot came up. He was a good shot and cranked off two or three rounds and got two or three people around the gun. The rest took off.

So the gun was out of the way and we were moving forward and at the edge of this clearing when a machine gun opened up on the other side just opposite of where the gun was. It put off a couple of blasts, but nobody was hit. The gun was firing into one of the platoons. I was up close, right behind the scouts, and crawled up behind a large coconut tree where I thought I was safe and was thanking God. I started yelling, "*Bakuo!*" I picked up the word from our interpreter. On the trip overseas, I asked him for a word that would be an insult like "you bastard," "shithead," whatever. The insult translated into something like, "You son of a turtle." [laughs] That was as close to a dirty word or insult. Every time I hollered it, I got a blast, and dirt on each side of me was flicking up. Just to my right, they were getting the ricochets. But now we could see the gun and where it was firing from, and we were distracting them. So I signaled one of my men to circle. He got the message, and his squad flanked the gun, and I kept them busy in the front. It went on for a couple of minutes. Two of my men riddled the machine-gun crew, knocking it out. We were able to move on. It was the last organized opposition before we moved into Tasimboko.

At Tasimboko we found lots of supplies. Medical supplies, and strange almost fishbowls filled with fluid of some kind. As far as we could tell, it was a type of firebomb. You light it, throw it, it breaks, and there's a blast. There was a lot of food, some saki, and brown bottles of beer. The food was particularly inviting: anchovies, sardines, crab, and lots of rice. We took whatever we could and destroyed the rest. Most importantly, we found a trove of valuable documents.

We destroyed everything we couldn't take. One way of despoiling the food was to urinate on it. We peed on it. Another gun was found, and we along with the other two took the breach block off and threw them away into the ocean. One of the other companies also destroyed an antitank gun. Eventually the boats came to pick us up. Anything we didn't take we threw overboard.

I can never understand why they didn't react better. After we landed, more of our ships arrived. Maybe they thought a major landing was taking place and pulled back, but that isn't in the Japanese character. I just can't understand it. They had a perfect opportunity to overrun us just after we landed.

ROBERT YOUNGDEER
1st Raider Battalion

Like Joshua Lawrence Chamberlain's last stand at Gettysburg's Little Round Top seventy-nine years earlier, the battle for Bloody Ridge was the crucial land battle for Guadalcanal. On the night of September 12 and 13, 1942, most of Major General Kiyotaki Kawaguchi's converging battalions were not in their assigned places for the attack on the ridge. As darkness fell, Kawaguchi's haphazard first attack fell on the Raiders' C Company and attached machine-gun platoon from E Company, forcing several platoons to withdraw. Robert Youngdeer, an E Company scout-rifleman, was manning a strong point along the main approach of the Japanese attack that night.

We heard them splashing across the river. They weren't very quiet. We could hear them jabbering away. They weren't attacking; they just were coming down the fire lane trying to find us. Soon they were all around our position. I could hear the bolts being pulled back on their weapons. Next they sprayed the bushes near us. We didn't fire because we knew if we did, we'd give away our position and they'd overwhelm us. So we threw grenades into them as they went around us, toward the ridge. We just kept throwing grenades. There wasn't the kind of fear you might think. There wasn't any panic or anything.

They came back through us again. Like I said, they weren't very quiet. They were making a lot of noise, talking, yelling to one another, and I heard someone getting beat up on the left. I can still hear the screams. He was begging for mercy. They [the Japanese] were berating

Bloody Ridge and Hill 120 looking out from the perspective of the Japanese attack.

him. Later on, I found that it was one of my friends, Ken Ritter. I'd seen him the day we went into our position. He had dysentery and was in bad shape, laying alongside the trail. As I went by, he looked up and smiled real weak-like. He didn't have anything to say. I heard from people later on that they bayoneted him.

When daylight came, well, a few more people were hit and killed by snipers. I was wounded in the morning.* I finally got out of there. I was flown off the island. They were flying the wounded off.

I have a granite memorial in the garden where I live. It says "Red Mike and his gallant men, Edson's Raiders, South Pacific, WWII, Semper Fidelis." I have an American and Marine Corps flag behind it. It's my way of remembering those who didn't return.

JOHN SWEENEY
1ST RAIDER BATTALION

John Sweeney's B Company held the center of the line, the vortex of the battle for Bloody Ridge during the main attack on the nights of September 13 and 14. He was the third B Company commander in twenty-four hours.

As we were pulling back, Edson came up to me and said, "Monville is being evacuated, and you're now the B Company commander." I had no officers—they were all gone. But the NCOs [noncommissioned officers] were all strong. At the time I was too tired to realize the situation I was handed, but as the sun was going down, I realized more and more what was given to me.

As darkness fell, Edson came back again with his binoculars and was looking down the ridge. I remember he said to me, "John, this is it. We are the only ones between the Japs and the airfield. You must hold this position." And he walked away with Burak [Edson's runner] trailing behind. It brought it all home.

One of the things that bothered me was leaving the 1st Platoon down where they were going to be the first hit. They knew it also.

Shortly after darkness fell, this platoon and Haines' platoon were hit by the full weight of the Japanese attack. They just ran through the position. In the dark, those that survived were pulling back to the ridge, firing, throwing grenades.

---

* Youngdeer was shot in the face while trying to rescue a wounded Marine.

They were twenty yards or thirty yards away down the ridge and also fortunately firing over our heads. At that time, there were several banzai charges up on the ridge preceded by flares. The flares gave them direction, and some had smoke. Some thought it was gas. I think it was the Marines themselves hollering, "Gas!" I heard this in the distance. It contributed to some temporary panic because we didn't have any gas masks then. It became individual and unit small-arms fire.

About that time, I got a call from Edson on my SCR [radio] that Maddox handed to me, and he said, "What is your situation down there?" Before I could answer, a voice broke in: "My position is excellent, sir." Apparently they had gotten the C Company SCR and were on the channel. It was the Japanese—of course, the hair goes up! Right after he said it, I caught my breath and realized what had been said, and I'm sure Edson did, and I said, "Cancel that last information, here's my situation." I gave them in vague terms because they were listening.

They were moving into position in the ravine in my rear and also to the front, and at the point he acknowledged the information and then came back with, "Can you take over spotting for artillery?" I gave him the affirmative because we were quite prepared. That was what we needed. When I said "Yes," I handed it to Maddox, who had been in mortars and artillery in his career, and said, "I can handle it." I gave it to him, and he relayed it to [Thomas] Watson [11th Marines forward artillery observer], who was a corporal up on the ridge with Edson. For us it was most effective. He began firing 200 or 300 yards in front of us and fired across until he brought it down. I think it was about 100 to 150 yards in front of us. I remember him saying, "That's right, now walk it back and forth across the front." That's what they did. They fired, fired, fired, fired barrages, and that I think broke up the people in front of us that we were almost eyeball to eyeball with.

After this interruption on the radio, Edson himself apparently got Burak to come down on the nose of the big ridge across from where I was and hollered, *"John Wolf! This is Burak. Do you hear me?"* I called back, "Affirmative, affirmative, John Wolf." Then the next call came through the cup of his hands. *"Red Mike says it's okay to withdraw!"* Believe me, that was a welcome message to get. After that, I told Maddox to move back from the paratroopers on the left of the message and then get at the pass where the road cuts in the ridge and stop our people there to regroup. Then I told him we'd pull the withdrawal in about five minutes after he departed.

Shortly after that, we got some probes in close. In the meantime, artillery fire that was going on was close. I think it broke up the major who was commanding the battalion. The artillery fire caught them on the ridge and on each side. I think it killed him.

My group was now around sixty or so people. We had some people who disappeared, and that's something that I think needs to be said. We had stragglers. The 1st Parachute Battalion had stragglers—not stragglers in the sense they were lagging behind but a few men that were leading a charge to the rear. That's where Edson [Bailey] and, I hope, myself, and NCOs were able to quell any panic in the sense that once one or two start, then pretty soon you get others following. I had a brief flare-up of that. We quelled it by shouting, challenging, cursing. "Act like Marines! You call yourself Raiders? Get back there!" What we ended up with was reorganizing them on the reverse slope. This was during the process of some of the messages that were going on. I had one lad who reported earlier. I never met him before he reported to Maddox. He was replacing a runner, a messenger. He was a young fellow, and where he came from I don't know. He was ordered up from the battalion to report to us. Shortly after dark, Maddox came over to me and says, "The new runner doesn't have a rifle." "What'd he do with it?" "Threw it away." "What!?" I went back, grabbed the kid, and his whole body was as stiff as that piece of metal, rigid, trembling. He was scared shitless. As a runner, as a Marine, as a fighter, he was worthless.

This was the height of the battle. We moved back on that cut [on the ridge], and "Horse Collar" [Jim Smith] was ordered by Edson to bring up what he could of the headquarters people. My eyes widened when I saw him and said, "Deploy your company over here." Smith responded, "We're not a company—just seven men." I said, "Oh, shit!"

DAVE TABER
1ST RAIDER BATTALION

Dave Taber was one of "Horse Collar" Smith's communicators who fought bravely among Sweeney's men. Six of the seven men were casualties that night.

We were on top of the ridge near the command post. Major Bailey came up and made an eloquent speech. He said something like this: "All you fellows have buddies and friends that have been wounded and killed, and it will all be in vain if we lose the airfield. Now let's get out, hold the line, and save the airfield. If we lose the airfield, we're going to lose the island." That was about the gist of it. It was quite dramatic and got everybody moving. I thought to myself it was almost like something out of a movie.

I was with a close friend of mine, Ike Arnold. (Ike's name was really Herman Arnold, but I called him Ike.) We each had five or six grenades. We went out. I'm not sure what happened, but somehow we got separated from some of the other guys. In fact we were a little too extended, I guess. When the Japs attacked, we were throwing grenades. There was a lot of shooting going on, a lot of action: rifle fire, grenades moving so fast. Anyway, we were throwing grenades down the ridge, and then all the sudden Ike talked to me. [Choking up, Taber said, "I'd rather not go through this," but then continued.] He called me Tabe. He said very calmly, "Tabe, I've been hit." I turned to him. He was off to my side a little, and I said, "Where?" He said, "In the throat." He no more than said that, and he was dead. He must have been hit in the jugular vein or an artery. Blood just gushed out. I had my arm underneath him, across his back, and I lowered him down to the ground. [crying] There's nothing you could do. He was a very good friend of mine. I looked around, and I was all by myself.

I thought to myself that I better get back and make contact with the others. I didn't know whether to crawl back or walk back because there was danger both ways. We'd been told what to do in these cases. I acted without even thinking. I decided to stay on my feet. It was pitch dark. I was walking a little bit, and all the sudden I heard something behind me and along comes a grenade right through the air and the fuse is burning! Before I knew what I was doing, I fell on my face away from it. As I was going down, I turned to see where the grenade was falling; it fell in between my feet. I had sharpnel between my feet and legs. I was a little stunned but got up. I was in shock, and nothing was bothering me. I'm walking along slowly and heard a Japanese voice behind me and he was talking to me. He must have thought I was a Jap going up in front of him. I had a .03 rifle and I swung around and shot, and he dropped as I kept on going. I finally got back [to the CP], and one of the first people I ran into was Horse Collar Smith, who was wounded.

IRA GILLIAND
1st Raider Battalion

Ira Gilliand recalls his night on the ridge.

It's tough to talk about this stuff. It's been fifty-eight years. It gives me the chills thinking about it.

The Japanese were trying to outflank us and looked like they were going to overrun our position. I remember their screams. They screamed a lot, especially when they were charging. It made you alert in a hurry even after being up for two days and you're ready to fall asleep.

They kept charging, but that's where the grenades came in. We threw grenades all night long. I remember rolling the grenades down. We were up on the hill and they were below us. They kept feeding us boxes of grenades. I remember the sound of Plante's BAR. He kept it going all night long. A lot of guys spent a terrible night out there.

The 1st Parachute Battalion was with us. I remember one of the paratroopers got shot. The corpsman came over because of his cry for help, and he [the corpsman] got shot right through the heart. His name was Smith, so when I saw Smith go down, I grabbed him and carried him down the hill. I didn't think he was going to die. When I got him down to the first aid station, I saw one of our doctors cry. [chokes up] Old Smitty was my friend, a real nice guy, and I broke down also.

JOHN MIELKE
1ST RAIDER BATTALION

About three hundred Marines gripped the side of the small knoll, Hill 120. The horseshoe-shaped line was the last defensive position before Henderson Field. John Mielke recalls their last stand.

We got together and were holding a position on the reverse slope of the ridge. At that time, there was a moment of panic. Around the base of the ridge, some paratroopers were retiring from their position because they knew we were there. They were calling out the password. One of the things you fear more than anything else is panic. We were cussing them out and giving them a real hard time. As they moved along, I felt sorry for them. I wasn't afraid. Fortunately, they were turned around [by the officers], and many of these men returned to their holes and died there.

Then they [the officers] said, "Fix bayonets! And move up." We were going to cover the spot they were evacuating. I was the low man on the squad. I was an ammunition man, so I followed the men up the ridge. The squad leader set up his position, and the other ammunition man who was a bit older than me said, "John, I'll take care of you." That wasn't the case. We left together, but I saw him for just a few moments, and we lost each other in the darkness making it up the ridge. I got up there and had this rifle with no sling on it, and this was awkward.

Most people were down in a prone position facing the ridge, throwing grenades as fast as they could throw them. As I came up there, I saw two men struggling. One was a big guy and the other was a small guy. I tackled the small guy. Like a bag of newspapers, I threw him down the ridge, and he went tumbling off into the darkness. The guy that was on top was a paratrooper. He had been bayoneted by the Japanese.

We were bringing in cases of grenades. I spent the night bringing

grenades to the men and throwing them. It was like a bad dream: men firing BARs, Springfields; there were cases of empty grenades all over the
place. There weren't many of us left standing. By daylight there were
wounded and dead all over the ridge.

TOM LYONS
1st Parachute Battalion

*Outnumbered and running out of ammunition, Edson's three hundred defenders
faced their gravest threat when a large element of the Japanese III Battalion, 124th
Infantry seemed poised to overrun the left side of the knoll. Edson ordered the Marine parachutists holding that side of the knoll to counterattack immediately. But
the parachute battalion's commanding officer was nowhere to be found. He was relieved on the spot by Edson, and Captain Harry Torgerson was placed in command. Torgerson assembled two companies of parachutists and launched them in
a desperate counterattack, saving the left flank of the line. After the Marines regained the line, the fighting became hand-to-hand, as parachutist Tom Lyons
vividly remembers.*

When they started raking us with a machine gun, that pissed me off, so I
got up and crawled through the grass. The grass was about a foot and a
half tall off the side of that hill, and I crawled up and around to the side of
the machine gun. Bullets were flying everywhere, but the grass was high
enough that it would partially hide you. I got almost to the machine gun
before I was detected. They didn't see me until I stood up. There were so
many people running around you couldn't shoot anybody. I stood up and
threw a hand grenade, and just as I threw the grenade, they swung the
gun around and ripped me up through the middle. I took several bullets;
most of them went all the way through, and one missed my heart by
about a half an inch. It knocked me ass over tin cup down the hill. The
first one stung like hell. It really hurt. But the others after that didn't hurt
at all. It seemed like I just left my body and was floating up in the air looking down at everything going on.

I saw a Jap come out, and he stepped on my stomach and he stabbed me in the throat with his bayonet. It went through the side of my neck and into the ground behind me but it didn't hurt. Jesse Youngdeer [Robert Youngdeer's brother] was coming up the trail with a box of hand grenades, and this Jap stepped off me and instead of finishing me off, he made a thrust at Youngdeer. [Youngdeer] stopped it with the box of hand grenades, and then he grabbed the Jap's rifle and was trying to wrestle it out of his hands. The Jap had stabbed him just above the knee. Another Marine ran up with his bayonet, and he tried to stab the Jap, and he got confused and stabbed Youngdeer right in the leg.

My eyes were wide open. I could see everything that was going on. I thought I was seeing it from fifty feet above. When they started firing the 105s [artillery] right in my area, I got some shrapnel in the right side of my chest. The bullets and shells were passing right over where I was floating around up there, and I was afraid they were going to hit me.

Morning came, and they came around, and all the Japs were gone. There were dead Japs all around me. They were picking out the Marines and throwing all the bodies on a truck, and they cut all our dog tags off. They hauled us down to the cemetery in the coconut grove, and they dumped our bodies out. I ended up at the top of the pile. The driver came around close to the tailgate and thought I was coming alive, so he started running into the jungle screaming, and he didn't come back.

An hour or so later, two corpsmen came by in a jeep, and they put me on a stretcher and hauled me to the hospital. They put me under a palm tree. From the stretcher, doctors told them to take this one out and bring in someone they can save. So I was there under a palm tree, and fresh troops started coming up the road. A ship came in with reinforcements, and an officer came over and said, "Take all the people out of the field hospital and put them on my ship and I'll take them back to Buttons [Base Buttons in Espíritu Santo]." And he said, "And that one under the palm tree, put him in my cabin and call the ship surgeon." He said, "You're going to be on the bridge all the way back to Buttons." I was conscious but couldn't talk. My mouth was full of caked blood. I was wearing the same clothes for almost two months.

This ship surgeon got my lung uncollapsed, and he pumped all the blood out of it and had me all cleaned up. After we made port, they put me on a plane to New Zealand. My mother got a check from my insurance saying I was dead the same day she got a letter from me written by a nurse at hospital in New Zealand.

JAMES SMITH
1st Raider Battalion

On September 27, the 1st Raider Battalion would help launch an attack near the mouth of the Matanikau River. Poor intelligence greatly underestimated the strength of the Japanese defenses facing them, turning the operation into a disaster. The Japanese halted the Raiders and 5th Marines' advance at the mouth of the river and nearly wiped out the amphibious landings by another Marine battalion at Point Cruz. Jim "Horse Collar" Smith recalls the battle.

We were on this narrow trail along the east side of the Matanikau River, a steep cliff on the other side. As we snaked up the side of the trail, a guy named Ed Mertz had a kidney stone. And here we are plastered alongside the trail with Japs on the other side of the river and this guy Mertz goes down screaming, clutching his gut. I remember thinking, "Oh, God, we are going to get it." It was just a little farther along there that C Company was just a little ahead of us. Ken Bailey [the battalion executive officer and Medal of Honor recipient for his actions on Bloody Ridge], with his runner right behind him, was dashing across a log footbridge, caught a Nambu [machine gun] between the eyes and went down.

A little later in the day—I guess we were still heading south—Sam Griffith got shot in the shoulder at about 300 meters. That left us with a bunch of young 1st lieutenants (who had just made 1st lieutenant), and there was actually a discussion at the CP as to who was the senior officer. Edson was in a state of shock after Bailey was killed. It affected [Bailey's runner] more than anything else. He had been Major Bob Brown's runner until the ridge, and Brown was killed coming off the ridge. Someone said to him, "You must be a jinx, because this was the second major you lost." The poor kid became unglued. It was a terrible thing to say.

I remember when we pulled Bailey into the aid station in a poncho. Aid station [sigh]—a couple of guys sitting on logs and doctors treating them. There was a kid by the name of Dobson who had been shot right in the groin. His face was absolutely dead white, you couldn't believe it. He just sat there and held his stomach. Everybody knew he was going to die, and he knew he was going to die. Not a murmur out of him; talk about stoicism. He died shortly after that. He just slid off the log and was dead. A man next to him had a flesh wound and was crying like a baby. Talk about a contrast.

Eventually they pulled us out of there because the Japs were well entrenched on the other side of the footbridge.

FRANK GUIDONE
1st RAIDER BATTALION

The 1st Raider Battalion served as a reserve force after the Second Battle of Matanikau, but it was decimated by sickness and losses. Nevertheless, A Company and a machine-gun section from E Company got the call to move up into the line for what has become known as the Third Battle of the Matanikau. After probing the Japanese defenses during the day, the men dug in for the night. A pocket of about 150 Japanese soldiers was trapped on the Raider side of the river and that night led a breakout, wiping out most of the American mortar squad, as Frank Guidone remembers.

About dusk the Japanese came roaring out. It was frantic; at nighttime everybody was in their holes. There was a half-track firing across the river. Japs were coming out of the pocket. I didn't move in my foxhole that night. I just waited for somebody to jump on me. That's the kind of night it was.

The Japanese came through with their bayonets and hit the mortar squad. There was one guy, Bill Dodamead, the Jap jumped into his fox-

Elements of Carlson's 2nd Raider Battalion on the "Long Patrol," which covered over 150 miles of ground on Guadalcanal and lasted nearly a month.

hole, and he grabbed a machine-gun barrel, and he just beat the pulp out of this Jap.

I looked up seaward toward the wire, and the Japanese were stuck on it. They hit that wire, and it really busted them up. They got hooked up in the barbed wire, and the tracers were just cutting them down. They were on the wire silhouetted. Tracers do the damnedest thing—it's not pretty, it's deadly. It was pitch black, and you could hear the moaning and the groaning. I think about Gettysburg; it was probably nothing like it. But I think about the men lying out in those fields not getting any treatment.

I knew that whole mortar squad. That's one time I really felt it. That next morning, I went up on a short patrol, and I saw these guys laying in their foxholes dead. Joe Connolly, Neldon French, Don Steinaker, and Denny Thomas. I just had to walk away. The whole mortar patrol was gone, nine or ten guys. They were all in their outpost positions. This one guy, Joe Connolly, was an Irishman from New York, and he was older than us and we called him "Pop." I drank many a beer with him in Quantico, and I was in a boxing tournament in Samoa and Joe was my corner; that was the worst feeling I ever had. Gunnery Sergeant Cliff McGlockin, our acting platoon leader, put his arm around me and said, "That's the way it is, you know." I said, "Yeah, I know." The thing is, I was one of the first ones up there. We went up on a patrol because we didn't know if the Japs were around there again or not. I got to that spot, I just stopped, I couldn't believe it. I never forgot that.

We had a guy named Steinaker; he was in the mortar platoon. On our way up, before we left the camp area for Matanikau, he got word from the Red Cross that his wife had given birth to a baby. I can't remember if it was a boy or girl. But he was ready for it. He was passing out cigars. We were marching down this trail heading toward Matanikau. He was carrying a base plate for a mortar, and he was smiling. We called him "Pop." "Hey, Pop, how ya doing?" He was very happy. All these guys had ships named after them, destroyers.

Then we came back to the beach. A couple of days later, we went aboard a transport and we were gone, but that was a hell of a way to go. That made their deaths even worse—being so close.

DEAN WINTERS
2ND RAIDER BATTALION

Shortly after the departure of the 1st Raider Battalion, the 2nd Raider Battalion disembarked at Aola Bay. Its task was pursuing three thousand hungry and exhausted Japanese soldiers retreating from the eastern side of the island to rejoin elements of the Japanese 17th Army on the western side of the Matanikau. The Raiders spent a month pursuing the Japanese on what was called the Long Patrol.

It seemed like it was raining all the time. We also had to cross many rivers. We had to climb a steep ridgeline dividing the Lunga and Tenaru valleys using ropes that we each carried and then linked together. We found an artillery piece that had been shelling Henderson Field. It was nicknamed "Pistol Pete." Several men took it apart and threw it over a cliff.

We came upon a Japanese field hospital and bivouac area. We killed a lot of Japs. We bayoneted and shot anything that was still moving. It was a series of grass huts. They were on the ground wounded. Several had broken legs. It didn't look like they had proper medical attention, because some were bent on a 45-degree angle. They weren't sticking straight out. We were back in Japanese territory and didn't want to make noise, so we used bayonets. I was pretty angry. We had a patrol, and they captured one of our men and tied him over a log and used him as a woman. They rammed a bayonet up his butt and he bled to death. That made me angry! So whenever I'd get into action, I'd get angry. I wasn't afraid when I was angry. We all felt that way after what we had seen.[8]

After we left the area, we went up around Mount Austen. They ambushed us on the top. We had one man wounded. We carried him out; it was a long way down the mountain. We had jungle rot on our crotch and down our legs so bad that we had to stop every once in a while to empty the blood out of our shoes. It was painful. When you're in the field like that, you go, and you can't worry about pain.

The Raiders were a very special group. They're all volunteers. They were very select. We were interviewed by Evans Carlson or Jimmy Roosevelt. Roosevelt interviewed me and asked me if I was afraid to die. I said, "Anybody not afraid to die is a fool. But I would if it came to that. I wouldn't hesitate." He passed me.

RAY BAUML
2ND RAIDER BATTALION

Ray Bauml recounts the Long Patrol.

You dragged your ass all the way. With our training using rope and pulling up hills and all that, it sure came in handy there. Christ, it was raining, of course. When didn't it rain in the hills? We climbed up on this hill; well, you couldn't walk up it, it was almost perpendicular. We'd tie the rope to a small tree, boost the guys—we got over. You can imagine the time involved.

I'd been the point man four or five hours. That puts a strain on you. A native was leading us and said, "I smell'm Jap." I forgot his name, but let's call him Tonto for now. We worked on hand signals, and his hand went up to signal everybody to stop. You'd look back and everyone else's hand went up down the line, motioning the people behind them to stop.

I feel somebody tap my shoulder, and it's the guy next to me. He points to me and he points up: "You go and check." I looked at him incredulously and said, "What?" I'm thinking to myself, "Here are all these Navy Cross tough guys I'm with. Why aren't they doing it?" So I'm crawling up. I get near the base [of a ridge]. I motioned the rest of the squad to move along and spread out. We start crawling up the hill on our bellies. There was a bunch of dead leaves, and every leaf would crackle when you moved across it. Ten feet from the top were the remains of a Jap bivouac.

I slipped the muzzle of my weapon into my helmet and raise it expecting a burst of fire. Nothing happened, so I crawled up and began exploring about six or seven foxholes. They were there not too long before, because in the jungle meat doesn't last too long, and there was fresh meat just starting to rot, which has an intense smell. I'm looking around, I'm the only one, there's no one backing me, no one protecting my butt— that's what bothered me. I'm looking around at all these foxholes, stepping lightly. My weapon went into the foxhole first, and I'm thinking, "Why the hell am I doing this?"

I was about to go back to tell them I couldn't find anything, and behind us our officer [Miller] and his runner must have walked up along the trail, come around, and crashed through like a herd of elephants. I almost shot him. I said, "Holy Christ!" He was pissed off. He said, "Where the hell is everyone? What is taking so long?" I said, "They're laying over here about fifteen yards, I'm guessing."

Then I was going to step in front of them to lead them, but they train the officers to go first, so I stepped right behind them. I was about a step behind him. We took two steps, and a Jap machine gun went off and almost blew his entire head off. All his teeth were knocked out, and his tongue was like strips of liver; his whole lower jaw was almost missing.[9] I said, "Lay low." It's amazing how you react, and I said, "Lay low, lieutenant."

I started backing up, and Putnam said, "Cover me. I'll get him." He was about five, ten feet behind me. I said, "Okay." So I raised my rifle and I'm thinking to myself, "Who the hell am I covering? I don't see anybody. Where the hell is everybody else? Why aren't they firing?" [The firing] came out of a tree. I raised my weapon. [The runner] left, and another burst came. I'll tell ya, they were so damn close that machine-gun smoke was enveloping us. I patted Miller's leg. "Lay still." I don't know if he heard me or not.

What saved my butt were these ironwood trees in the jungle. They are so tough that you take the sharpest machete, swing all you've got, and barely put a crease in there. Above my belly, near my chest, were two slugs that would have got me if the ironwood tree hadn't stopped them. Then a few minutes later—Christ, I thought ten years had passed—I heard a shot and it turned out that [the runner] got shot in the arm going back to the group and lost his arm. [One other man] was the one who saved our ass. He said, "I see them." He was being smart because despite all this training, a lot of these bastards are trigger-happy. He said, "I see them." He opened up with his BAR, stops, opens up again, and he said, "I got them, I got them." I'm guessing there were two.

The next day Miller died. He suffocated from his own phlegm. It wasn't a pretty sight.

CHAPTER THREE

Up the Solomons: Strangling Rabaul

The cherry is the first among flowers
as the warrior is the first among men.

—AN ANCIENT JAPANESE SAYING

KILL JAPS. KILL JAPS.
KILL MORE JAPS.
You will help kill the yellow bastards
if you do your job well.

—SIGN POSTED AT THE HEADQUARTERS OF
ADMIRAL WILLIAM "BULL" HALSEY

R ABAUL WAS A MIGHTY JAPANESE air and sea bastion located about 640 miles northwest from Guadalcanal on the northeastern tip of New Britain Island. About 100,000 soldiers were stationed there. Its airdrome could handle a thousand planes, and its well-protected harbor could easily shelter the entire Japanese navy. It was prime military real estate that menaced Allied lines of communications from the United States to Australia, blocked Allied advances up the east coast of New Guinea, and placed the Japanese in an excellent position to move south. After the Allies secured Guadalcanal in early 1943, reduction of Rabaul became the primary mission of the Allied forces in that area.

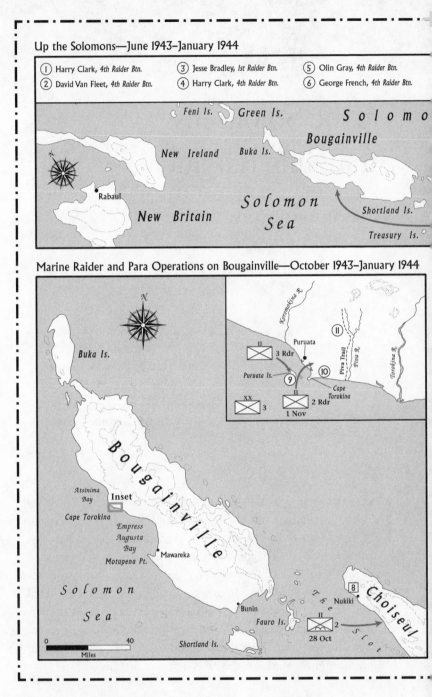

Up the Solomons—June 1943–January 1944

1. Harry Clark, *4th Raider Btn.*
2. David Van Fleet, *4th Raider Btn.*
3. Jesse Bradley, *1st Raider Btn.*
4. Harry Clark, *4th Raider Btn.*
5. Olin Gray, *4th Raider Btn.*
6. George French, *4th Raider Btn.*

Feni Is. Green Is. *Solomo*
Bougainville
New Ireland Buka Is.
Rabaul
New Britain *Solomon Sea* Shortland Is.
Treasury Is.

Marine Raider and Para Operations on Bougainville—October 1943–January 1944

Buka Is.

Koromokina R. Puruata 11
3 Rdr
Puruata Is. 9 10 *Piva Trail* *Piva R.* *Torokina R.*
Cape Torokina
XX 3 2 Rdr
1 Nov

Bougainville
Atsinima Bay Inset
Cape Torokina
Empress Augusta Bay
Motupena Pt. Mawareka

Solomon Sea
Bunin
Fauro Is. 8 Nukiki *Choiseul*
2 *The Slot*
28 Oct
Shortland Is.

0 40
Miles

Marine Raider Operations on New Georgia—June–August 1943

Attack on Bairoko

NLG Positions   NLG Final Attack
Line 20 July

Enemy Outpost Line   Enemy Defense Line

Inset

Western
Landing
Force

Eastern
Landing
Force

Attack on Viru Harbor

○ Bivouac

American Advances

Allied Advances

Japanese Airfields

During the spring of 1943, the Joint Chiefs had devised Operation Cartwheel to isolate the enemy fortress. The plan called for General Douglas MacArthur, in charge of the Southwest Pacific Area, to approach from New Guinea in the west. At the same time, Admiral William "Bull" Halsey, theater commander of the South Pacific, closed in on Rabaul from the southeast by advancing up the Solomons from Guadalcanal.

Halsey's first major target was New Georgia Island, two hundred miles up "The Slot" from Guadalcanal.[1] (The Solomon chain is about 500 miles long, and the water between the islands was referred to as "The Slot" by the Americans.) Halsey felt it necessary to secure New Georgia for fighter bases to support air bombardment on Rabaul. No Marine divisions were available for the operation, so the bulk of the task fell on the Army.

The Raiders, however, had made contributions even before the main operation began. On June 21, 1943, half of the 4th Raider Battalion was put ashore by high-speed destroyer transports called APDs at New Georgia's Segi Point. This group, the Eastern Landing Force, would be responsible for clearing that portion of the island. After rescuing an endangered coast watcher, the Raiders made an arduous trek through jungle and swamp considered impassable by native scouts. They eventually destroyed a Japanese strong point and 140 mm coastal gun position at Viru Harbor. After consolidating their hold on Viru, the Raiders were reinforced by Army units and on July 9 were withdrawn to Guadalcanal.[2]

Meanwhile, on June 30, the other half of the 4th Raider Battalion (Companies N and Q) and the 2nd Battalion of the 103rd Infantry swiftly seized Vangunu Island and the valuable supply point of Wickham Anchorage.

On July 5, the main assault on New Georgia, Operation Toenails, began. The 1st Raider Battalion led the two Army battalions of Halsey's Northern Group in an early-morning landing at Rice Anchorage, on New Georgia's northwest coast. Once ashore, the 1st Raider Battalion was to cross more jungle and a swamp known as the Dragon's Peninsula, then seize the Japanese barge bases at Enogai and Bairoko.[3] The goal was to sever Japanese supply lines while the Southern Group, led by the green 43rd Infantry Division, went after Munda Airfield, where the Japanese had concentrated most of their forces on the island.

The trek through the swamp was herculean, and the Raiders faced not only the elite Japanese (*rikusentai*) but the punishing environment. Leeches, oversized insects, and parasites thrived in the pesthole. Fungus that attached to the body created open sores known as jungle rot. Malaria, dysentery, and dengue fever were rampant in the weeks the Raiders spent fighting on the island. Steamy humidity combined with temperatures of over 100 degrees drained the health and the combat effectiveness of the Raiders. But the men pushed on.

After capturing the village of Triri, the Raiders reached Enogai. Several hundred *rikusentai* and elements of the Japanese 1st Battalion, 13th Infantry Regiment bitterly defended the village. The final machine-gun nest was cleared on the morning of July 11.

About two miles west-southwest of Enogai, on the opposite side of the Dragon's Peninsula, lay the port of Bairoko, the main Japanese supply point for New Georgia. Anticipating an attack after the fall of Enogai, the Japanese beefed up their main defenses around Bairoko. Opposing the Americans would be four fortified lines of coconut log and coral bunkers containing mutually supporting automatic weapons hidden under palm fronds and branches. Marine Colonel Harry "the Horse" Liversedge, in charge of the Northern Group, had the difficult duty of breaking through the Japanese fortress.

The attackers had been bolstered by the 4th Raider Battalion, but they had already suffered serious losses on New Georgia and remained understrength. The 4th Raider Battalion was short two hundred men, and the 1st Raiders were down to what amounted to two companies. The lightly armed Raiders also lacked the equipment for bunker busting: their heaviest weapon was a 60 mm mortar. And after Enogai, the Japanese knew they were coming.

The attack on Bairoko began the morning of July 20, 1943. The survivors in the 1st and 4th Raider Battalions remember it painfully. As the Raiders advanced on the Japanese defenses, they were peppered by 90 mm mortar and automatic fire, taking heavy casualties. Nevertheless, the

Raiders and the Army battalion broke through the first two defensive lines. By late afternoon, however, with no reserves and having suffered over 25 percent casualties, Liversedge had no choice but to order a withdrawal.[4]

The next day, the Raiders made the long march across the Dragon's Peninsula to Enogai, where they remained in defensive positions for the rest of July.

In the southern part of the island, near Munda Airfield, things weren't going much better. The Japanese put up fierce resistance around the airfield and wore down the 43rd Infantry Division; its commanding general was sacked, and the 37th Infantry Division, along with elements of the 25th Infantry Division, had to be called in to complete the job.

By August 4, Munda was finally in U.S. hands, and the Southern Group pushed north, linking up with Liversedge's Northern Group and bringing the battle for New Georgia to its final stage. Hoping to trap the bulk of the island's defenders, the Army overran a token Japanese rearguard at Bairoko—but it was too late. The Japanese had completed a masterful withdrawal, evacuating thousands of troops to nearby Kolombangara Island. At best, the battle of New Georgia was a pyrrhic victory for the Allies.

On August 28, the Raiders sailed for Guadalcanal. For them, New Georgia had been expensive real estate. The 1st Raiders had just 245 men out of about 900, and of the 4th Raiders, a mere 154 were fit for combat.

With New Georgia secure, Halsey continued pushing up the Solomons chain toward Rabaul, seizing the practically undefended island of Vella Lavella, with the assistance of the 2nd Parachute Battalion, and neutralizing the Japanese stronghold at Kolombangara.

Bougainville, the northernmost island in the Solomons, was the next objective. The island and the nearby Shortlands were defended by about 27,000 troops and contained several large airfields. Here the Japanese concentrated their forces, hoping to reverse their losses elsewhere in the Solomons.

On October 28, the 2nd Marine Parachute Battalion landed on Choiseul Island as a diversion from the main invasion of Bougainville. The parachutists harassed the Japanese until November 3. The raid had a slight effect on the Japanese high command, prompting them to shuttle troops from the Shortland Islands to deal with the paratroopers.[5]

On November 1, 1943, after a bright dawn, the I Marine Amphibious Corps reached Bougainville's Cape Torokina. The main landings were made by elements of the 3rd Marine Division. Assisting the 3rd, the 2nd Raider Battalion assaulted Green 2 Beach under machine-gun and rifle fire. Once ashore, the Raiders blasted bunkers apart and moved inland. In conjunction with the main landings, the 3rd Raider Battalion hit nearby Puruata Island.[6]

Over the next few days, the Marines expanded their perimeter and met sporadic resistance from the enemy. Mud, swamp, and jungle seemed to be more of an obstacle than the Japanese.

The Marines pushed forward, and the Raiders' 2nd and 3rd Battalions (organized as the 2nd Raider Regiment) had some tough fights in November, helping to repel several attacks. At the end of November, they would be joined by the 1st Parachute Battalion, followed by most of the 1st Parachute Regiment. Throughout December, the Raiders and Marine paratroopers held defensive positions along the perimeter or were in corps reserve. Then, in the middle of December, the Army poured into the Bougainville beachhead, relieving the Marines. The last parachutists and Raiders left the island in the middle of January.

It was not the end of the fighting on Bougainville. The Japanese continued to put pressure on the beachhead and in March made an all-out assault. The Army held, causing roughly five thousand Japanese losses, and at the end of March broke out of the beachhead, neutralizing Bougainville and isolating Rabaul from the south.

Bougainville was the last battle the men would fight as Raiders and parachutists. After returning to base camps, both units were disbanded. Most Raiders would join the newly formed 4th Marine Regiment, while the majority of parachutists became the core of the 5th Marine Division.

The changing nature of the Pacific war reduced the need for specialty units. Once standard tactics had been developed—massive amphibious assaults, followed up by the destruction of Japanese strong points by heavily armed units—the need had diminished for light units

Raiders cross a river during the New Georgia campaign. (USMC)

that could strike deep into enemy territory. Another factor was the un-precedented expansion of the Marine Corps. Two divisions, the 5th and 6th, had to be formed, and men were needed to fill the rolls. Finally, many senior officers within the Marine Corps never were comfortable with the idea of an elite unit within the elite Corps.

Yet the elite troops made their mark in the Solomons, a campaign that had proven decisive. Unable to drive the Americans out of Guadal-canal, New Georgia, and Bougainville, the Japanese found themselves embroiled in a battle of attrition that they could not win. This precluded their implementing offensive operations in areas such as New Guinea. The Allies continued their drive west from the Solomons that pointed like a dagger into the heart of the Japanese Empire.

HARRY CLARK
4TH RAIDER BATTALION

On June 21, 1943, before the main operation to capture New Georgia began, half the 4th Raider Battalion landed at New Georgia's Segi Point. This group, known as the Eastern Landing Force, was responsible for clearing that portion of the island and destroying a Japanese strong point and a 140 mm coastal gun position at Viru Harbor. To gain the element of surprise, the Raiders trekked through swamp and jungle. Harry Clark describes the capture of Viru.

Something I will never forget is the dank stink, the rotting odor of a jungle on a dark night. You couldn't see diddly-do, but you could smell that thing. I have an active imagination, I admit it, but it was like it was brooding, waiting for us. We were told that we were going to go to a place called Viru Harbor.

To get there, we had to cross jungle and swamp. This was one of the thickest jungles on earth . . . vines, banyans, chest-deep water, insects were all over the place. We had to ford several rivers. It went on forever, and every step was a bitch. Roots as slimy as could be. Men had jungle rot on their feet.

At the edge of this swamp, there was a fifteen- or twenty-foot bank to get out and on dry ground. It was a nightmare. We used toggle ropes to scale it. Every now and then, somebody would lose it and fall back down into the swamp. Eventually we got out and the two companies split. One company hit another small village, and we hit Viru.

We took Viru Harbor. A lot of boom boom and bang bang . . . it was a blur. It was kind of bewildering to say the least. There's nothing orderly about modern combat. I'm sure you've been told that enough that you are about to vomit in your wastebasket. It's a blur of sound. The only thing you're whittled down to immediately is the base person you are. You know what you're supposed to be doing. [sigh] I shot this guy; thank God, he was Japanese and not American, or I would have made the biggest mistake in my military career. [sigh] Being a scout sniper, I'd been cautioned over and over to look for papers, look for documents, this, that, and the other thing. This [soldier] was about six feet, clean as a whistle. Most were starving to death and filthy and dirty. This guy was as clean as a whistle, and around his neck he had the most gorgeous miniature painting of himself in Shinto robes. I took his dog tags and papers he had in a side pocket and turned them over to military intelligence. They are the ones that told me his name, something that has haunted me for my entire life. They said, "This is a second lieutenant. They don't call them that, but he's like a lieutenant in their Special Landing Forces, their marines, and his name was Ryuki Yanigara." I'll tell you I cannot remember the names of so many people to whom I owe so much, but I remember his name. It's terrible to find out the name of somebody you killed. Later I was in Japan with the Dow Chemical Company, and I ran an article in the newspaper: "Anybody interested in knowing about Ryuki Yanigara, Special Landing Forces in WWII please contact Harry Clark at such and such a hotel." At my age I'm forgetting so many things, but the last thing I'll ever forget is Ryuki Yanigara.

DAVID VAN FLEET
4TH RAIDER BATTALION

On June 30, half of the 4th Raider Battalion (Companies N and Q) and the 2nd Battalion of the 103rd Infantry seized the Japanese barge base at the tiny village of Kaeruka on Wickham Anchorage. The small base was on Vangunu Island, located on the east side of New Georgia and in position to interdict Allied communication and transportation.

We were on an APD—a World War II destroyer converted for troop transport. The seas were so high that the water was coming over the deck, and it was raining pretty hard. The Higgins boats were bobbing up and down next to the destroyer. We had to jump into them. This friend of mine tried to jump into the Higgins boat, and his foot got caught between the destroyer and the Higgins boat, crushing it.

We finally landed, and it was mass confusion. At the time, we didn't know we landed farther down the bay, and I had to carry this man with a crushed foot. It was terrible. I walked him down the beach and reached the others, where they put him on another Higgins boat and they brought him back to the ship. We walked all the way across the island that at times was waist- and knee-deep with water. Mosquitoes were everywhere.

It was near dark when we got to the Japanese outpost. It was right on a river. As we approached it, they opened up with quite a few snipers and machine guns. There was a lot of activity. We secured the outpost. We bivouacked the river, and that night somebody told us to go down to the beach. We were pissed off because we were dug in. At about 2:00 A.M., the Japanese tried to land several metal barges on the beach. We started opening up on them, and we got them mostly with grenades. Bill Flake got shot, and the boy next to me was killed, and our first sergeant was hit; he was hit in the shoulder, the face . . . he got hit in three or four places.

The next morning, I went down to look at them, and surprisingly there was a chicken coop on one side of the barge. I thought this was odd. I don't think they knew we were there. There were over a hundred dead bodies at the barges. The grenades didn't make it a pretty sight. A few Japanese got into the water and tried to swim away. We started to walk back across the swamp to the other side of the island. I never could figure out why the ship never got us on that side of the island. I suppose it was because they were afraid the Japanese controlled the water over there.

We had several wounded and killed and I was told I was going to be a litter bearer. I had to carry Johnson, the first sergeant, who weighed over two hundred pounds, plum across the entire island and back through the swamp. I thought he was dead, but he was unconscious. He looked like hell with wounds in the face and shoulders. I was never more tired in my life. They brought the Higgins boats in and took us back to the ship.

JESSE BRADLEY
1ST RAIDER BATTALION

On July 5, the Northern Landing Group arrived at Rice Anchorage, located in the northern portion of New Georgia, as a lead element in the main invasion of the island. Once ashore, the 1st Raider Battalion crossed a jungle and swamp known as the Dragon's Peninsula to attack Enogai and Bairoko, the supply bases for the Japanese force in the southern portion of New Georgia.

We landed in the dead of night in what seemed to be the darkest day of the month; there was no moon. After the first boats went ashore, they came out and got our platoon. You couldn't see your hand in front of your face it was so dark. We actually used fluorescence that came off the plants in the jungle to mark the beach. Our mission was to knock out a battery of pretty good-sized guns. Some of them were in turrets. After we got on shore, we moved into the undergrowth. It was daybreak before we started out on the operation. We went down one or two trails that our advance people, with the help of the natives, cut through the jungle. To get to them, we had to go up and down the coral ridges through swamps filled with banyan trees; it was a pretty rough go. As an example, to get up and down the coral ridges, it was raining continually, and to climb the ridge you had to dig in with your fingernails to get to the top. Plus we crossed a river about three different times. On our way to our first objective, we ran into a couple of Japanese outposts, and we lost people during firefights.

We finally got to Enogai late one afternoon and set a perimeter up. We maintained that until daybreak the next day. That morning we assaulted the guns. I wasn't involved in the main attack. We went in after our first platoon helped spearhead the breakthrough and cleaned out the area where the guns were at. We came down on the left facing the sea to the north, and we ran into a defensive area where they had a couple of heavy machine guns plus an antiaircraft gun. We had a hell of a time taking that, and we lost a lot of men. In fact, I was wounded there in the process of trying to take out the antiaircraft gun. I came down through our battalion area where the battalion headquarters were at, and I saw a Johnson [light] machine gun lying on a pile of weapons. Generally when somebody gets knocked down, [fellow Raiders] pick up their weapons and bring it back to headquarters. I knew who the weapon belonged to— one of the sergeants from B Company—so I put my M-1 down and I picked up the Johnson plus the four mags [magazines] of ammo next to it, and I went down into where the four machine guns were at. We were close enough that I could see smoke coming up from the guns. Japanese heavy machine guns have an oiler system. The top of the receiver is where strips of ammo pass through them, and they clean the strips and oil it. As a result, they smoke like hell when they fire. So I aimed the Johnson light machine gun at the nest and pulled the trigger and "clack"! The gun had a broken firing pin. That stopped me from doing anything. The bolt rammed home on their machine gun, and they laid into us. There were four guys laying at my feet behind me, and they were hit, plus myself. We were all wounded. We threw in a couple of grenades, and they threw one back at us. We finally silenced all the guns. By that time it was getting dark, so we pulled back around the perimeter that we established near the big Jap guns.

HARRY CLARK
4TH RAIDER BATTALION

With Enogai secure, the Northern Landing Force turned its attention to Bairoko. The attack began on the morning of July 20, 1943, led by the 1st and 4th Raider Battalions. As the Raiders advanced on the heavy Japanese defenses, they were peppered by 90 mm mortar and automatic fire. The Raiders broke through the first series of strong points, only to be gored by the bastion's inner defenses. Harry Clark recalls that day.

I came upon a little opening in the jungle as we began our advance on Bairoko. Machine-gun and mortar fire seemed like it was coming from everywhere. Our sergeant major, who I secretly wished I looked like and was built like and he had a great brain to boot, not just a military brain, was possibly one of the first wounded. His jaw was completely shot away, blood all over the place, and he was obviously in hellish pain. He was still conscious, leaning up against a tree with a basic bandage put on him.

I fell, stumbled, leaped, crawled, and stumbled some more to get across this clear area. I saw a lot of our fellows were dead or wounded. As I was moving forward, I saw the body of a Japanese marine who had a tree limb impaled through his body. He had been blown on that tree spike. It went through his uniform and out the other side of his body. It was the grotesquerie, macabre of war. Eventually, I fell down next to a young guy about my age. I don't know his name. I swapped a cigarette with him. He looked over his left shoulder at me—I was at his right—and he said, "Shitty, isn't it?" I looked up and over and around; there was a lot of fire coming all around us. The leaves on the trees were being clipped by the machine-gun and rifle fire. I grabbed him by the arm and said, "Do you want to follow me, or do you want me to follow you?" I shook him and he never turned around to look at me, and I said, "Come on!" I rolled him over, and his brains were coming out of his mouth. This is something I have never spoken to anyone about.

OLIN GRAY
4TH RAIDER BATTALION

By the afternoon of July 20, the area around Bairoko resembled a slaughterhouse; nearly 250 Raiders had been killed or wounded. With no reserves, Colonel Harry Liversedge had no choice but to order a withdrawal. The next day, the Raiders made the long march across the Dragon's Peninsula to Enogai.

I'm not too crazy about talking about the war. When somebody gets decorated, it's because a lot of other men died. They don't hand them out because you were a good guy or whatever. If the rest of the men up there hadn't died, I would have walked out of there with nothing . . . which I would have much rather done.

We moved in further [toward Bairoko], and our machine-gun squad was held in reserve. There was a lot of action going on up in front of us. There wasn't much to see; it was pretty well overgrown jungle. Pretty soon the word came down for our squad to move up. So we moved on up to the front, and [an officer] was supposed to take our squad around the left flank and hopefully outmaneuver a couple of machine guns that had us pretty well pinned down. We'd gone maybe 100 yards, and all of the sudden we hit kind of an open area. We were going straight ahead, and

Raider casualties from Bairoko being evacuated in a PBY Catalina floatplane. (USMC)

we no more got in that open area when the machine guns cut loose on us. They sprayed us pretty much from the right and from twelve o'clock and ten o'clock. Corporal Bob Taylor was leading the squad. Number one gunner William Regan and Dale Massen were behind me, along with a runner. They killed the lieutenant and his runner and shot off Taylor's hand, part of his hand. He was an architect. That made it that much worse; it just ruined him for the rest of his life. They killed Regan behind him and missed me. Dale Massen was just a few steps behind me. He was just a big overgrown Iowa farmboy, just a wonderful kid, and he hollered, he said, "I'm hit!" There was a little spot of blood right in the middle of his chest. I didn't have time to stop. One of my friends was on stretcher detail, and he told me when he picked him up he was dead. He had a hole in his back you could put your hand in. [The Japanese] sometimes used wooden bullets. They would go in and splinter, and if they don't kill you, they have a hell of a time getting the splinters out. Whatever hit him must have gone crazy inside of him and busted everything.

I found myself alone with a machine gun in my hand and no tripod.

Raiders perform a jungle service honoring the fallen at Bairoko, August 1943. (USMC)

From the stories I've heard, I just went right up in the middle of God and everybody. I fired that damn thing 'til I was damn near out of ammunition. By that time, it was almost dark, and I just slipped back into the edge of the jungle. It was dusk when all the firing stopped.

I had two thousand rounds of ammunition when I went in, and I had about one hundred when I was finished. I was credited with taking out two nests. You fire where you think it's coming from. When they quiet down, you know you've done your job. I remember reaching over and the gun was so hot from all the rounds that went through it.

I spent the night up there by myself shaking like a leaf. The next morning, I made my way back to the main line, a hundred yards or whatever. They said, "Gray, you bring up the rear." I thought to myself, "What have I done now?" and we pulled back to Enogai.

I think about those other fellows a whole lot. I made myself promise if I ever went to Iowa, I would stop and look up Dale Massen's family and pay my respects. Three years ago, I did. I talked to his brother. For some reason, they never asked for his body to be retrieved, and I never understood that because I wanted to visit his grave. He was more than a good friend. He was such a great person that always had a smile on his face. I also received a letter from a lady who was going to marry the lieutenant after the war. I told her how he died that day.

GEORGE FRENCH
4TH RAIDER BATTALION

George French relives the bloody attack on Bairoko and the long withdrawal to Enogai.

When we landed, there were dead Japanese on the coral rocks. We weren't able to bury them, so we just covered them with brush and threw a shelter half over them. But during the night, the land crabs would eat the dead. That smell, the smell of death, is something you'll never forget.

More bullets in the air than you can possibly imagine. They just had too many . . . too much. They kept throwing 90 mm mortars at us. You could see the 90 mms hitting the trees. It was absolute murder. Men were dropping all around us. I don't know how many I helped carry out of there. We had so many. I lost four or five close friends, maybe more. I put one on a PBY [seaplane] and he got shot down five minutes later.

I had to bury one man myself. We had a spot that was soft enough to dig. The doctor told us to bury him. The situation was different. Ordinarily you'd be all shaken up. It had to be done so it didn't bother you so much. I didn't know the man I buried, but he had a nice ring on him and I was going to take the ring off him and send it to his parents. It [the battle] wasn't over, and I was afraid the Japanese would end up with it [if I were captured or killed], so I just left it on him. I thought about telling his parents what happened, but I never did. After the war, I managed to dispose of those feelings—maybe because I'm a little older than the rest of the fellows. I'm ninety right now. A few years ago [Army Central Identification Laboratory] found him when they were looking for the remains of our men.

I remember we had to carry a lot of the wounded back after dark, and that was terrible. It was so black you couldn't see anything. The communication guys ran a wire, and we used that to feel where we were going. We kind of spread out as we moved back. The dead and wounded were all over the place. I brought back three or four.[7] We put them on makeshift stretchers made from ponchos and tree limbs. The blood poured into the ponchos and leaked on the jungle floor. That added to the smell. That smell of blood is horrible. Blood and smoke mixed together, you never forget it.

HARRY CLARK
4TH RAIDER BATTALION

After the failed attack on Bairoko, the 1st and 4th Raiders moved to Enogai, where they remained in defensive positions for the rest of July. Harry Clark recalls their plight.

When we got back to Enogai, we were always hungry. We had airdrops that dropped blood plasma and cigarettes. Thank God for the cigarettes. [laughs] PT boats tried to drop off food, but that never worked that well. They had a hard time getting through because they were sunk by fast Japanese destroyers. There was one that did get through with the unusual assortment of supplies and two letters. One letter was addressed to Colonel Currin and the other was to Harry Clark. That was a mistake of course, because my letter was stuck to the back of his. However, for those of us that were left, I was very popular because the letter was from Patricia, an ex–girl friend from high school. Everybody owned that letter. It may have been written to me, but it was to everybody because it was from the real world—a female from the real world. So around the campfire, I was given a small flashlight, and I read it out loud. I almost died.

I'll close this out by telling you I had dozens of ulcers on each leg, and they went right down to the bone. Our medic used to keep us going by putting cotton on a pencil and putting it down and taking the pus out. We were all ill from every illness you can get from the jungle. I weighed ninety-seven pounds. Eventually we went back to Guadalcanal, and I was later admitted to a hospital on Espíritu Santo.

MIKE VINICH
2ND PARACHUTE BATTALION

After the Raiders' failed attempt to take Bairoko, the Japanese realized that the garrison's days were numbered. By the time Halsey's Southern Group punched north and overran Bairoko, the Japanese had withdrawn most of their troops. With New Georgia secure, Halsey continued driving north. The northernmost island of the Solomons, mountainous, heavily defended Bougainville, was the next major objective. To confuse the Japanese on where the Allies would strike next, Victor Krulak's 2nd Parachute Battalion was given the mission of executing a diversionary attack on nearby Choiseul Island.

There was only about six hundred of us; it was kind of a suicide mission to draw the Japanese attention away from the landings at Bougainville.

Our squad nearly got trapped on the island. It was a strange thing. If everything went wrong, we were supposed to assemble at Nukiki Village. We were guarding the radio that was used by the XO [executive officer] of the battalion. We went through a torrential rain, and it drowned our radio out and we didn't have any communication. So the order was to head for Nukiki. That night we stumped it on to Nukiki on this well-used trail. When we got to Nukiki, our sergeant said, "Form a perimeter." I looked up at the skyline, and I saw these jagged rocks, coral rocks, and moved into the rocks so I wouldn't be seen.

I got up into the rocks, and all night long, I don't know how many [Japanese] barges landed in that vicinity. There were about nine of us in these rocks about twenty yards from this landing area. In the morning, I looked across the inlet, and there were all kinds of Japanese over there. Pretty soon, we saw two LCP(R)s [landing craft] appear in the inlet. I was the only one in the squad who knew semaphore [use of flags to signal ships]. I went out on the rocks as far as I could and I started signaling, *Urgent! Come get us! Urgent, come get us!* I guess the Japanese thought I was one of them because no one shot at me. One of the boats peeled off and came right straight toward us. As the squad was wading out in waist-deep water and scrambling aboard the boat, Sergeant Tom Siefke and Private First Class James Moe turned around and opened fire on the Japanese. We all climbed into the boat. They turned their guns on the Japs over there, and they picked off several of them. The boat took us back to our base camp. Down there part of our platoon boarded a PT boat, which was commanded by John F. Kennedy, after one of the LCP(R)s hit a reef and started sinking. There was a kid by the name of Schell who was dying that Kennedy put in his bunk. He got shot through the midsection. Schell later died on the boat. Eventually, we made it back to Vella Lavella.[8]

JOSEPH McNAMARA
3RD RAIDER BATTALION

On November 1, 1943, the 2nd and 3rd Raider Battalions along with elements of the 3rd Marine Division helped seize a beachhead along Torokina Bay in the main assault on Bougainville. Heavy surf swamped scores of landing craft. Japanese resistance was strongest in the southern beaches that the Raiders attacked. The 3rd Raider Battalion (less M Company) was tasked with the separate mission of seizing Puruata Island, located just off the beachhead. Once Puruata was cleared, the Raiders were attached to the 3rd Marine Division and moved inland. Joseph McNamara recalls the battle for Puruata.

It was a terrible place, the worst place I'd ever been on. The conditions— the jungle and the rain and the insects and the stuff you pick up. It rained every day.

We landed on an island, Puruata. The 3rd platoon was on the right flank, and actually we bore the brunt of what was on there. There were three pillboxes there; I never saw them they were so camouflaged. They were in a triangular shape so that they covered each other. In the afternoon we brought in two half-tracks [75 mm self-propelled guns], and they knocked those out. The guys on the guns in the half-track were both killed. We hadn't learned to work with the tanks or half-tracks. The half-tracks were out in front of us about thirty to forty yards, and we actually went up with them to cover them.

I had two close shots on me. I had my pack on, and the bullet went through my bedroll. When I took my poncho off that night, about every four inches there was a hole—and this was on my back. Then there was another one where I had crossed an open area and got behind a coconut tree. I decided I better look around and see where I was because the platoon had gone off and left another guy and I. We had caught up with them, so I raised my head up and looked around the coconut tree, and the instant I raised my head to the right, a shot rang out. I firmly believe if I hadn't moved at that time it would have gone right through my helmet. The bullet barely shaved the coconut tree, and it sent off slivers that hit my throat and I thought I was shot. I was perspiring heavily and called to my platoon sergeant who was off to my right, "Red, I think I'm hit!" He said, "Just stay there, Mac." He got up and took off, and I thought, "Son of a gun." After a while I'm feeling this juice running down me and I thought, "Well, I better see what the heck is wrong." I finally inched my arm up, and it was just perspiration. The bullet did go through. I had a K-BAR hunting knife attached to my pack, and it shot the handle off of it.

Finally, I got lined up with the skirmish line they had a little distance away. We're facing where we think everybody is. I'm lying there waiting, and there was a 1st lieutenant—I can't think of his name—he was out in front of us about thirty yards with some other guy. Finally he turns around and shouts back at us, "I want a BAR man up here!" Well, I looked to my left and right, and nobody's jumping up, and I thought, "Well, I better get my ass up there before somebody starts screaming at me." So I got up there to where he was, and I was just standing there and he starts pointing out these different coconut trees he wants me to shoot at the tops of. We're standing there, and he is looking at me when all of the sudden a shot rang out. It sounded like it was an explosion in front of

Raider light-machine-gun team in a water-filled foxhole,
typical of the miserable conditions on Bougainville. (courtesy of Frank Cannistraci)

us. We both hit the ground, and then we got up and he says, "Are you hit, Mac?" I said, "No." He looked at me and said, "Are you sure you're not hit?" And I said, "No, I'm okay." "All right, then. Clear those coconut trees." I stood there and shot at about three coconut trees. That was actually all the firing I did on Bougainville.

In the meantime, as I said before, we bore the brunt of all this. We had several guys killed, and we had about twelve or sixteen guys wounded, little wounds—hands, arms, this and that. Finally those half-tracks came up in the afternoon, and they knocked everything out.

That night we were facing the water on the other side there. We were digging in, and on the other side of us was the 1st platoon. Each group was 15 or 20 yards apart with their backs to each other. Well, somebody got up to take a leak, and one of the sergeants [from the other side] saw the guy standing up and shot him with a Thompson submachine gun. Then the corpsman got up to help the guy, and the [same] guy shot him. They were both killed. The sergeant was later killed on Okinawa.

FRANK FITZ
3RD RAIDER BATTALION

Frank Fitz reveals his most vivid memory of Bougainville. For his actions, Fitz was recommended for the Navy Cross.

My squad had the point. Edward J. Sinning was on the flank and without knowing it walked about ten to fifteen feet in front of a Japanese position. There was a platoon of Japs there, and he got hit near them. Corporal Wheeler tried to get him out first, and he was killed. They fragged him with grenades. Next, a private was killed trying to get him out. I was the new man in the company and didn't know people that well. As Sinning called out, I saw these three Japs come out with bayonets, and I sort of lost it. Instead of shooting them, I charged them, shot from the hip [with a BAR], and killed them. I got my arm under [Sinning's] and grabbed him by his pack. I was firing wildly all over the place, but this kept their heads down. I got to a depression. I was telling my wife the other day, I can still remember vividly a strange bug crawling in the grass while all of this was going on. Why this is frozen in my mind, I don't know. I started to fire back, and this stopped some of their fire. How many I hit, I don't know. I

Raiders capture the strain of battle during a lull in the fighting on November 1, 1943. (USMC)

know I remember hearing them scream when they got hit and then the firing stopped. Then all of the sudden, a grenade landed between Sinning and myself. It got my hand, and my thumb was dangling. They hit Sinning again and took part of his jaw off, and I couldn't stop the blood. I had this little first-aid kit and tied it around his face. It was just turning red and blood was dripping all over. I said, "I can't carry you and my weapon too. I can't use my left hand. If you want me to stay with you and whatever happens . . . happens. If you want me to take a chance, I'll leave you alone a few minutes." I can remember saying that just as clear as I remember talking to you. It stays with you until the end. [chokes up] "If you want me to get help, I need somebody else. I can't do it by myself." I said, "Blink your eyes if you understand." He blinked so I said, "Blink your eyes if you want me to go get help." And he blinked again. I ran out, and the first guy I ran into was Wheeler, and he was dead. I saw many other Marines wounded. I got to Charlie Biddle, and I said, "I need help. I think I can get Sinning out of there." And he said, "Lead the way, kiddo." So we ran back to him. I threw the BAR over my head and let it hang down and got Sinning with this hand [the hand that wasn't wounded] and Biddle got his other arm and we ran like hell with him out of there. We got back and one fellow said, "You crazy SOB. When you went back with Biddle, following you were tracers going right behind your head. I figured they were going to blow your head off." *

I was written up for the Navy Cross, and years later Colonel "Stormy" Sexton asked if I ever received the Cross and I said no. I was out, I was alive and happy, and I had a family. He recommended it again and sent it in, and they knocked it down to a Bronze Star. I said, "Why?" They said, "It was a routine thing, and you had to go get help." They asked, "Why did you get help?" I said, "Because I was wounded." They didn't know I was wounded. It wasn't in the report, so they resubmitted it for the Navy Cross but they already issued the Bronze Star and let it go at that.

CHARLES MEACHAM
3RD RAIDER BATTALION

Charles Meacham remembers that the fight on Bougainville was as much with the environment as it was with the enemy.

Mud, mud, mud, and more mud. The swamp and mud were knee deep at times. On occasion when we were quote "sleeping" at night, sometimes we'd have to hold our buddy's head up in our lap as he slept because you were floating in mud and water. When it came your time to sleep, he'd hold your head up. The foxholes were totally filled with water. There were

---

* Edward Sinning survived the attack.

bugs and critters, but you didn't pay much attention to them. We conducted a raid and lots of patrols. The main thing was to stay alive. When we finally left Bougainville, the skin on my feet was peeling off. You could literally pull pieces of your foot off. I wasn't the only one. We were all in very bad physical shape when they finally moved us off that island.

KEN O'DONNELL
4TH RAIDER BATTALION

In early 1944, the Marine Raiders and paratroopers were unceremoniously disbanded. Most Raiders went to the 4th Marine Regiment, and the majority of Marine paratroopers would form the core of the 5th Marine Division. Ken O'Donnell remembers the day they were disbanded.

They brought us out into company formation and told us that we would be disbanded. We were all disappointed. It was really something to be a Raider. It was not a welcome thing, but they took the sting out of it by telling us that the Raiders would be given the honor of re-forming the 4th Marines.

We were a cocky group. For the most part, the rest of the Marine Corps resented the Raiders. They felt you don't need an elite force within an elite force. Some of the better battalion commanders during the war echoed these sentiments. The general making the announcement closed by saying, "Welcome back to the real Marine Corps."

CHAPTER FOUR

Burma:
Merrill's Marauders

With the blood-stained flag of the rising Sun,
I'd like to unify the world.
As I urinate at the great Walls of China,
A rainbow rises above the great Gobi Desert . . .
Now we are in Chicago, once terrorized by gangsters,
Where our grandchildren pay homage
to our Memorial Monument.

— "WORLD CONQUEST" BY KIROSHI SHIMOSAKA,
A JAPANESE SOLDIER KILLED NEAR NHPUM GA

THE CHINA-BURMA-INDIA (CBI) THEATER was a backwater. Of all the World War II areas of operation, it received the fewest ground troops and the least matériel. Today, the CBI's overgrown jungle battlefields are little changed and are largely forgotten—except by the men who fought there.

By 1943, most of China's ports, major cities, and farmlands were under Japanese control. The rest of the country was divided between the Nationalists and the Communists, and the Nationalist-controlled areas were divided further among warlords. Nevertheless, China's soldiers tied down a significant portion of the Japanese army. Allied strategy in China boiled down to feeding China enough Lend-Lease matériel to keep the country afloat until Japan could be defeated.[1] A key element to these plans was a campaign in northern Burma to reopen China's last overland link with the outside world: the Burma Road.[2] To connect the Burma Road with India, the Ledo Road would have to be built.[3] Once completed, the highway would be capable of carrying supplies to help augment China's armies.[4]

After the Allies were driven out of Burma in 1942 by the advancing Japanese army, the British took the offensive in western Burma, below the Indian border. Lack of resources, rugged terrain, and a strong Japanese presence doomed their attack, making the British and Chinese leery of further offensive actions. Burma and the road, however, would remain a constant preoccupation with American theater commander Lieutenant General Joseph "Vinegar Joe" Stilwell.

Interest in Burma was revived in February 1943 when an eccentric brigadier named Orde Wingate launched a raid deep behind Japanese lines. Wingate's force, known as the Chindits, a nickname drawn from the winged stone lions that guarded Burma's temples, conducted hit-and-run attacks on Japanese bridges and communications for three months. The raids were hardly a masterstroke, but Winston Churchill hailed them as a success and even brought the articulate Wingate to the Quebec Conference in August 1943. Swayed by Wingate's arguments, the U.S. Joint Chiefs of Staff approved a long-delayed offensive into northern Burma. General George Marshall agreed to supply Wingate with a special U.S. raiding force.[5]

The American force that emerged for the job was called Galahad, or the 5307th Composite Unit (Provisional). Determined that the 5307th would not serve under Wingate or any other British officer, General Stilwell prevailed on Lord Louis Mountbatten, the chief of the newly formed Southeast Asia Command, to place Galahad under his command. It was the beginning of a relationship that would produce one of the worst cases of troop neglect in U.S. Army history.

The 5307th sounded more like a street address than a special raiding force, and the men quickly took to the name given to them by the press: Merrill's Marauders, after their new commander, Brigadier General Frank D. Merrill. The Marauders made their combat debut in February

1944, advancing ahead of Stilwell's Chinese 22nd and 38th Divisions and the 1st Provisional Tank Group. Screening the Marauders' movements were native mountain tribesmen known as Kachins, who were organized under OSS (Office of Strategic Services) Detachment 101. The Marauders pushed through the punishing jungle and enveloped the right flank of the elite Japanese 18th Division at the small town of Walawbum.[6] The Japanese launched several furious counterattacks on the Marauder roadblocks. Using only mortars and small arms, Galahad inflicted several hundred casualties before the 18th slipped away into the jungle.

Stilwell resumed the offensive on March 12, 1944, with Galahad acting as the spearhead for Stilwell's Chinese troops. Negotiating steep slopes and hacking through dense underbrush, the Marauders again established roadblocks to stop the Japanese as they tried to retreat south. On an isolated ridgeline known as Nhpum Ga, the Marauders' 2nd Battalion set up defensive positions hoping to outflank the Japanese. Instead, the Japanese quickly surrounded the battalion, shelled it, and launched a series of attacks against the besieged Marauders. The situation became desperate. The Japanese attacks grew in intensity, water ran out, and the stench of rotting mule carcasses filled the air. The 2nd held out for over ten days until Galahad's 1st and 3rd Battalions broke through Japanese lines and relieved it on April 9.

The long marches, battles at Walawbum and Nhpum Ga, and numerous other skirmishes reduced Galahad from its original strength of around three thousand to about fourteen hundred exhausted men. They anticipated a lengthy rest; instead, Stilwell ordered the Marauders to seize a key airfield at the strategic town of Myitkyina, which served as the main rail and road terminus for northern Burma.

With orders in hand, the remaining Marauders, two Chinese regiments, and some elements of OSS Detachment 101 began a grueling sixty-five-mile march over the 6,000-foot sawtooth Kumon mountain range. Mud made the trails treacherous, and smothering heat, disease, and clashes with the Japanese further thinned the ranks. The men were stretched to the limits of their endurance, but Stilwell's promise that they would be relieved after the capture of Myitkyina kept them going.[7]

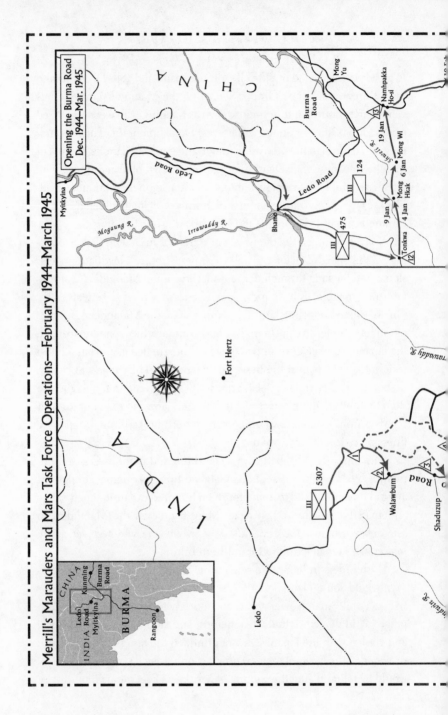

Merrill's Marauders and Mars Task Force Operations—February 1944–March 1945

Opening the Burma Road
Dec. 1944–Mar. 1945

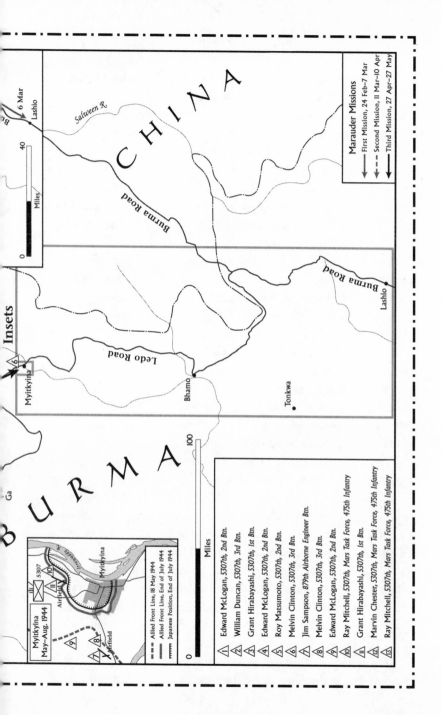

CHINA

BURMA

Ga

Lashio • 6 Mar

Salween R.

Burma Road

Ledo Road

Burma Road

Bhamo •

Tonkwa •

Lashio •

Insets

Myitkyina

6

Miles
0   40

Miles
0   100

Marauder Missions
→ First Mission, 24 Feb–7 Mar
⇢ Second Mission, 11 Mar–10 Apr
→ Third Mission, 27 Apr–27 May

Myitkyina
May–Aug. 1944

III 5307
II
II
Airfield
Myitkyina
Irrawaddy R.
5307
9
8
Airfield

--- Allied Front Line, 18 May 1944
— Allied Front Line, End of July 1944
~~~ Japanese Position, End of July 1944

△ Edward McLogan, 5307th, 2nd Btn.
△ William Duncan, 5307th, 3rd Btn.
△ Grant Hirabayashi, 5307th, 1st Btn.
△ Edward McLogan, 5307th, 2nd Btn.
△ Roy Matsumoto, 5307th, 2nd Btn.
△ Melvin Clinton, 5307th, 3rd Btn.
△ Jim Sampson, 879th Airborne Engineer Btn.
⑧ Melvin Clinton, 5307th, 3rd Btn.
△ Edward McLogan, 5307th, 2nd Btn.
△ Ray Mitchell, 5307th, Mars Task Force, 475th Infantry
△ Grant Hirabayashi, 5307th, 1st Btn.
△ Marvin Chester, 5307th, Mars Task Force, 475th Infantry
△ Ray Mitchell, 5307th, Mars Task Force, 475th Infantry

Despite the obstacles, the Marauders and a Chinese regiment surprised the Japanese and captured the airfield on May 17. The poorly trained Chinese troops probed the town but turned back in confusion after getting into a firefight with each other. Meanwhile, more Chinese troops were flown into Myitkyina to reinforce the airfield.[8] The Japanese, however, soon recovered from the initial shock of losing the airfield and also rushed more troops into the town. The Chinese launched several uncoordinated, piecemeal attacks on the town but were repulsed each time. Heavy monsoon rains stalemated the situation. Myitkyina became a city under siege.

By the end of May, the Marauders were losing seventy-five to one hundred men every day to malaria, dysentery, and scrub typhus.[9] Marauders cut holes in the seats of their pants so that dysentery would not interrupt their firing of their weapons. British and the Chinese troops were also pressed into the line. Stilwell was in an awkward position politically: if he relieved the Marauders, he could be accused of favoritism. So the men fought on, with the sick and wounded who could still walk pressed into service. Engineers and service personnel who had not fired a rifle since basic training were flown into Myitkyina airfield and put on the line. Morale plummeted. After the war, congressional hearings were held to investigate the Army's poor handling of the men.[10]

Yet the men continued to fight on. By June, the Allies had tightened their grip on Myitkyina, and on June 8 the Marauders cut a main supply route into the city. Harassment by the Marauders and Detachment 101, as well as pressure from the other Allied units, forced the Japanese to slowly withdraw from the besieged town. On August 3, 1944, the Chinese 50th Division made the final assault, securing Myitkyina later that day.

The few original Marauders left to see the city fall were cobbled together with replacement troops and formed into the 475th Infantry Regiment. Combined with the 124th Cavalry Regiment and support units, the new unit was designated the 5332nd Brigade (Provisional) and dubbed Mars Task Force.

The Allied offensive in Burma resumed on October 15. Pushing on multiple fronts, the Allies drove the Japanese back. Mars, with several

Chinese divisions, advanced south, toward the Burma Road. In December, the 475th held against repeated assaults from the Japanese 18th Division at Tonkwa, forcing it to withdraw farther south. After making a grueling march through cloud-topped mountains, the "Marsmen" outflanked the Japanese and took up positions along high ground over the Burma Road. From here, they controlled the road with artillery and patrols, threatening the Japanese line of retreat. This, combined with Chinese divisions that attacked from the north, and thousands of Kachins organized under Detachment 101 that operated behind the lines, forced the Japanese to withdraw toward Lashio. On January 28, overland supply with China was reestablished when the first Allied convoy rolled from Ledo to Kunming. With the Burma Road open, Mars Task Force was disbanded in July 1945.[11]

The capture of Myitkyina and the reopening of the Burma Road made an expansion of the supply effort for China possible. But by January 1945, only eight months remained until Japan surrendered. After the near collapse of its armies in 1944, China's continued contribution to the defeat of Japan was limited. Thus, the reopening of the Burma Road had little effect on the eventual outcome of the war. What should not be forgotten is the courage and sacrifice of a few thousand Americans who accomplished so much when they were given so little.

EDWARD McLOGAN
5307TH COMPOSITE UNIT, 2ND BATTALION

In February 1944, the men of the 5307th began their first mission, moving through the Hukawng Valley, important because the Ledo Road would have to cross it to reach the main rail, road, and air terminus of northern Burma, Myitkyina. Two regiments from the elite Japanese 18th Division held the valley. Pushing through dense jungle, the Marauders hoped to trap the Japanese by hitting the town of Walawbum from the rear while several Chinese regiments advanced from the north. Ed McLogan remembers a day on the march to Walawbum.

We'd wake up at the first hint of dawn after spending the night in two-man foxholes. You were laying flat on your back, and the light would stream through the jungle canopy. You'd get right up and put on your helmet and boots, sprinkle a little water in your hand and splash it on your face, and you were ready for another day.

I remember watching the steam from my urine wafting up from the jungle floor and saying to myself, "What the hell am I doing in the middle of Burma? A nice guy like me."

Breakfast was the same every day: K rations. After putting on an ammo belt, rifle, helmet, pack, and canteen, you were carrying more than 60 pounds.

Next we'd take a quick check of the mules and start walking fifty minutes and stop for ten minutes. At the time, I was twenty-two or twenty-three years old and very healthy, but you might have a recurrence of malaria. Many men had diarrhea. We lost weight. I lost about twenty-five pounds. But we pushed forward.

WILLIAM DUNCAN
5307TH COMPOSITE UNIT, 3RD BATTALION

After marching through the Burma jungle, the Marauders set up roadblocks at the small town of Walawbum, and the Japanese furiously counterattacked. William Duncan recalls the battle.

We had a few skirmishes going down the trail to Walawbum. When we got there, we ran into a bunch of Japs in the village. My lead scout looked around and saw a guy about to shoot. He fired and got him, but the guy shot me right through the side. The bullet went between the skin and the fat. The doctor fixed it up, and I went back down with the platoon.

We dug in along the bend in the river on some high ground. The Japs came out of the tall grass. There were hundreds of them, like something out of the Civil War. They came in on us in massive waves yelling and screaming "Banzai!" They had bayonets and swords and machine-gun crews. Bodies were piling up by the river's edge from our fire.

We killed hundreds of them before they broke it off. That night, we went down toward the lower part of the hill, and we heard them coming in on trucks, so we were ordered to get out of there. As we circled around to get out of there, the area had been booby-trapped, and we had some of our own men injured by our own traps. The next day we pushed forward.

GRANT HIRABAYASHI
5307TH COMPOSITE UNIT, 1ST BATTALION

Resuming the offensive, the Marauders again tried to trap the Japanese. Grant Hirabayashi, one of the Marauders' Japanese American interpreters, recalls the 1st Battalion's actions around Shaduzup and the long march to Nhpum Ga. His recollections begin with a trip to visit his family, who, like many other Japanese Americans, were locked in an American internment camp. They were at Tule Lake; Hirabayashi was already in the military on this visit.

When I first approached Tule Lake, I was shocked you could see rows and rows of the tarpaper barracks behind barbed wire. I looked up and saw a sentry on a watchtower with a machine gun facing inward. That was quite a shock. Soldiers took me halfway to the barracks where my parents were assigned. My parents were waiting. We smiled, but inside we were crying. I was quite devastated. They were deprived of their comfortable home and their life and were placed behind machine guns and barbed wire. It was very difficult. [sigh]

My stay was brief, and when I got on the train to go back, I was in deep thought. I said to myself, "I'm in uniform and I have my freedom, yet my family is behind barbed wire. Their only crime is they look like the enemy and were of Japanese descent." I was quite confused as the train left the station. Here I am fighting for peace and freedom, and I found my parents and siblings behind barbed wire. While I was in deep thought, I heard someone call out, "Corporal." It was the conductor. He tipped his hat and said, "Can I see your ticket, please?" He was very courteous and seemed to genuinely respect my uniform. It had a kind of soothing effect to know that there was someone out there that paid re-

Marauders crossing a bamboo bridge. (U.S. Army)

spect to my uniform and me. It changed me. It made me realize I was a soldier and I had a mission to fight the enemy. I thought my loyalty to this country was being questioned. I also thought that perhaps I had to prove myself. After six months of intelligence school, I volunteered for the Marauders.

My most vivid memory of combat was the evening that we got to Shaduzup and were being bombarded by Japanese artillery. I was in a foxhole, and there is nothing you can do but count the number of artillery shells that pass over the hole. The fifth shell is the one that landed so close that it shook the ground. The dirt in my foxhole went down my spine. I said to myself, "I had it." I said my last prayer. Fortunately I survived.

The following morning, the 1st Battalion divided into two columns—

one White and one Red. I was with the Red column. The White column crossed the river and caught the enemy by surprise at dawn. [White] came across a Japanese telephone wire and tapped the line. We were ordered to cross the river to join them. The water was chin high. I had my gun in the air and a heavy pack. In midstream a sniper took three shots — *choo . . . choo . . . choo.* Somehow I made it across safely. The unit covering us aimed at the sniper in the tree. The firepower was so strong — a lot of automatic weapons — it cut the tree down. I got to the phone line, but it was dead.

From there we had to make a forced march to Nhpum Ga. Since India, every time I ate, my whole body broke out with hives. My lips were swollen. Back in India, I had realized I was allergic to the K rations on my first training maneuvers when I suffered a fractured elbow. I had my arm in a sling and ended up in the aid station. The battalion medical officer said, "You are unfit for front-line duty." I pleaded with him. I spent six months training at the Military Intelligence School and long-range penetration training. He said, "Well, you have to face the consequences if you want to go." I said I was ready to do so.

Every day was a daily struggle for survival. I had amebic dysentery and the allergic reaction to the food. I remember thinking, "Should I eat? If I eat, I'll have to go [defecate], and I'll have to catch up with the column and miss the ten-minute break." I was so weak that the medical officer took my pack and put it on a mule, but it suffered a shrapnel wound so it had to be destroyed. So it went on another mule. It was the longest five minutes of my life. The mule had my pack, and it collapsed, and when the ten-minute break was up, the men started walking and disappeared. I knew in my condition I was not able to take the pack and double time with everybody. The mule skinner cursed up and down and said, "Damn it, you volunteered, too!" He made a desperate pull, and the animal got to its feet. It saved my life, so to speak. I followed the mule and had to hang on to its tail. You're so weak but you had to hold on. We were also fighting the enemy the whole time. I made it to Nhpum Ga and was evacuated in a small plane, an L-5 [comparable to a Piper Cub].

EDWARD McLOGAN
5307TH COMPOSITE UNIT, 2ND BATTALION

As the Japanese retreated, Stilwell pursued, using the Marauders as a spearhead for his Chinese divisions. More roadblocks were established, but each time the Japanese managed to slip away south toward Myitkyina. Finally, on an isolated ridgeline known as Nhpum Ga, the Marauders' 2nd Battalion set up defensive positions hoping to trap the retreating Japanese once again. Instead, the Japanese quickly surrounded the battalion. Ed McLogan recalls the fourteen-day battle at Nhpum Ga.

We had just hit the trail when their shelling began. We hadn't experienced artillery or anything like that in the past. I was more than frightened, carrying the wounded and knowing we had to go farther on an open trail.

It was probably 10:00 when we got into the village of Nhpum Ga and Merrill was there. He and McGee [Colonel McGee, battalion commander] laid out a defensive perimeter for us. Later that night, the Japanese hit the southern part of our perimeter. We were dug in our foxholes on the north end, which was a bare hill. We sent out patrols to make contact with our other battalions. It was day three that we were surrounded by a Japanese regiment. It turned out to be about 3,000 men. Our strength was about 700, down from about 850.

Every day they made attacks or probes. The mules were tethered in small defoliates here and there. And each morning we'd experience artillery. We'd hear a "plunk," and the animals would fall over after they were hit. We were in foxholes; they weren't. After about three or four days, the odor was just unbelievable. In addition, there were dead Japanese bodies. The odor was so intense you had to breathe through your mouth instead of your nose. It was the odor of death and rot . . . rotting animals and bodies. I remember not being able to eat, it was so intense. The water hole was contaminated. We had to get our water from swampy areas before the water drop. There was never enough water.

That night I could hear this rumbling. It was like a theater was letting out. They were mumbling a couple hundred feet from the hill. It kept on and on. I told McGee, and he said, "Send Matsumoto down there."

Staff Sergeant Roy Matsumoto, hero of Nhpum Ga. (U.S. Army)

Roy Matsumoto listened but couldn't understand anything, so he handed me his ammo belt and carbine and said, "I'm going to crawl out there." It was maybe 10:00 at night. We figured out a password and off he went. I guess maybe he was gone twenty to thirty minutes and said, "You're not going to like what I'm going to tell ya. They're going to concentrate and attack this portion of the hill."

I got McGee on the radio. He said, "Keep Matsumoto with you and vacate your foxholes, booby-trap them, and move back on the hill 100 feet or so and dig in. That will give you a better field of fire." In the morning we heard whispering first. We could sense they were gathering, and then they were yelling and screaming at the top of their lungs and running forward.

More than half of the platoon was on top of the hill. We had a dozen foxholes. We held our fire, and they started coming. They never quite reached the line. There were a couple of Japanese officers, and they retreated back down the hill and all was quiet. I guess maybe a few minutes went by, and then they launched a second charge, and this time they jumped into our foxholes. I'm not sure if any of the booby traps made a difference. That's when Matsumoto called out to them *Charge! Charge!* in Japanese, and we mowed them down again. Then Colonel McGee came up to tell us what a good job we had done. The Japanese opened up with small-arms fire of such magnitude that I had never believed was possible. There couldn't have been millions, but it seemed like millions of bullets. We jumped in our foxholes. The bullets sounded like a Chinese New Year. They were popping and cracking when they'd go right over your head. You could see them literally hitting the trees and bushes. There was a twig the size of my thumb right in front of me, and it just disappeared when a bullet hit it.

The next day was Easter Sunday, and we were told that they were gone and the 3rd Battalion had fought their way into us. What a joy that was. Then we disposed of the dead. We put lime on the dead bodies, and the flame throwers burned the bodies as best they could. We gathered up the wounded. We had a lot of men wounded and killed.

ROY MATSUMOTO

5307TH COMPOSITE UNIT, 2ND BATTALION

Matsumoto recalls his role during the battle of Nhpum Ga.

I volunteered in the Marauders, like the rest of them. We didn't know where we were going, but they told us it would be a dangerous and hazardous mission. We expected an 85 percent casualty rate.

I was born in Los Angeles. My father was born in the old country. I was a second-generation American, yet they classified me as an enemy alien, 4C. I'm not an enemy . . . I'm an American citizen. That's what made me so mad. I tried to get out of the [internment] camp so bad, any way possible. It was in Jerome, Arkansas. Fortunately, a recruiter came around and asked us to serve the country, so I volunteered to get out of camp. At the time I was so mad I didn't know what to do.

Around the first week of April, we'd been surrounded. The trail was sealed. In the meantime, we got our food and ammunition from airdrops. The waterhole changed hands several times. Finally we couldn't get any more water since they [the Japanese] occupied it. Every day we were getting bursts from mortars and were under small-arms fire. The Japanese would attack our position daily. There was not a place to bury the dead. Their stomachs were so swollen, juice and maggots would ooze out from the dead Japanese. And the stench!

Something was going on in McLogan's sector, so I was sent there by Colonel McGee. I couldn't figure out what was going on because there was too much noise. I was ordered to go to this area where they were hearing noise like a theater letting out.

Nobody understood all these people talking, so I went out there. I took my field jacket, pistol belt and carbine, and helmet off and left them there. I went down there to find out what they were saying. I crawled down the side [of the hill]. It was in the evening, total darkness. I got to their position and listened. I found out that the following morning at dawn, they were going to attack McLogan's sector. I reported this to McLogan. They thought they got us, but it turned out the other way. When they attacked at dawn, they were charging and yelling and everything: "Death to Americans! Die! Banzai!" They got no response because we were not there. [laughs]

They came further up the hill, and we opened up. They tried to retreat, so I issued an order to countermand that order that said to charge. I told them to charge in Japanese. Then they jumped into the foxholes, which were booby-trapped. Grenades go off and we're throwing hand grenades after that and firing. The dead were scattered all over.

There was a certain dialect from this area of Japan. My folks came from Hiroshima so we had this Hiroshima dialect. The people that were attacking came from the 18th Division. I learned their dialect because twice a week when I was younger, I was a delivery boy. I delivered groceries in the United States, but the people I delivered to came from the same prefect as the men from the 18th Division. When they heard my voice in their dialect, they charged. According to many of the men, I saved six hundred lives twice—once at Walawbum and then at Nhpum Ga. That's why the people of the 2nd Battalion know me. But I was just a cog in the wheel. Actually McLogan and the colonel deserve a lot of credit. If it wasn't for them, we would have all been wiped out.*

---

* At a recent reunion, Roy Matsumoto was greeted by a fellow Marauder who hugged Roy and said to me, "He saved all of us. If it wasn't for him, none of us would be here today." Matsumoto humbly assigned the praise to the other men in the battalion.

MELVIN CLINTON
5307TH COMPOSITE UNIT, 3RD BATTALION

The veterans who survived the attacks at Nhpum Ga and the Mauraders' other battles made a grueling sixty-five-mile march over mountainous territory to capture Myitkyina airfield, as Melvin Clinton recalls.

As of this date, as far as I know, I'm the only one left alive from my platoon.

After we had been in there for several months, I was fortunate to still be on my feet. I developed malaria real bad. For two or three weeks, I was running a high fever almost every day. The other men were weak, malnourished. Our food just wasn't keeping up with the requirements of our bodies. I went from 180 pounds to about 118. I was still on my feet, but I was barely hanging on. We were ordered on a long march before we captured Myitkyina Airfield.

At times the trail was very, very slippery, and some mules would slip and fall. So we'd have to carry their loads ourselves and maybe make two trips up the mountains. On a few occasions, it was so steep you couldn't walk carrying that stuff up, and you'd hand it to the next person, and we'd pass it up the mountains.

We got orders to set up near the airfield since it had fallen; the airfield had been taken by the 1st Battalion. We were ordered to get close because they figured the Japanese would counterattack. I remember hanging on to a mule's tail most of the last ten miles because I just didn't have enough strength to stay on my feet, so I just grabbed the mule's tail and let him pull me along. Fortunately, the [malaria] medicine began to take effect. The next day I was somewhat better. I fought on for three more weeks, but I was getting weaker all the time.

I've heard stories that the morale was real low in different units and things, but I can't say that about my unit. We knew that was going to be our mission, and we were looking forward to getting out of there. If we captured that airfield and held it, they'd relieve us—that's what we were told.

The thing that began to worry me wasn't the morale of our people; it was the health of our people. We finally got to Myitkyina. I crawled from hole to hole at night checking on my guns and my buddies, and they were just totally exhausted. We'd fend off the attacks. You're so fragile. Some men cut holes in their pants so they could relieve themselves from the dysentery. We were afraid to sleep since they'd [the Japanese] walk in on us. They seemed like they were everywhere.

JIM SAMPSON
879TH AIRBORNE ENGINEER BATTALION

"Merchant of Venice" cracked over the radio at General Stilwell's headquarters. It was the prearranged code signal that meant Myitkyina was secure and the process of reinforcement could begin. Standing by were ten gliders loaded with engineers from A Company of the 879th. Jim Sampson remembers the glider landing.

I never talked about it [the war], and it wasn't until a few years ago that I discussed it.

We took off in ten gliders towed by five C-47s. We were fully loaded with our airborne equipment.

I sat in the copilot's seat of the second glider that was being towed by the first C-47. I was sitting there with a Thompson submachine gun on my lap . . . why, I don't know. I would have never done anything with it. [laughs] We had several fighters flying escort.

The pilot was kind of scared, and he had us behind the slipstream of the C-47, and it was shaking the daylights out of the glider. I told him to pull it up out of the slipstream and level off the glider, and the ride smoothed out. We also had a newspaper photographer with us, and he was leaning out of the crash door because he was sick to his stomach, it was so bad.

As we approached the clearing, the other glider pulled loose, and he went straight down and crashed into the jungle. My pilot put the glider into a steep dive and then came down. I said, "Are you going to straighten this out?!" At this time, we were getting our wing shot full of rifle bullets and just about everything else coming up at us. The pilot got kinda frozen at the controls and held there. We crashed, and one wing tore off. We spun around three or four times on the runway. I looked back, and all I could see was a red cloud behind us, and I remember thinking, "Oh, boy, there goes the gasoline we're carrying in the glider." It was red dust on the runway that was doing it.

We had to tear loose the front of the glider to get our equipment out. Mortar and rifle fire were coming down around us.

We started filling in shell holes [with small bulldozers] so we could bring in additional troops. That night, the place was like the Fourth of July. They were firing across the field. Everything was going . . . mortars, rifle, and machine-gun fire. But the planes came; first with ammunition, and later troops.

MELVIN CLINTON
5307TH COMPOSITE UNIT, 3RD BATTALION

After the airfield was secured and reinforcements were flown in, the battle for My-itkyina turned into a protracted siege. One Marauder even referred to it as "our lit-tle Gallipoli."

You're afraid, there's no ifs, ands, or buts about it. If you can't let go of the fear, it will overcome your ability to fight. During the constant attacks, some guys panicked and maybe should have stayed put . . . but that was the only thing I always tried to tell myself. Every little battle that came up that was . . . if you panic, you're in trouble. That's the way I saw it. I saw that happen a time or two. Somebody panicked, and it cost them their life.

I never had the feeling that I wanted to get out of that hole and run or anything. I just wanted to stay and fight it out. That was just the way I felt about it. But anybody who says they're not scared, there's something wrong with them. It seems as though the Japanese had their minds made up that they could overrun us from frontal attacks, and it just didn't hap-pen that way. We just stayed put, and the boys in the machine-gun sec-tion that I was in, they took a toll on the Japanese army.

There were five of us out of the fourteen. There were five of us left
. . . we all came out together. I didn't see them ever again. I never cried at
the time, but I did since then when I thought about different guys that
didn't come back. They had assigned a group of them out there to me.
Orders came down on the 29th day of May, and I got on a plane and flew
out of there. They were flying Chinese troops in and flying us out. That
was one of the happiest days of my life. I was sick and weak. I can remember going into the hospital, and a British nurse was cutting my
whiskers with a pair of crooked scissors because I had so many sores on
the side of my face. After that for the next twelve hours, I don't remember
anything. I guess I passed out.

One of the hardest things I ever attempted to do was to go to schools
and talk with children. I'd take a set of maps, and then things would flash
back. That's the hardest thing—remembering the war—because you relive it. I finally stopped speaking to schools and children. The questions
little children will ask get to you, because they watch a lot of TV and they
think that's the way war is. People that weren't there don't understand.

EDWARD McLOGAN
5307TH COMPOSITE UNIT, 2ND BATTALION

Edward McLogan recalls his last day at Myitkyina.

On the day we came out, I had ten men out of thirty-six. I had red streaks
running up my legs from blood poisoning. We just had the feeling that
when we got to Myitkyina, that would be it, and we'd be pulled out.
There were lots of men with dysentery and malaria. Wounded men
stayed on the line. One of our officers even passed out on the last day. We
didn't have contact with the enemy, and we didn't know where the
enemy was at the time, so I was ordered to take my men out 'til I found
them. We moved out, and a chap named Michael—he was walking six or
eight feet from me—each of us at the same instant saw this Japanese on
an outpost rise up. He was already practically standing in his foxhole aiming his rifle. At that moment I don't know if he was aiming at me or

Michael, but Michael had a huge red beard, and he shot [Michael] right in the middle of the forehead and his helmet went up and tumbled right down to my feet. He sank in a cross-legged position, and he went down over his knees, and as he was going down, he just looked at me. I could see the bullet hole. The air went out of him just like a balloon . . . *hssssssssssshhhhhh*. We knew we were going to be taken out of there, so nobody wanted to be a hero. We organized an attack on that outpost, knocking it out.

The next day I was on just about the last plane to come out. When I think back on it, it was not so much a *Gung Ho* shoot-'em-up sort of thing. It was walk, walk, walk, stopping for a break and then walk, walk, walk.

RAY MITCHELL
5307TH COMPOSITE UNIT, MARS TASK FORCE, 475TH INFANTRY

Ray Mitchell remembers how, in desperation, poorly trained replacements were thrown into the line around Myitkyina.

I kept this thing [the war] locked up so tight. I was sitting in a Rotary Club meeting. And one of the men in the meeting, who was also a doctor, said he saw something about a Marauder reunion in a retired officers' magazine. I debated whether or not to go, but decided to attend. But I said to my wife, "If we are there thirty minutes or a day, and I say we have to leave, we are going to leave." I did not want to go back to the war. I've changed since I fought in those jungles, and the men I served with were some of the meanest individuals I'd ever known. She said, "Okay. But I think you should go." It had been thirty-five years since the war was over, and when I got there, I didn't see anyone I knew.

The next morning, somebody came up to me and said, "Are these seats taken?" I recognized his voice. It was an officer I knew. I began to talk to people and relive the war. It started flowing and flowing and flowing. It's almost impossible to stop. I'm glad, but I'm also sorry it started. I would have preferred to keep it locked up. I'll take you back.

There was a group of us that came into Myitkyina at the end of May. We became Marauders. We were not an organization, but we became an organization. We were a group of replacements that were thrown in as a unit. It was probably one of the worst things that could possibly happen. Seven days from when the ship landed at Bombay, we were in combat. There was confusion; we lost so many men before we became acclimated to combat and the jungle. There was a stalemate for two and a half months at Myitkyina. You can learn a whole lot in two and a half months, especially when the Japanese are the teachers.

I was the battalion sergeant major for the 2nd Battalion. I was promoted because a lot of men were killed. We had two real severe things happen to us. We had an entire company ambushed and lost over two hundred men in F Company; seventeen men came back. That's the day I took over as acting sergeant major. I had four hundred men missing in action out of one battalion. I went back to the area where they were ambushed and took some fellows with me. We went through the remains— bodies were everywhere. You know soldiers, and you don't know soldiers. There were many men I knew, some of them that I had volunteered with and knew quite well.

The military method of identification, so you would not lose your clothes and all, was to put the initial of your last name and the last four numbers of your serial number on your stuff. Mine was M-4305. The Japanese were souvenir hunters, and they went through the bodies and took rings, watches, and dog tags so we found dog tags on practically no one. We picked through the bloody remains and took the numbers off jackets, belts—anything we could find. I worked for quite a while tracking people. I had the list of everybody who was missing in action. Every man that came back from the hospital went through that list. I finally got the list down to about twenty-five men missing in action, which was way too many. Eventually, we buried the remains. I was dead to it. After I came home and had been home for a while, I began to realize I wasn't smelling anything. For seven years, I totally lost my sense of smell.

Another incident that comes to mind most vividly is when the B-25s came over. They bombed from 5,000 feet. They dropped as many on us as on them. They came back later and bombed us again. Nobody said they were sorry. I even wrote several letters in the CBI newsletter asking for information. I got a number of letters back from a pilot of an observation plane who saw the whole thing happen and realized the bombs were dropped on us. But there was nothing he could do since [the bombers] were on a different radio frequency. We had to dig those men out. That was the most horrifying experience of the war, digging men out. We were digging men out that had been suffocated, buried alive. We had a few that were still alive and badly wounded. There were an awful lot that we didn't get out. That had a tremendous effect on us.

GRANT HIRABAYASHI
5307TH COMPOSITE UNIT, 1ST BATTALION

The siege at Myitkyina created a desperate need for more men. Even the hospitals were emptied of men who could walk. Grant Hirabayashi was one such man flown into Myitkyina.

I was convalescing at the 20th General Hospital in Ledo, and orders came down for anybody that could walk to report to Myitkyina. Again I took an L-5 [light aircraft]. I was assigned as an interrogator, working on prisoners. The Japanese tried to kill themselves before they were captured, so when they were captured, they were at a loss. When I first got them, I would ask, "Do you need medical attention? Have you heard from your parents?" Then I would share a cigarette with them, and I would start my interrogation. They were shocked and would often ask, "Aren't you going to kill me?" I said, "No, I'm a soldier." Some would ask to be shot. Most would break down and have tears in their eyes.

I did have trouble with a lieutenant. He was captured and made an attempt to escape but was bayoneted in the hip, arm, and leg. He was brought in on a stretcher, and his bandages were full of blood. One of the GIs that brought him in said, "That son-of-a-bitch killed my brother!" He wanted to kill him. I said, "Wait a minute!" I stopped him and said, "The information I get from him may save your life. I'm the interrogator; leave everything up to me." He finally understood. It was late so I said, "Give him first aid, but I want to question him in the morning." He was brought in first thing in the morning. I asked him if the first aid was satisfactory, and he looked at me and said, "You're a traitor!" I said, "Wait a minute. If we were to cut our wrists, maybe the same blood would flow out, but I'm an American. I'm an American soldier. You're a Japanese officer. We are both fighting for our country. Let me make this point clear: I'm the interrogator, and you are the POW." He kept on saying, "You're a traitor!" And he failed to respond to any of my questions. So I was getting hot under the collar. The officers in charge were expecting me to come up with good information. Finally, he refused again, so I told the MP [military police] to put him in the center of the enlisted men's stockade.

I went around talking to the other POWs. Now and then, I would walk by, and he would call me: "Mr. Interpreter, I want to die." I would say, "How do you want to die?" "I want you to shoot me." I said, "I have no bullets to waste on you." But I did tell him I had a captured sword that he could use to demonstrate how to commit *seppuku* [suicide]. With that I left him.

On my second round, he pulled my trousers and said he had a change of heart and answered my questions. That was the only time I had received feedback. Captain Chan, who was on General Stilwell's intelligence staff, said that was the information he was looking for. Usually we'd write a report, submit it, and wouldn't get any feedback.

We captured several comfort girls. The guard called my name: "Grant, come on over." I saw the women in a makeshift British tent with barbed wire around it. I said to myself, "I know how to interrogate a POW, but comfort women—that's not my line." So I called Captain Chan—I called him Charlie Chan (to myself)—"I need help." He said, "Okay." And he recruited several other interrogators, and the four of us went to the tent. Chan was anxious to get information, but what can you expect from comfort girls? They had very little knowledge. Chan had photos of the commander, and one identified the commander of the Japanese regiment.

When it got dark, we left. It was a full moon, very bright, as I left the stockade. I thought to myself, "These are innocent victims." And I reflected on my family at Tule Lake, who were also behind barbed wire.

MARVIN CHESTER
5307TH COMPOSITE UNIT, MARS TASK FORCE, 475TH INFANTRY

Marvin Chester reflects on the closing days of the battle for Myitkyina and the subsequent fighting to the south, at Tonkwa.

When I got home, I'd wake up at night, and the artillery shells would come in. A lot of guys lost their lives, but I was spared. I still feel guilty about that. In this nightmare, I could see Kornfeld, who was a sergeant, lose his leg, and the radio operator was ground up into hamburger meat. You couldn't tell he was a human being; you couldn't tell what he was. The same nightmare would occur over and over until the shell finally made a direct hit. I relived it at night. I'm reliving it here with you.

I had my runner with me, and I was trying to keep up with the other guys, and we got to a bomb crater. I told him, "Let's stop here and get our breath." We waited a minute or two, and we started to move out. He grabbed me by my field jacket and said, "I want to go first." As he crested the top of the bomb crater, a sniper bullet went right through his heart. Blood splattered, and he quivered and collapsed. I felt so guilty about that since I was the one that should have been leading him. He and I had been through a lot together; we had been good buddies.

My other friend got killed in that field. The night before we started the attack, he told me, "I'm going to get killed tomorrow." I said, "You're not going to get killed." He said, "Yes, I am. They sent me new replacements, and I'm going to get killed trying to get them out of their foxholes." That's exactly what happened. He was killed the next day.

As a grown man in my early twenties, I sat down and cried. [crying] I'd never cried before that since I was a child, but that's how much it af-

Members of the 475th marching through a rice paddy to Mong Wi,
Burma, January 1945. (U.S. Army)

fected me. When we finally ran the Japanese out of there and were back
at camp, I sat down and wrote his wife a letter and told her what happened. They just had a baby, which he never saw.

August the 3rd, Myitkyina finally fell. I remember because it's my
wedding anniversary (at the time I wasn't married). It was mostly the
Chinese that took the town. When the town fell, I had two guys in my
platoon that couldn't wait to hunt for souvenirs. One was from Chicago,
and the other was from New York. They were going to command posts to
try to find all the jewelry and stuff, so I called them the gangsters since
they pulled gold teeth out of the bodies. The guy from Chicago was
eventually killed.

I didn't think much of it then, and I don't think of it much now, especially after I saw the things the Japanese did. They'd stake them [the natives] out, legs spread, arms spread, stripped of all their clothes. This one native, they cut his penis off and put it in his mouth, and stuck bullets in his eyes and up his nose. This galvanized our hatred, and it made it easier not to take prisoners. We were ordered to take no prisoners because we had nowhere to take them. However, not many of them tried to surrender. A few did, but we had to shoot them.

When the battle for Myitkyina ended the first week of August, a group of us that had been known as the 2nd Battalion pulled back and deactivated the Marauders. Combat ended around the 3rd of August. We built Camp Landis. As the 5307th was deactivated, the 475th Infantry was activated, and then within a month or two the 124th Cavalry came in straight from the States and they called us Mars Task Force. Several artillery and other units were also included. We had no vehicles; all we had were mules and our backs. We were fed and kept going by the Air Corps. For supplies, every third day we hoped for an airdrop.

We started out from Myitkyina and headed south, covering anywhere from fifteen miles in the mountains to thirty to thirty-five miles in the flatlands. We would set up drop zones, and every third day the Air Corps would drop food, ammunition, and medical supplies.

[Our first big battle was at Tonkwa.] About 2:00 A.M., someone woke me up and said, "Sergeant, they're out there. We can hear them talking but we don't know what they're saying." We had a Japanese American who was an interpreter, and he went up there and listened to what they were saying and told me what was going on. They were preparing to attack at dawn. This officer was about ten yards in front of me and yelled, "Banzai!" They all yelled and started charging. I carried a Tommy gun, and I put thirty rounds in him. Then the rest charged. I knew our men; I knew we could hold. Time sort of stopped. It seemed like an eternity. It became mass confusion after the officer was killed. They didn't know where to go or what to do.

I was wounded when they threw mortars at us. A piece of shrapnel hit me in the head and gave me this big scar. I didn't know I was hit until I felt something running down my neck and it was blood.

There were dozens of dead bodies in front of our position. We found orders [on the officer] that directed him to kill us at all costs; don't let anyone out alive.

My radio operator was in contact with the Air Corps, and they said, "What do you need?" He responded, "A bulldozer." "What the hell do you need that for?" Then my radio operator responded, "So we could shove all the bodies out of the way."

After the battle, I sent out a few men to see if any were still alive. Most of them were dead. But we finished off any still alive.

RAY MITCHELL
5307TH COMPOSITE UNIT, MARS TASK FORCE, 475TH INFANTRY

Ray Mitchell remembers cutting and eventually helping open the Burma Road.

We hit the fringes of the mountains and continued to head south. That's where we cut the Burma Road. The 475th hit it first, and the 124th Cavalry came in next and took up positions.

We first had to take a ridge that overlooked the road. Then we were cutting off supplies to the Japanese who were driving up the Burma Road toward Kunming. Kunming was where most of the supplies were coming from India and were entering into China. We later cleared the Japanese from the area and helped open the road.

When we took the ridge, we sent patrols down to block the Japanese transportation coming down the road. The first week we were there, we'd go down at night and destroy anything on the road with bazookas. We also put 45-pound charges of TNT under rocks and touched them off when their trucks rolled down the road. We even destroyed a small Japanese tank that tried to escort one of their truck convoys.

The battalion commander and I, as sergeant major, stayed in contact all the time. One night I was in his bunker talking with him about everything that needed to be done. At about 11:30 P.M., he said, "Let's go to the observation post overlooking the road so we can see what's going on." It

Members of Mars Task Force firing on Japanese positions near the Burma Road,
January 1945. (U.S. Army)

was a bright moonlit night. We got up there and climbed into the observation post.

I was a heavy, heavy smoker, and I explained to the colonel that I was going back to my foxhole to get some cigarettes and I'd be back in just a minute. He went into the observation post, and I went into my foxhole about ten yards away. I had a friend that was there, so I opened a pack of cigarettes and pulled one out, and the first shell came over. The Japanese would play psychological games with artillery and were shelling every hour on the half-hour. I lit a cigarette. He asked me what I was doing, and all I said was I was getting ready to go to the observation post with the old man. He asked what time was it, and I said 11:30 and said, "I can beat the next shell." He said, "You better wait." These were 150 mm, which are huge shells. When it slacked off, I jumped out of my foxhole, and I saw the next one. I saw the dust and debris from the observation post. It was a direct hit. The colonel was killed. When I got there, I pulled a couple of fellows out. Body parts were everywhere. We had a Jewish sergeant, Kornfeld, who was in there and had a leg that was practically blown off. It was dangling by a small piece of flesh and muscle. The leg was trapped. The medics and the surgeon just reached over and pulled a trench knife out of one of the fellows' scabbards and cut the leg off and then tied it off. Kornfeld was still lucid. If it weren't for that pack of cigarettes, I would have been there too.

CHAPTER FIVE

New Guinea

"We're none of us the same!" the boys reply.
For George lost both his legs; and Bill's stone blind;
Poor Jim's shot through the lungs and like to die;
And Bert's gone syphilitic: you'll not find
A chap who's served that hasn't found some change.

— SIEGFRIED SASSOON, *"THEY"*

GENERAL DOUGLAS MACARTHUR, commander in the Southwest Pacific, was responsible for the American campaign in New Guinea. Since mid-1942, MacArthur had conducted a "hit-'em-where-they-ain't" leapfrogging campaign up the spine of New Guinea. Weaving together an American air war with a ground war waged mainly by Australians, MacArthur's forces bypassed Japanese strongholds, neutralizing them through a series of amphibious assaults. Slowly, MacArthur's troops were gaining control of the world's second largest island.

The amphibious assaults that underpinned the operations were collectively known as Cartwheel, designed to lead to the capture of the main Japanese base at Rabaul, which sits on New Britain Island, off New Guinea's east coast. (Allied planners eventually chose to isolate Rabaul rather than attack it, a fortunate decision.) The general plan was for MacArthur's Sixth Army, along with the Australians,[1] to move up New Guinea's coast and seize the Bismarck Archipelago, while Admiral

William F. Halsey's forces closed in on Rabaul from the southeast by way of the Solomons.

The Japanese stronghold at Lae, located on New Guinea's northwestern coast, was an essential stepping stone in this plan, and one in which the elite troops played a key role. The 503rd paratroopers were the airborne component of a land, sea, and air operation to capture Lae. On September 5, 1943, the 503rd dropped onto the abandoned Japanese airfield at Nadzab, about twenty miles from Lae. All three of the regiment's battalions accurately hit the drop zone, making it the U.S. Army's first successful mass parachute drop of the war. The troopers' only battle was with the man-size kunai grass that covered everything. The next day, the Australian 7th Infantry Division began air landing at Nadzab.[2]

With Nadzab in Allied hands, Lae was attacked from three sides. The bastion fell on September 16, clearing New Guinea's Huon Peninsula. The paratroopers' only significant action occurred when fleeing Japanese units ran into elements of the 503rd's 3rd Battalion. Several paratroopers were killed, but the Japanese attack was halted and the Japanese withdrew into the hills.

MacArthur's leapfrogging continued, and by May 1944 his forces had clawed thirteen hundred miles up New Guinea to the meathook-shaped westernmost part of the island, the Vogelkop Peninsula.

Lying in the Allies' path was Biak Island, site of three airfields needed to secure the Vogelkop. After taking two smaller islands, regiments from the 41st Infantry Division assaulted Biak on May 27, 1944. Shrewdly, the Japanese commander allowed the 41st to advance inland, then counterattacked from caves and dug-in positions overlooking the beaches. One of the 41st's regiments was forced to fall back to the shoreline and reinforcements were brought in.[3] At last, the 41st secured the beachhead, but the bitter struggle for Biak continued. The Japanese were able to prolong the battle by secretly bringing in their own reinforcements at night from nearby Noemfoor Island. In response, the Allies assembled Cyclone Task Force, consisting of over seven thousand men, primarily from the 158th Regimental Combat Team, to cut off the Japanese reinforcements and capture Noemfoor's three airfields.[4]

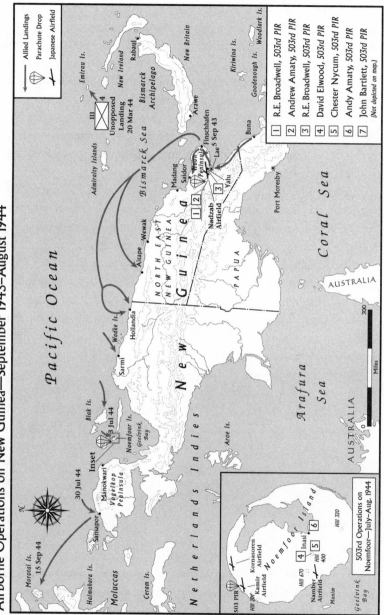

Airborne Operations on New Guinea—September 1943–August 1944

Legend:
- Allied Landings
- Parachute Drop
- Japanese Airfield

1	R.E. Broadwell, 503rd PIR
2	Andrew Amaty, 503rd PIR
3	R.E. Broadwell, 503rd PIR
4	David Elwood, 503rd PIR
5	Chester Nycum, 503rd PIR
6	Andy Amaty, 503rd PIR
7	John Bartlett, 503rd PIR

(Not depicted on map.)

Pacific Ocean

Bismarck Sea

Bismarck Archipelago

New Britain

New Ireland

Rabaul

Emirau Is.

Admiralty Islands

Unopposed Landing 20 Mar 44

Kiriwina Is.

Goodenough Is. Woodlark Is.

Arawe

Buna

Finschhafen

Lae 5 Sep 43

Huon Peninsula

Saidor

Madang

Wewak

Aitape

NORTH EAST NEW GUINEA

Yalu

Nadzab Airfield

Port Moresby

PAPUA

New Guinea

Coral Sea

Hollandia

Wadke Is.

Sarmi

Geelvink Bay

Biak Is.

30 Jul 44

3 Jul 44

Inset

Noemfoor Is.

Manokwari

Vogelkop Peninsula

Sansapor

Halmahera Is.

Morotai Is. 15 Sep 44

Moluccas

Ceram Is.

Aroe Is.

Netherlands Indies

Arafura Sea

AUSTRALIA

Miles
0   300

Inset: 503rd Operations on Noemfoor—July–Aug. 1944

Noemfoor Island

Hill 320

Hill 400

Inasi 5

4

Hill 670

Number Airfield

Manim

Kamir Airfield

Kornasoren Airfield

Hill 201

503 PIR

6

Geelvink Bay

On July 3, 1944, the 1st Battalion of the 503rd Parachute Infantry Regiment, commanded by Colonel George Jones, jumped on Kamiri airfield on Noemfoor to reinforce the 158th's assault.[5] Altimeters on the lead planes were incorrect, and the men jumped from far below the prescribed 600-foot level. They came down hard on Japanese construction equipment and an unforgiving coral runway. The result was seventy-two injuries, including thirty-one with broken bones. The next morning, the 3rd Battalion dropped, with similar problems. Scores more men were injured on the runway. Fortunately, the 2nd Battalion was spared the jump and was brought in by sea.[6]

After Colonel Jones' regiment assembled, it marched inland to confront the remaining Japanese defenses on the island. The combat was brutal: the paratroopers faced a green morass of snake-infested jungle, insects, tropical disease, and a weakened yet determined enemy.

Food supply became nonexistent for the Japanese when they were driven into remote areas of the island by the Americans. Faced with this impossible situation and the human need to stay alive, many Japanese soldiers resorted to cannibalism. The Japanese primarily ate their own dead, but also cannibalized several captured 503rd troopers.[7] The nightmare was over by the end of August when the 503rd and 158th cleared the Japanese from the island.[8]

Aided by fighters and bombers that took off from Noemfoor's Kamiri airfield, MacArthur was able to seize the Vogelkop Peninsula. New Guinea was secure. After landing at Morotai in the Moluccas, north of New Guinea, in September, the Allies turned their gaze northward toward the Philippines.

R. E. BROADWELL
503RD PARACHUTE INFANTRY REGIMENT

At 8:25 A.M. on September 5, 1943, the first C-47 roared down the runway carrying the 503rd Parachute Infantry Regiment for a drop on the abandoned Japanese airfield at Nadzab. R. E. Broadwell recalls the jump.

On our way to Markham Valley, a fighter nearly hit our plane, putting us into a dive. We hit the top of the ceiling; I felt like we were glued to the ceiling for five minutes, but it was actually only a second or two. Eventually everyone hit the floor. One of the sergeants cut his head open. I thought the plane was going down, so I was standing in the door looking out. They said, "Don't jump!" I really thought that I'd be the only one that would survive. The plane leveled off, and the pilot came back, apologized, and said, "The plane would have been cut in half, and we'd all been killed if I hadn't dove." Anyway, several men had cuts. They told us and told us a hundred times what the plan was and where we were going to jump, the approach, etc. We were all excited when we came to this field and leveled off. We had a green light, and we were supposed to jump after the lieutenant. We were passing the field, but the planes in front didn't jump. I knew that this was the field, but we were passing it. I told the lieutenant, "Goddamn it, jump! Get out of the way; I'm getting out! This is it! This is it! Either jump or get out of the way! This is it! This is it!" They were waiting for the plane in front of us to jump. I don't know if he [the lieutenant] panicked or what, but we finally jumped and landed in grass as high as this ceiling.

ANDREW AMATY
503RD PARACHUTE INFANTRY REGIMENT

Andy Amaty describes his first night in the jungle outside Nadzab. *

We landed in kunai grass easily as high as this ceiling. The underneath part was impossible to walk over—kind of like deep snow when you're trying to walk on it in the winter. Finally, we got off the kunai and onto the trails that were well used by the natives and Jap patrols. We shot azimuths with our compasses and moved according to our maps.

We were on a five-man patrol. It was starting to get dark, so we got off the trail. In the jungle at night, you can't see two inches in front of your

* The day after granting me this interview, Andy Amaty died, joining the over eleven hundred American World War II veterans who quietly slip away every day.

face. It's not dark; it's black. And when it rained in the jungle, you were freezing. The bugs! I never liked bugs, so you'd button up everything—tuck your pant legs in, tuck your sleeves in—and try to keep them out of your ears.

I had my Tommy gun across my lap and a flashlight in my hand. I'm laying there, and I finally start to fall asleep, and I hear in my left ear, *sniff, sniff, sniff.* I say to myself, "Son-of-a-bitch, *what is that*?!" I take the flashlight out, and I point it at the sniffing, and it is a bandicoot, a large, furry, ratlike creature. According to the book we were given, under "bandicoot" it says "edible." When it saw the light, it let out a high-pitched squeal, *"eeek!"* and took off.

R. E. BROADWELL
503rd Parachute Infantry Regiment

The 503rd's only significant contact with the enemy at Nadzab came in mid-September, when the 3rd Battalion ran into a Japanese column at Yalu, located east of the airfield, as R. E. Broadwell recalls.

We were told the Japanese were escaping along a trail, so they force-marched us nearly double time. We marched and carried full field equipment. We were exhausted. It got to the point where some of the guys couldn't make it. We had some of the older men in the battalion in my squad. We sat down. One of the lieutenants said, "Get up!" I said, "Lieutenant, I'm not getting up." I said, "If these men get up there [to the trail], one man [Japanese] could whup all of us. I can make it, but they can't make it. They have to have some rest. Go on in front of us, and we'll meet you with the rest of the men. We'll all be together. Just give the men some rest." One of the men was so mad that he put a round in the chamber and was going to shoot the lieutenant. I stepped right in front of the lieutenant, and the other man and said, "No, don't do that!" You're mad as hell and tired, and I believe he would have shot him. I told him, "I'm not going, lieutenant! When we get there, we'll be ready to go into combat." We made it up to the trail, and that night they put us in foxholes.

Troopers from the 503rd in the jungle outside Lae, New Guinea,
September 1943. (courtesy of Jack Herzig)

We were in a native village, and someone yelled, "Knee mortar!" I was there with Lieutenant Colonel Tolson. I got behind a tree and, goddamn, the men jumped up and were running like quails. They were running together, bunched up—something you are not supposed to do. This general [Tolson was later promoted] called several guys by name and said, "At ease, at ease, men." Everybody just settled down and relaxed and spread out. Everybody respected him. It was the first time we'd ever been shot at.

That night we dug foxholes and set up a machine gun. The Japs started crossing a creek, and we started throwing grenades. They were stragglers. One of the men started getting out of his foxhole. Anyone that got out of his hole, we'd shoot them, because anyone in the open at night was considered an enemy. He said to one of the men, "This is Steve. I'm out of hand grenades, and I'm coming back. Don't shoot." The next day, a guy by the name of Wells shot one of the Japs in the back, and he crawled into some bushes trying to hide. Wells pulled him out; he was still alive. The lieutenant said, "Don't shoot him." [An officer] came by and said,

"We will take no prisoners, we will not surrender, and we will not retreat." So one of the men shot [the Japanese] right between the eyes.

DAVID ELWOOD
503rd Parachute Infantry Regiment

With Nadzab secure, the next obstacle facing the elite infantry was Noemfoor Island. On July 3, 1944, the 1st Battalion of the 503rd Parachute Infantry Regiment jumped on Noemfoor's Kamiri airfield to reinforce the 158th Infantry, whose commander believed the Japanese defensive force was larger than it actually was. The 3rd Battalion jumped the next day. Throughout July and August, both units pursued and engaged pockets of Japanese scattered throughout the island. David Elwood describes his most vivid memory of the fighting on Noemfoor.

There was a small hill, thirty feet high. The Japanese had snipers picking at us, and automatic weapons were spattering the area. It got so bad that the company commander said, "We need to get them off the hill; they're picking us off one by one." We were along the base of the hill.

I was the first scout, and my squad went around to the left side of the hill, and the rest of the platoon hit the front side of the hill and I started up first. "Grenade!" It came over the top at me. I was lucky. It was a concussion grenade, and he [the Japanese] threw it right after he activated it, so it rolled further below me. I curled up, and I got the full blast on this leg. It kind of numbed me. Time seemed to pass for an hour, but it was only a few seconds. I was still conscious. That's when Eubanks started moving up the hill. A man who had a BAR charged with him but froze. Eubanks grabbed the BAR out of his hand, and he sprayed the top of the mound. He just charged over the top and opened up with the BAR, killing just about everyone up there. As he charged, his right forefinger was blown off by a bullet which also hit the BAR, rendering it useless. Eubanks charged several of them with his useless rifle and beat four Japanese soldiers to death with the stock of his gun before he got hit. Lieutenant Van de Voort was with him the whole time. He just had a pistol. They were both killed. Posthumously, Eubanks received the Congressional Medal of Honor, and Van de Voort got the Silver Star. There were about twenty dead Japanese soldiers with automatic weapons plus snipers.

Afterwards, the hill was covered with dead bodies and blood. A couple of them were still alive, barely alive and badly wounded. One was holding his gut, doubled over, blood squirting all over the place. One of our men, I won't tell you his name, put a pistol to his head and pulled the trigger. They were suffering—it was out of mercy. We couldn't get them to the aid station in time. Others were killed in the same manner. I still wake up at night reliving that day.

CHESTER NYCUM
503RD PARACHUTE INFANTRY REGIMENT

The Japanese on Noemfoor Island ran out of food, and many resorted to cannibalism. Chester Nycum recalls one such incident on the daily patrols on Noemfoor.

The Japanese had dug in on a coral hill and were waiting for us. We took whatever cover we could find, moved into firing positions, and battled throughout the day and into the night. Daylight came, and we put feelers out to see if the Japanese were still there. They had moved out. We moved up the hill into the evacuated Japanese positions. There, we found [our scout's] body; it had been carved as though he were a piece of beef. All the flesh was gone from his legs, arms, buttocks, and chest, and his heart and kidneys were missing. We had no doubt that they were eating our dead. We vowed right then never to take another prisoner!

[Before], we did take a few prisoners, but we had no way to take them with us. So someone devised a holding technique, which we called the Indian death lock, to hold the enemy prisoners until we returned—if we returned. We would find a tree approximately six to eight inches in diameter, slide the prisoner up the tree, with his arms tied around the tree. Then, crossing his legs around the tree, we would force his left foot inside and over his right knee. Using his Japanese belt of a thousand stitches [a cloth belt] as a hangman's noose, we would fasten it around his neck with a slipknot and tie the other end higher up to the tree trunk. As long as the prisoner had strength in his legs and arms, he could hang on. If his strength gave out, he was choked to death. I only knew of this happening once.

[Several days later] I received one of the most dreaded orders I was ever given. I was told to take two men and to cut a trail to our left, making as much noise as possible. We were to try to draw fire from the Japanese. Luckily they didn't fire. We journeyed out about two hundred yards, hacking and banging on rocks and trees. Then we were ordered back. Rejoining the squad, we moved cautiously forward into and through the Japanese positions of the day before. Initially [we moved] with caution, then rapidly to get away from the awful odor of rotting flesh. Our route took us out of the rain forest and into an open area where the trail followed a ridge. Walking single file, we pressed forward. Suddenly, approximately three hundred feet ahead of us, a grenade exploded. Moving forward to the point of the explosion, we found a Japanese soldier with his guts blown out, lying between the thin roots of a large tree. We assumed he was chicken and took the easy way out [committed suicide because he was afraid]. Within a mile further down the trail, the same thing happened again: another Japanese blew himself up.

Someone in our group determined our assumptions of the Japanese taking the easy way out was all wrong. These were actually death outposts. Each exploding the hand grenade was sending a message to the main force, letting them know exactly where we were. The soldiers who were sacrificed apparently were too sick to keep up with the main body of troops. After making this determination, our tactics changed. We would watch the trail ahead for anything large enough to hide a Japanese soldier. Then we would send a man around to the flank. If he spotted one, he would slip up on him, take the soldier from the rear, and cut his throat before he had time to detonate the grenade. When I had completed my time out front, I was relieved and placed next to the last man in the squad.

We were moving through fairly open country, along the base of a hill, when the man behind me fired. Turning to see what he was shooting at, I saw a Japanese soldier starting to bend forward. He fired a second shot, and the Japanese fell to the ground, face forward with his knees pulled up against his chest. He was gasping for breath. I walked over to him, pulled my .38 revolver from its holster, and put one shot through the top of his head. This stopped his suffering. Then, grabbing his feet, I straightened him out on his stomach, crossed his legs, and rolled him over for inspection. The lieutenant in charge of the patrol came over and commented, "Just like shooting hogs." I thought to myself, "Oh no, hogs don't kill and eat humans."

ANDY AMATY

503rd Parachute Infantry Regiment

Andy Amaty recalls the barbarity on Noemfoor.

[The Japanese] were cannibalizing their own until they got two Americans from our 3rd Battalion. [The paratroopers] got hit late in the afternoon. Fire was intense; the Japanese must have had a big Nambu machine gun. They were covering the area, so I figured, I guess, that they'd wait 'til the morning to pick up the bodies. Come the morning, the bodies were decimated. Up until that time, we were reporting to corps headquarters that these bastards were resorting to cannibalism. They were like, "You're full of shit." The next morning, we recovered the two bodies, carried them and put them on a truck, and sent them down to corps headquarters and said, "Here's the proof!"

Up until then, it was quite common to G-2 [interrogate] a man, search him, and we'd often find smoked fingers. Fingers, all of them, from an entire hand. If they had anything, they had fingers. Their regimental surgeon was showing them what to do. Our interpreter got this from prisoners.

It was a rarity, but we did capture prisoners. I'm one of the few to capture them alive. One of them was an officer who was taking care of a corporal. To say they didn't care for life was a fallacy. He [the corporal] had gangrene. For Christ's sake, it was the color of your shirt [dark blue]. We walked into an area where they had been camping for a few days. You could smell something about the odor. They had been cooking. You didn't have to be a damn Indian to know that people were cooking. The area looked like it had been lived in.

I had my Tommy gun, and I walked into the clearing, and about ten yards in front of me, peeking through the brush, were two Japs. The guy behind me yelled, "Enemy, enemy in front of you!" You can't shoot because some of the men were moving around in front of me. We had about fifteen guys. I fired . . . *rrrrp rrrrp* . . . eight shots. I hit two of them. They were petrified. By the time the last shots went off, I was charging into them. One was hit in the arm. The bullet went clean through it. The other was hit in the leg. I bandaged them up, and one of my guys said, "Let's shoot the sons-of-bitches." This was after the cannibalism, but I said, "No!" I threatened one of the men by pointing my Thompson at him and told him that I'd kill him if he pulled the trigger. I'm not a large person, but he listened and backed down.

I remember sitting there in the cold, in the dark that night and thinking, "Jesus, I hope nothing happens to me." I got this terrible fear. Most of it was psychological. You had to bite your tongue or do something to keep your cool, to maintain your senses; otherwise, you're liable to get yourself killed. I often tell people there were two wars: one in the Pacific and one in Europe. They were two absolutely different kinds of wars. The jungle, disease, and the Japanese were all your enemy. Most of it was psychological. Initially, we believed that the Japanese were supermen. Eventually, we caught on to their behavior, and we let them know that we could cope with any bullshit they were going to give us. We had better weapons, were physically stronger, and we started to understand their tactics.

For many fellows including myself, the dogs at night got the guys incensed. I'd tell them not to lose your heads. The natives had dogs, and when they didn't have enough food to feed them, they'd let the dogs go into the jungle. When there were bodies laying out, you'd hear the dogs, and you'd know what they were doing . . . eating the bodies.

Things like this, if you dwelled on them too long, you'd go nuts. I tried to mentally dismiss them so that I didn't go bananas. I don't know how I did it. I seemed to be able to shake it from my mind, especially when the dogs were eating those bastards. After that, we had open season on the dogs. As soon as we saw a dog, Christ, we'd fire shots. We tried killing every dog we saw, which was fine by me. I don't like to kill anything, but sometimes you'd see a Jap who was just buried within six inches of soil with a few stones thrown over him, and there'd be a son-of-a-bitch dog there sitting on the mound waiting for it to get dark to start chewing on the body.

JOHN BARTLETT
503rd Parachute Infantry Regiment

The savage and relentless fighting in the Pacific had no parallel in Europe. The racist attitudes on both sides helped to create a war of annihilation. John Bartlett reveals his last days on Noemfoor and his feelings toward the Japanese.

I vividly remember the miserable conditions on Noemfoor. We were constantly thirsty, hot, and tired. Water was a problem. Dysentery and jungle rot were a problem.

I had dysentery so bad that I'd take some pills for it, and it would be gone one day and back the next. Finally, they sent me back to a field hospital, which was a tent and some stretchers used as cots. The doctor approached me about the dysentery. As I was about to leave, I asked him if there was anything he could do for my foot. I had a massive infection on it. He said, "Why didn't you show that to me earlier?" He wanted to evacuate me back to New Caledonia, but I begged him not to send me since I wanted to be with the unit. So I spent about eighty days in a general hospital trying to get rid of that.

I never thought in my own mind that I killed another human being. They were Japs . . . just Japs. I thought about the war and how if we ever landed on Japan, I would have killed every man, woman, and child on the island. During the war, it wouldn't have bothered me a bit. [After the war] we went to Alaska, and there were all these cute Japanese kids with their families. Now, I have no animosity towards the Japanese.

CHAPTER SIX

Into the Marianas

There was never a good war or a bad peace.

— BENJAMIN FRANKLIN

VETERANS RECOGNIZED MANY OF THE MEN they fought with on Makin, Guadalcanal, New Georgia, and Bougainville as they boarded transports and set sail for their next major battle. The men's faces were familiar, but their unit numbers had changed. The old Raider veterans now formed the nucleus of the new 4th Marine Regiment. Joined by the 22nd Marine Regiment, the force became the 1st Provisional Brigade. They were part of Admiral Nimitz's drive through the Central Pacific.[1]

During the early summer of 1944, the 1st Provisional Brigade, the 3rd Marine Division, and the Army's 77th Infantry Division headed toward Guam, the largest island of the Marianas and the first major U.S. territory that American forces would try to recapture.[2] The capture of Guam, Saipan, and the remainder of the Marianas would put U.S. bombers within range of Japanese cities, so the islands were vigorously defended. At sea, the Japanese Combined Fleet sortied into the Philippine Sea and met the U.S. Navy in what has become known as the Great Marianas Turkey Shoot. During the course of the battle, the Japanese lost over 350 planes to the Allies' 30. American submarines also sank two large Japanese carriers.

The ground campaign was not as lopsided. Early on the morning of July 21, 1944, the 1st Provisional Brigade stormed Guam's western beaches. As the Marines crossed the beach, they were hit by heavy fire from Japa-

The 4th Marines on Guam—July–August 1944

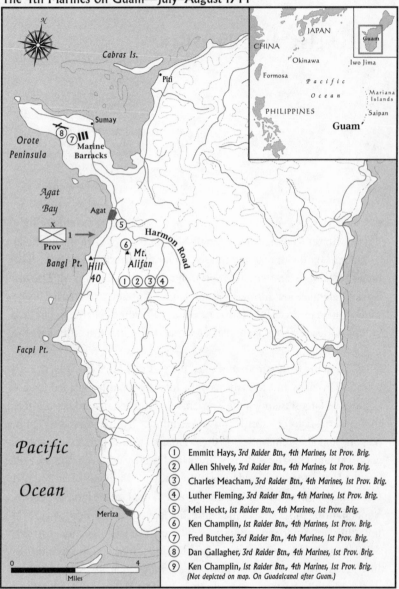

Pacific

Ocean

① Emmitt Hays, *3rd Raider Btn., 4th Marines, 1st Prov. Brig.*
② Allen Shively, *3rd Raider Btn., 4th Marines, 1st Prov. Brig.*
③ Charles Meacham, *3rd Raider Btn., 4th Marines, 1st Prov. Brig.*
④ Luther Fleming, *3rd Raider Btn., 4th Marines, 1st Prov. Brig.*
⑤ Mel Heckt, *1st Raider Btn., 4th Marines, 1st Prov. Brig.*
⑥ Ken Champlin, *1st Raider Btn., 4th Marines, 1st Prov. Brig.*
⑦ Fred Butcher, *3rd Raider Btn., 4th Marines, 1st Prov. Brig.*
⑧ Dan Gallagher, *3rd Raider Btn., 4th Marines, 1st Prov. Brig.*
⑨ Ken Champlin, *1st Raider Btn., 4th Marines, 1st Prov. Brig.*
(Not depicted on map. On Guadalcanal after Guam.)

nese artillery that had survived a massive thirteen-day Allied naval and air bombardment. About eighteen thousand Japanese were dug in along the rugged mountainous spine of the island. After heavy fighting, the 4th Marines carved out a beachhead about sixteen hundred yards inland.[3]

That night, the Japanese counterattacked. The weight of the Japanese attack fell on Hill 40, only three hundred yards from the beach. Here the 3rd Battalion of the 4th Marines repelled several banzai attacks. The next morning, hundreds of Japanese bodies were counted at the base of the hill.[4]

On D-Day plus one, Japanese tanks hit the 4th Marines. The Marines stopped the attack, then counterattacked, capturing Mount Alifan.[5]

The 4th Marines continued moving up Guam's Orote Peninsula. The advance was tough, with the Japanese contesting every yard. On July 29, Marines captured Guam's main airfield and raised the American flag over what was left of the old U.S. Marine Corps barracks.[6]

Yet the Japanese fought on. By August 10, however, General Hideyoshi Obata was forced to radio Tokyo that there was no hope of holding the island, and organized resistance on Guam ended. Nevertheless, mopping-up operations continued until 1945. Long after the war ended, small groups of Japanese soldiers refused to surrender. Only in 1972 did Guam's final holdout, Sergeant Shoichi Yokoi, become the last soldier of the emperor to surrender. Guamanian fishermen stumbled on him trying to set shrimp traps.[7]

By the end of August, the 4th Marines had left Guam, turning occupation duty over to the Army. The Marines returned to Guadalcanal, where another new Marine regiment joined them. The 29th, the 22nd, and the Raiders who made up most of the 4th Regiment were reassigned to the new 6th Marine Division. From here, the division and Admiral Nimitz's other forces would continue to move west through the Central Pacific toward Japan, while General MacArthur mounted his return to the Philippines.

EMMITT HAYS
3RD RAIDER BATTALION,* 4TH MARINE REGIMENT, 1ST PROVISIONAL BRIGADE

On the morning of July 21, 1944, the 1st Provisional Brigade stormed Guam's western beaches. That night, the Japanese counterattacked the 4th Marines. The focal point of the Japanese attack was Hill 40, only three hundred yards from the beach. Here men mainly from K Company repelled several massive banzai attacks, as Emmitt Hays remembers.

The war has been difficult for me to forget. I'm going to a reunion in a few weeks. When I go to a reunion, it's to see the guys, and we sit around and talk. Very seldom do we talk about battle. It's like just going to visit brothers. There's a few battles that are refought, but most of it is the comical stuff. If we talk about the combat, it reawakens things that have been buried for all these years. I get to a point where I can't even talk if we talk about it in depth. [crying] I'm about the youngest, seventy-five, in the outfit. There are very few of us left. There were a few hundred that I knew by name, and most are all gone now. The ones that I still know are walking with canes.

I enlisted just before my sixteenth birthday and had my sixteenth birthday in boot camp. You're supposed to be at least seventeen, but I lied about my age. And I'm glad I did. My mother knew. I talked her into it. I had my seventeenth birthday just before Bougainville.

We scrambled down the cargo nets to the boats, where they took us up to the coral reef where we got in the amphibious tractors. We had to jump from the boats over to the amphibious tractors.

As we approached the beach, we were getting sporadic machine-gun and sniper fire. The artillery and mortars were directed at the tractors.

---

* The Marine Raider and parachute battalions were disbanded in early 1944. The author chose to include the original elite unit each veteran started out in to provide a context for this chapter and the chapters that follow.

They knocked out a few while we were going in, but they destroyed a lot of them out in the earlier assault wave. It was a day landing and one of the few times I got ashore without my socks getting wet.

At the end of the day [on Guam], we set our defense in some old Japanese trenches. We thought we were going to spend the night, but our company commander, Captain [Stormy] Sexton, he moved us. After dark, we moved out of the trenches and went out on a right angle near a dry creek bed that came out on a forty-five degree angle. We set up. I was a BAR man, and we had an automatic weapon of one kind or another in every foxhole—either a Thompson or a BAR or a .30 caliber machine gun.

The Japs pulled an all-night assault. They hit our position hard. I had one and a half units of fire, which would amount to several hundred rounds; I used it up and nearly burned out the barrel on my gun. I couldn't touch it, since it was red hot. We had visible targets for an hour. They were in our faces. They came up that close. I ran out of ammunition, and someone passed machine-gun belts up the line so each BAR man got a machine-gun belt. We transferred those into magazines. I'd find three or four of them together and give them twenty rounds and hope that you hit them. We had flares all night. We could see them moving forward; their helmets would throw a shadow on their faces. But the way the flares were going up, you weren't sure if you hit that group or another group that was moving up. It was nothing personal until the next morning.

The next day we went out there. [chokes up] There were hundreds of bodies lying out in front of us. You feel guilty about killing guys that were wounded. I cut a guy's throat with my knife. That hurts. [chokes up] I've never really talked about this to anyone. The only reason that I am now is if someone doesn't relate it the way it actually was instead of the Hollywood version, it's going to be lost.

[The wounded man] was an officer. He had a collar insignia and a sword and a pistol. I took both of them. He was helpless but alive. He was not a danger to me; that's why I feel bad about it. If he'd been threatening me and I killed him in self-defense, I wouldn't have felt bad about that at all. But I hated that I killed a helpless man. At the time I felt I needed revenge because several of my close friends had been killed. Bob Swanson and I were tent mates before Bougainville, and he was killed that night.*

ALLEN SHIVELY
3RD RAIDER BATTALION, 4TH MARINE REGIMENT, 1ST PROVISIONAL BRIGADE

Allen Shively, a few foxholes down from Emmitt Hays, recalls how the battle for Hill 40 deteriorated into a hand-to-hand struggle.

They threw a grenade in first, but we couldn't find it, so we just hunkered down. It exploded. Then a Japanese officer charged in through the trench to our foxhole. There wasn't anybody behind him, luckily. I stood up, and he attacked me with a saber. He kind of lunged at me with it. That saber went in my britches near the right-hand pocket. As I was twisting, it went out the back of my britches. He came at me again, and I got a hold of his hand. I cut myself a little bit on the wrist, but I wrestled the sword away from him. About that time, another flare went up, and I saw him reach for his chest and pull out an automatic pistol. He fired it at me, and I [grabbed his arm and] had it pointed up in the air. I took it away from him. Then I literally beat the hell out of him with my hands. When I got him on the ground, I took his saber and rammed it through him about five times. I looked around for my buddy, and he was dead, and I was alone.

* Emmitt Hays was nearly killed by a mortar round about a week into the battle for Guam. He was comatose for ten days and still carries a sizable piece of shrapnel near his heart.

Japanese soldier killed on Hill 40. (USMC)

CHARLES MEACHAM
3RD RAIDER BATTALION, 4TH MARINE REGIMENT, 1ST PROVISIONAL BRIGADE

Charles Meacham remembers Hill 40.

As the night wore on, the Japanese started coming. We could look down and see these guys wiggling through the grass. They looked like brown maggots wiggling through the grass. There we were, approximately thirty of us on this hill, and we took it straight on, all night long.

They massed for one banzai attack after another. They just came in bunches, one right behind another, yelling and screaming with swords and rifles. We backed up and got off the base of the hill and moved up until we got to a steeper area on the hill. Here, most of the brush and trees were blown away. One man and myself ended up in a shell hole. That was a fourteen-inch shell hole that was just like a funnel. We got inside of that where we could maneuver. It was just never quiet; those damn guys would come up, and you'd knock them down. Hundreds were hitting the hill, and you'd knock them down again. It was like shooting fish in a barrel; it went on all night. They were trying to get through our defensive line; it was either kill them or get run over.

The first time you kill a man is one feeling. The first time you look him straight in the face and shoot first and kill him, that's another feeling, and after that it doesn't make much difference. As a human being, you feel all of this. Shooting someone from a distance, that's one thing, but when you look him in the face . . . that's a bit different. Hill 40 had everything, but they were mainly right there with you.

The next morning, we went down to check out what was going on, and there were some of these guys still around. There were hundreds of bodies and body parts all over the place. The next morning, I think the count was [several hundred] dead Japanese. I came around one place, and I did not see this guy, and he had a dead drop on me. He was about two coconut logs ahead of me, and the next thing I heard was a *rrrp* . . . *rrrp*, and my friend saved my butt. We lost a lot of good boys on that hill. Many died in their foxholes.

I don't think about the war a great deal. Those things are pretty much behind me. When I got out of the service, I had to pretty much make up my mind that I didn't want to be poor. So I got the war behind me and got on with it. I married my high school sweetheart and started college without a high school diploma and went four years and three double summer sessions. I came out with a wife and two children and have been going ever since.

LUTHER FLEMING
3RD RAIDER BATTALION, 4TH MARINE REGIMENT, 1ST PROVISIONAL BRIGADE

Luther Fleming remembers his night on Hill 40.

The first night they launched a huge banzai attack. We were about a good mile from where the attack was taking place and had a clear view of things. Tanks were being blown up, men scurrying across the field, star shells, the whole bit—in fact, it was more like watching a battle scene on TV. Later on that night, a runner came in and said he needed men to fill in gaps in the line. So Lieutenant Plock volunteered his platoon, which included me. We walked almost a mile down that beach.

We got into the trenches that were facing this field where Japs were coming across. We crawled hundreds of yards up Japanese-dug trenches, dropping off in pairs as we went. The trenches were full of Japanese bodies. Most of them were dead, a few were alive. There was one dead Marine, and we put him behind us. I found a machine gun and pulled the lever back to see if it was still cocked. Some Jap jumped right up in front of the machine gun and fired about twenty rounds right between [my buddy's] and my heads. All we got were powder burns and ringing ears. We lucked out again and took care of him. We fired our weapons all night long as they charged across the field, but you could never tell if you hit one or not.

Our platoon was the first one out on the field. There were hundreds of bodies. Arms, legs, and body parts were everywhere. We had to shoot those in the head that weren't dead yet. We had to finish them off. If you thought they were breathing, you shot before they got you. There was banging up and down the line. You learned that early in the war that one would be laying there with a hand grenade underneath him waiting to take you out.[8] I'd seen it happen way down the line from me. You hated to do it, but, hell, you couldn't risk your life or your buddy's life.

MEL HECKT
1ST RAIDER BATTALION, 4TH MARINE REGIMENT, 1ST PROVISIONAL BRIGADE

In the early morning hours of July 22, the rumble of tanks was heard above the din of battle. Four Japanese light tanks and supporting infantry assaulted the 1st Battalion's position, attempting to break through their lines. Mel Heckt describes the Japanese tank attack and the 4th Marines' advance to Mount Alifan.

I was a machine-gun gunner at the time, and we set up my gun on the right side of Harmon Road to form a roadblock. That first night, four Japanese tanks came about ten yards from my machine gun. Before they got that close, we were firing at the side of the tanks, knowing that .30 caliber machine-gun bullets don't do any damage to the tank. I remember my teeth chattered and my knees shook. I was more than slightly scared.

They got within ten yards, and a bazooka man named Bruno Oribiletti knocked out at least two tanks before our tanks got up there. After he destroyed the second tank, he was killed by a shell from one of the tanks. His actions saved all of us. Otherwise, the tanks would have run right through us.

The next day we advanced. It was raining and miserable, but we found lots of Japanese sake, which wasn't half bad, and salmon. We climbed the mountain [Alifan] and sacked in thick brush. We couldn't dig foxholes; there was too much brush. I didn't sleep much even though we weren't attacked. We thought they were all around us. One of my buddies even thought one climbed over him, only to realize it was just a rat. From then on, we were awake until dawn.[9]

KEN CHAMPLIN
1st Raider Battalion, 4th Marine Regiment, 1st Provisional Brigade

The 4th Marines advanced inland to secure Mount Alifan, overlooking the beach-head. Platoon Sergeant Ken Champlin describes his night on the mountain.

We landed on the extreme right flank of the invasion. We had been on ships for over fifty days without exercise. That's tough. There were about a thousand yards of rice paddies where we landed, south of the Orote Peninsula. We lost a few guys on the beach. Before the invasion, we picked up five new officers who were All-American football players from Southern California, Notre Dame, Michigan, Yale, and another—I can't remember the other college. We had a new lieutenant, Max Belko, who was one of these officers from Southern California. I still keep in touch with Frank Kemp from Yale. Kemp was probably the finest officer I ever served under outside of Lou Walt.

Anyway, we started up this hill. There was another hill and a valley in between, and the Nips were coming in all around us. I said to Max Belko, "Hey, Max, hit the deck!" He hadn't been in combat long, and when I hit the ground, I rolled so I wasn't in the same spot. Max didn't, and he raised his head up to see what was going on, and he took a shot right in the stomach. Within ten minutes, I gave him a couple of shots of morphine. That was about all you could do. [sigh, chokes up] He put his hand up, and I was holding it in my hand, and he said, "That's all she wrote, Champ." And he died.

We started up Mount Alifan, and I don't know just how far we got—I'd say a quarter or a third of the way perhaps—and we dug in for the night. I had no contact with my company or C Company, which was on my left. So we were stuck out there pretty much on our own.

We had fire from destroyers, and they were firing star shells and parachute flares and all kinds of things. We had dug in as best we could. It was pretty stony up there. I don't know when it was exactly, but I'll say it was

A wounded Marine displays his bullet-shattered helmet. (USMC)

twelve or one o'clock when the damn Japanese came down the mountain and pulled a banzai charge on us.

We were up on a kind of knoll on the side of the mountain, and we had machine guns set up on either side to create a cross-fire. Someone came down off the mountain from somewhere yelling and screaming. It seemed like over a hundred charged our position. It was a mass formation of men yelling and screaming. If you can keep your men settled and you can hold your position, you can knock the hell out of them. Between our fire and fire from the ships, over one hundred dead bodies were in front of our line of defense. We held them that night. As I saw our men in the morning, I remember seeing some of them had samurai sword cuts on their arms and chests.

FRED BUTCHER

3RD RAIDER BATTALION, 4TH MARINE REGIMENT, 1ST PROVISIONAL BRIGADE

Before the waist of Guam could be secured, the Marines had to clear the heavily for-
tified Orote Peninsula, which contained the old Marine barracks and an airfield.
Using a series of frontal and flanking attacks, the 1st Provisional Brigade secured the
peninsula by the end of July. Fred Butcher recalls fighting on the Orote Peninsula.

I don't know if you can call war a good experience, but I saw a lot of good
and some bad. One of my buddies [Rick] and I were talking about one of the
bad experiences. We had a guy in our outfit who you just couldn't trust—
ever. And one morning on Guam, we went on a patrol, and this guy was on
that patrol. All of a sudden, there was a few fire bursts, and it all got quiet.
This guy was dead on the ground, and there were a lot of bullet holes in
him, and we don't know if they were ours or theirs—somebody killed him.
We still don't know who did it. His dad was a bad cop in St. Louis and he
wasn't any better. We still question what happened. But there were hatreds.

We had been relieved by the 22nd Marines and told to move back to
the main area. As we were moving back, I spotted this gunfire coming out
of a pillbox. My specialty, I guess, was to put a magnesium grenade down
their ventilation shaft. I kind of figured out how their pillboxes were set
up. I was in the process of throwing a grenade down this one, and I saw
this guy come out and I thought I had my weapon on single fire but it was
automatic, and I ripped him.

We joined the main group near the middle of the peninsula, and we
were going through the old Marine barracks. We used a lot of ammo to
take the pillboxes. There was a weapons carrier a few hundred yards
back, so Rick and I went over to it to get a few bandoliers of ammunition.
On the way back again, with the bandoliers, we started taking mortar fire,
so we dove for a shell hole. As he was in the air, a tracer bullet hit one of
his bandoliers; he was blinded by the blast and wounded. I gave him a
pistol and the sword that I picked up. A year later after the war, he gave
me the sword but sold the pistol to a sailor for fifty bucks. We went

through a lot together. We were just kids. From my original platoon, there were only four guys left. Since Bougainville, Rick and I have brandy together every Christmas morning. Every Christmas morning, even if it's over the telephone, we have brandy together, to celebrate life and our friendship.

DAN GALLAGHER
3RD RAIDER BATTALION, 4TH MARINE REGIMENT, 1ST PROVISIONAL BRIGADE

After the Orote Peninsula was secure, the Marines and soldiers drove northward, clearing the rest of the island and finally securing it on August 10, 1944. Dan Gallagher reveals his most vivid memory from the closing weeks of the campaign on Guam.

That morning there was firing and artillery shells flying over our heads, and we were getting ready to shove off, and I saw two good friends of mine from the 1st Platoon, two very nice guys who were cleaning and oiling their rifles, getting ready. I always would bullshit with them and kid them about things. So I left their foxhole and . . . wham! A shell exploded and knocked me down. I turned around, and the first thing that accosted me was the smell of hot flesh. I still remember it . . . like you're barbecuing a steak. The foxhole was near the company commander's headquarters, and the first sergeant said, "Gallagher, bury the men." So I had to pick up a leg here, arm there, pieces of skull and eye sockets. Pick up body parts off bushes and put it in the hole. Other guys were helping.[10] We put them into a foxhole and started to cover it with dirt. We could not even find their dog tags. I was shocked to be talking to someone, and then they're gone.

Marine dead are prepared for burial in a hasty trench
excavated by the bulldozer in the background. (USMC)

KEN CHAMPLIN
1ST RAIDER BATTALION, 4TH MARINE REGIMENT, 1ST PROVISIONAL BRIGADE

After Guam, the 1st Provisional Marine Brigade was disbanded, and the 4th Marines became a regiment in the newly formed 6th Marine Division. Here Ken Champlin reflects on the aftermath of Guam.

From the couple I lost on the beach and on the mountain, I had nineteen killed and thirteen of us wounded. It is a pretty high casualty rate for a platoon. I often think about what I could have personally done not to have all those people killed. For a couple of years after the war, I had nightmares. A lot of guys did. I even almost strangled her [points to his wife]. I never forgot it. Guam was my most vivid memory of the war.

After Guam, I went home. [sigh] But before I went, we had several cases of suicide. Some of them you stopped, and some of them you couldn't stop. When it got to that point, it took about three people to hold him [a suicide case] down, and someone would run for the doctor to give him a shot. It was awful. You'd be sitting around talking and jeez . . . what's that . . . and someone had shot themselves. A good friend of mine, he was a quartermaster sergeant, just made warrant officer. One day he put his rifle in his mouth and blew his head off his neck.

I think it is part of my life that I'd want to trade. I don't know if I'd want to do it again, but I suppose I could. I wouldn't relish it. It was a little career when you're young. Having been in the Raider Battalion and with comradeship all these years and thinking next year we've been together for sixty years, it's kind of a nice thing to think back. You know these guys. It means a lot to me. I tell my kids that I don't have much money, but I don't have to go far in the United States and I have a friend. It used to be pretty true. These days they're dying off on me.

CHAPTER SEVEN

Leyte: The Return to the Philippines

In alien earth, across a troubled sea,
His body lies that was so fair and young.
His mouth is stopped, with half his songs unsung;
His arm is still, that struck to make men free.

—JOYCE KILMER, "IN MEMORY OF RUPERT BROOK"

IN A SMALL smoke-filled hospitality room in Nashville, Tennessee, on a sweltering weekend in July, several veterans reluctantly sat down to discuss their combat memories of the Philippines. Unlike most other reunion discussions, where funny incidents are often recalled and current events are discussed, this gathering was an almost joyless one. The men painfully relived experiences that have been buried since the war.

In a wood-paneled room, fifty-six years earlier, the Joint Chiefs had mapped Admiral Nimitz's drive across the Central Pacific, which was converging with MacArthur's advance up the northwestern shoreline of New Guinea. The officers debated where to launch the next major offensive to link the two forces. Admiral Ernest J. King, General George Marshall, and most of the other top-level commanders supported an invasion of Formosa (present-day Taiwan). Capturing the island would put

U.S. forces near China with the possibility of linking up with Chinese troops. The proposal outraged General MacArthur, who contended that the United States had a moral obligation to attack the Philippines and free the Filipino people and American POWs who had been under the brutal control of the Japanese since 1942. MacArthur also thought that the Philippines would be an essential staging area for future operations and that their loss would threaten Japanese trade routes between the home islands and the resource-rich East Indies. Finally, he wanted to make good on his famous promise to return and erase the bitter memory of his post–Pearl Harbor flight from the islands he failed to defend.[1]

Faced with these two options, the Joint Chiefs decided not to decide.[2] On September 1, 1944, the Chiefs agreed that invasions of Mindanao in the southern Philippines and Leyte in the central Philippines were prerequisites for a next step north to either Formosa or Luzon, the Philippines' main island.[3] In the end, logistics doomed the Formosa operation. The Allies wouldn't have enough shipping or troops in the Pacific until months after the completion of the war in Europe. Hopes for a link-up with forces on the mainland also evaporated with the near-collapse of Chinese forces in 1944.

Preliminary operations for the invasion of Leyte began at dawn on October 17, 1944. The green 6th Ranger Battalion landed on Dinagat and Suluan islands off Leyte's eastern coast to set up navigation lights for the main invasion three days later. Dinagat was unoccupied. On Suluan, the Rangers dispatched several Japanese defenders and captured a lighthouse with almost no casualties. A third island, Homonhon, was taken without opposition the next day. After accomplishing their mission, the Rangers served as guards for Sixth Army Headquarters for the remainder of the Leyte campaign.[4]

A-Day, or Assault Day (named to avoid confusion with the D-Day landings in France), began on October 20 with a four-hour naval bombardment. The Sixth Army's X Corps hit beaches between the Tacloban airfield and the Palo River, while the XXIV Corps moved inland between San José and the Daguitan River. By the end of the day, the beachhead was secure, and some units had pushed two miles inland.

The Return to the Philippines, Leyte and Mindoro—October 1944–January 1945

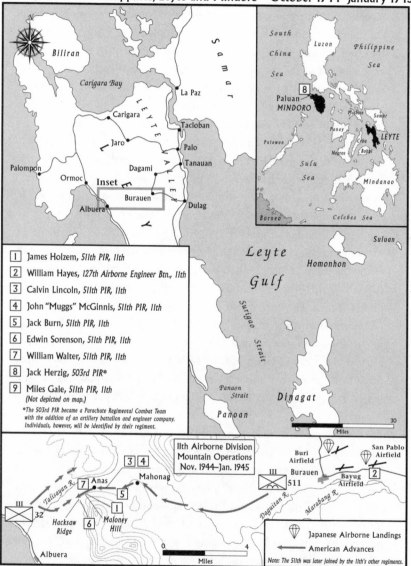

1 James Holzem, *511th PIR, 11th*

2 William Hayes, *127th Airborne Engineer Btn., 11th*

3 Calvin Lincoln, *511th PIR, 11th*

4 John "Muggs" McGinnis, *511th PIR, 11th*

5 Jack Burn, *511th PIR, 11th*

6 Edwin Sorenson, *511th PIR, 11th*

7 William Walter, *511th PIR, 11th*

8 Jack Herzig, *503rd PIR**

9 Miles Gale, *511th PIR, 11th*
(Not depicted on map.)

*The 503rd PIR became a Parachute Regimental Combat Team with the addition of an artillery battalion and engineer company. Individuals, however, will be identified by their regiment.

11th Airborne Division
Mountain Operations
Nov. 1944–Jan. 1945

Japanese Airborne Landings
American Advances
Note: The 511th was later joined by the 11th's other regiments.

151

To capture Leyte, the Sixth Army planned to build supply depots and airfields near the coast. Next, it would push through the Leyte Valley, a coastal plain near the landing beaches, advance over a line of uncharted mountains into another coastal plain known as the Ormoc Valley, and capture Ormoc, the island's largest port on the west coast.

The Japanese were determined to make Leyte one of the decisive land and sea battles of the war. Reinforcements poured onto the island with plans to exploit its mountainous terrain to bleed the Allies.

On October 23, the Japanese launched SHO-I, the largest naval operation of the war in terms of number of ships involved. The Japanese used their carriers as bait to lure Admiral Halsey's powerful Third Fleet away from the landing area, while three Japanese naval task forces converged on the vulnerable U.S. transport fleet in Leyte Gulf, with thousands of invasion troops aboard.

The transport fleet was guarded by elements of Admiral Thomas C. Kinkaid's Seventh Fleet, code-named Taffy 3, which had no large carriers or first-line battleships. Outgunned, Kinkaid's destroyers and planes from small escort carriers courageously engaged the Japanese. Believing that they were facing annihilation by a much larger force, the Japanese lost their nerve and broke off the attack, bungling their only chance for a major victory at sea. What was left of their naval strike force withdrew, only to be pummeled by U.S. airpower and submarines. Leyte Gulf was the last major engagement the Imperial Navy would fight.

On the ground, the Japanese buildup delayed the Sixth Army's advance through the Leyte Valley. To counter the Japanese reinforcements and attacks, the Sixth Army committed its reserve, including the green 11th Airborne Division. Once the units were ashore, General Walter Krueger, the Sixth Army commander, launched a double envelopment attack to surround the Japanese at Ormoc. Several infantry divisions formed the outer prongs of the attack, while the 11th Airborne Division struck the middle, slogging over the mountains toward Ormoc.

The mountain fighting deteriorated into a brutal and exhausting war of attrition. The paratroopers navigated deep gorges, climbed steep hills, and fought over narrow ridges defended by entrenched Japanese soldiers. Contributing to an already miserable combat situation were heavy rains that reduced visibility to a few yards and turned the jungle into a quagmire, cutting off food and other supplies for days at a time. Permeating everything was a putrid odor from rotting jungle vegetation.

While the painful advance on Ormoc continued, the Japanese tried to regain the initiative by launching a bold combined ground and airborne attack on the Sixth Army's airfields near Burauen, located near the center of the island. At dusk on December 6, 350 Japanese paratroopers from the 3rd and 4th Airborne Raiding Regiments, or *Katori Shimpei*, landed mostly on San Pablo airfield.[5] The Japanese paratroopers destroyed several planes, a jeep, and a fuel depot.[6] Support units, primarily from the 11th Airborne Division, contained the enemy paratroopers. Over the next few days, elements of the 11th, reinforced by other units, concentrated enough men to overwhelm the dug-in airborne troops.[7]

As General Joseph Swing's 11th Airborne was battling in Leyte's mountains, Colonel George Jones' independent 503rd Regimental Combat Team and the 19th Regimental Combat Team waded ashore on Mindoro, northwest of Leyte and about twenty miles south of Luzon. MacArthur wanted the island as a base for air operations in the invasion of Luzon. Mindoro was weakly defended except for small pockets of resistance, including a radio outpost located in the northern portion of the island. For one company of the 503rd, the outpost, carefully defended, proved to be a tough nut to crack. Nevertheless, within ten days after the main landings, an airstrip was operational, with several more under construction.

The beginning of the end of the Leyte campaign came when the 77th Infantry Division made an amphibious landing near Ormoc.[8] The port fell on December 10, and the two giant pincers of Krueger's double envelopment finally met on December 21, 1944.[9] A day later, after advancing through the mountains, the 11th Airborne's 187th Glider Infantry Regiment linked up with men from the 32nd Infantry Regiment, completing the operation after just over two months of fighting on Leyte.[10]

MacArthur declared the island secure on Christmas, but mopping-up operations would drag on until the summer of 1945. With victory in hand, most of the Sixth Army, including the 11th Airborne Division and the 6th Ranger Battalion, pulled out of Leyte and prepared for the invasion of Luzon.

JAMES HOLZEM
511TH PARACHUTE INFANTRY REGIMENT, 11TH AIRBORNE DIVISION

After preliminary operations against very light opposition on the small islands off the coast of Leyte, the real fighting began—and went on and on against an enemy determined to hold down as many Americans as possible. The 11th Airborne Division fought a bitter battle of attrition in the middle of the island, slogging over uncharted mountains toward Ormoc. James Holzem recalls the mountain fighting.[11]

My kids have asked me about it and I told them [sigh] that it was awful hard to talk about Leyte. I had a lot of sad experiences there. Luzon was a picnic compared to Leyte. I had to bury one of the guys that the Japs had eaten from B Company. There were two of them. Bill Hesselbacher had to bury one, and I had to bury the other. Then I had to bury Bill two days later, and it was equally sad. It wasn't like in Luzon where if we had wounded or dead, a jeep would come up and Graves Registration would bury the dead. It all began trying to take a hill.

We hit this one hill for several days. The Japs were dug in on it and firing their machine guns along the trail near the hill. I had to cross a trail that a Jap machine gun was firing at; I had to cross it six times in between bursts. The first day they sent the 1st Platoon to see if the Japs were still on the hill, and they got pinned down on one side of the trail.

The next day was when we really caught heck and had a lot of casualties. I knew where the machine gun that was aimed at the trail was po-

other people, and everyone said no. Finally, I was looking up at the sky between the corpses, and Bill wanted to go and get the sword, and I said, "Oh, I'll give you some cover, but you shouldn't do it."

First thing in the morning before we could go, I was put on water detail. They sent about ten guys with canteens about a half a mile down the mountain to a creek. I was sent down as a flank guard. So Bill went, and Iggy went with him. When I was down at the creek, I heard shooting, but I didn't know who it was. When I got back up about an hour later, guys were sitting around all sad. As soon as Bill went down to get the sword, there were five Japs hiding, and they shot him three times through the face and neck. Iggy ran back; it was only one hundred yards back to the platoon. The whole 2nd Platoon ran down there to get him. We had a little guy named Lorney DuBay. He was really fast; he could run like the devil. He was the first down there. As soon as he got down there, the Japs shot him through the chest. My platoon sergeant went down also. But he saw where the Japs were and shot all five of them. He got a Silver Star for it. When I got back from the creek, I went over to where the medics were, and I said, "Where's Lorney DuBay?" They said, "He's over there under that red parachute." The parachute was going up and down in the wind, and they said he was dying, drowning in his own blood. He died a few minutes later.

I went over to see Bill. He was lying by a tree on his back. There were a bunch of cigarette butts near him; he was a chain smoker. He was all bandaged up. I said, "How are you doing?" He said, "Light me up a smoke." I said, "You shouldn't be smoking." He said, "Look at all these butts!" I lit him a cigarette. The only thing he said to me was, "I lost my legs, didn't I?" I said, "No. Your legs are okay." He said, "Move them a little bit for me. I'm really tired. Do you mind coming back in an hour?" I left him. An hour later, I came back, and they were getting ready to bury him. I said, "Let's not bury him until the rest of the platoon gets back." When they got back, we had a little service for him. Iggy and I had to dig the hole. One of the men said some prayers over him, and then he said, "You and Iggy were the machine-gun team with him, so you bury him." We wrapped him in a parachute, dug the hole, carefully placed him in the hole, and had to throw dirt in his face. That was very hard for me. This is the first time I ever told this story and why I don't talk about Leyte. [crying]

WILLIAM HAYES
127TH AIRBORNE ENGINEER BATTALION, 11TH AIRBORNE DIVISION

As the Americans advanced on Ormoc, between 250 and 300 Japanese paratroopers mainly from the 3rd Airborne Raiding Regiment landed near the San Pablo airstrip and began destroying American equipment. The only troops in the area were a small detachment of airborne engineers and service personnel. William Hayes, a member of the 127th Airborne Engineer Battalion, remembers the desperate battle that night.

It was just about dusk—they had it timed pretty well—and somebody started yelling, "Those are Jap planes!" They surprised us; we didn't have any warning. We looked up and saw what looked a lot like C-47s, the same planes we jumped out of. Division headquarters was about one hundred yards from the strip, and I was in the motor pool at the time, which was just across from the headquarters. Our squad leader went back and had them issue us a supply of ammunition. He managed to get us each a bandolier. White parachutes were coming down, but we got it [ammunition] in time to shoot some in the air. I'm not sure if I hit anything, but I squeezed off a few.

We were told by division headquarters to set up a perimeter. They figured that they'd try to overrun the headquarters first. All night long, they were destroying things on the airstrip . . . planes and equipment. Shooting, grenades going off. It was chaos all night long. But nobody told the people near division headquarters that we were in front of [the Japanese]. [Headquarters personnel] were taking shots at us, and they killed one of my best buddies that night. I was so upset. We were ordered out there, and this was something that could have been avoided. I was made a runner to send a message back to the headquarters. As I was moving back there, they were [friendly fire] taking shots at me. Luckily, I wasn't hit.

During the night, our platoon leader got orders to attack the Japanese at dawn. There were about two squads. We didn't have a full platoon—about thirty altogether and some Seabees. We were the only ones attacking in the morning, which was pretty scary. We thought a battalion [about 650 men] jumped, but actually it was a little more than a company [between 250 and 300 men]. Still, there were only thirty of us, and we were completely outnumbered. So we were ordered to attack in the morning and run 'em off the strip if we could.

At that time, General Swing [11th Airborne Division commander] came up, and we were in a firefight with the Japanese. We exchanged fire for about twenty minutes, and we tried to set up two machine guns, and we managed to get a mortar set up. We just attacked head on. We lost about half of the men. The general came up and wanted to know where our battalion commander was. We told him he was probably in a dugout. So he said, "You guys follow me, and I want this machine gun." There were three of us. He said, "Bring that machine gun over here. We're going to flank them on the left side."

There was a berm on the far side of the airfield, and the Japanese were on the opposite side of it. Our platoon commander got hit in the legs and severely injured. Something also happened to a guy that got into *Yank* magazine. We were wearing fatigues with large pockets. Some of our grenades came in cardboard tubes, and he had the grenade in his pocket. Anyway, a bullet hit it and set it off. He wasn't scratched, nothing. He felt it, but by some quirk of fate, the shrapnel from the grenade didn't hit him.

CALVIN LINCOLN
511TH PARACHUTE INFANTRY REGIMENT, 11TH AIRBORNE DIVISION

The day after the Japanese airborne attack on San Pablo, the 2nd Battalion of the 511th Parachute Infantry Regiment moved out of Mahonag (located in the central mountainous area of Leyte), continuing the advance toward Ormoc by moving west toward the tiny village of Anas. E Company was left as a rear guard to cover the 2nd Battalion's advance. Calvin Lincoln recalls the fighting on December 7 and 8.

Members of the 511th take a breather and clean their weapons. (courtesy of Miles Gale)

We got down to this low ground where they [the Japanese] were digging for potatoes. They had their shirts off, and two or three officers were standing around, so we set up our machine guns. It seemed like a few sensed we were there and started moving toward the jungle. Within minutes, we opened up on them and killed most of them. As we walked up to see if there were any alive, a body was hollering in English. I carefully walked over to him since they were known for luring you in and they could shoot you or detonate a grenade. I could see his arms were out and he didn't have a weapon. He asked me in perfect English if I could get him a priest. That stunned me. I asked him, "Where did you learn to speak such good English?" He said, "I graduated from Catholic University in Washington." Our medic came over, and I told him what he wanted, and the medic gave him last rites. Then he asked me if he could have a cigarette. I gave him a cigarette, and he died within five minutes. It was the first incident where I came in contact with a Japanese soldier and talked to him. It put a human face on the enemy. You thought they were animals, and here he spoke perfect English and was more educated than I was.

It makes you feel bad when you kill someone. If they were shooting at me, I would obviously kill them first before they killed me. But I was never into killing. I was only nineteen years old, and you can be swayed pretty easy in your thinking.

After we secured the area, it was getting dark. We had to dig in for the night. Instead of going to higher ground, we stayed in the low area, which was a big mistake. We formed a perimeter like they formed when they circled the wagons in the West. All night long, we could hear them. They were hollering in Japanese. The next morning, we woke up to a banzai attack. Japs were everywhere; we were getting slaughtered. One guy turned around, and there was a Jap in the foxhole with him. They came in strength yelling and screaming. We were saved by one thing: their mortar shells wouldn't detonate. I could hear the Japanese mortar officer give orders to fire, and you could hear them [mortar rounds] sailing over the top . . . plunk . . . they would hit, and none of them would go off. Maybe they were up there so long that the powder got wet. They wouldn't detonate.

I didn't see it, but Private Elmer Fryar [who posthumously won the Congressional Medal of Honor for this action] was on the line directing machine-gun and mortar fire and killed a lot of them, breaking most of their attack.

JOHN "MUGGS" McGINNIS
511TH PARACHUTE INFANTRY REGIMENT, 11TH AIRBORNE DIVISION

Muggs McGinnis, a medic, has been away from the war and the men he served for fifty-six years. In July 2000, he was finally reunited with many of the men he helped save. Here he reveals his most vivid memory of Leyte: E Company's battle near Anas on December 7 and 8.

My first day my lieutenant got shot. He was my first casualty. We were up on a hill, and they were shooting at us, and I tried to give him blood plasma. I shook so bad I couldn't do it. Another guy gave him the plasma. This is war. I had to make a lot of adjustments. The training took over. As soon as a man was down, I was over there. I didn't even know who he was. I was interested in one thing: what's wrong . . . what can I do to help. I'm going to do what I can to get him out.

We went over the first ridge of mountains and were down in a potato patch, and we caught the Japanese out there in the open. We were between them. Stinky Davis was the platoon leader. He was a West Point graduate and a replacement. The first platoon leader got wounded the first day in combat, and Stinky Davis took over. We didn't know him too well. He was leading the platoon down this creek, and these other platoons [see Calvin Lincoln's story] started shooting at the Japanese in the open, driving them to us. There stood the 1st Platoon of E Company as the Japanese tried jumping across the creek.

When that was over, we stayed in the same area, and that was a mistake because we were in the same low ground where we ambushed the Japanese. The next morning we got hit. They dropped about four guys right away. They snuck up, and as we got up in the morning, they opened up on us. It caught everybody by surprise. Let me tell you, I don't know what the rest of the platoon thought, but, man, we had a battle. We got orders to pull out, and you had a log to go over or under to get out of there. All I know is that I'm going over the log. I just jumped. I got on the other side, and guys came underneath the log. The last guy that got out was acting as the rear guard, the last man. He was shooting and shooting, and he turned around and tried to make that log and they got him. I pulled him off the log and checked him out, and he was basically gone. He almost didn't have a pulse. I gave him a shot of morphine and said, "I can't carry you myself." No way in the world because he was just dead weight. But I wasn't going to let him get caught by the Japanese. No way. I waited around and nobody else came, so I tried to find a way out. I would never tell anybody, and I'm telling it to you now. It was one dose for pain and three or four to put somebody under. [He was the] only one I did that to. I did it on that one occasion. [sigh] But I had some guys I should have done that to maybe. These are judgment calls.

We finally got caught up to the end of the company and I said, "Man, this is hell!"

I treated guys that were good friends of mine, but I couldn't afford to get personal. If I did, I was going to tear myself apart. I'm an aid man first and foremost.

A day later, they moved our platoon to ambush positions, and the first night one of the guys got shot in the mouth. The bullet ricocheted around his mouth. I got him in my hole. I gave him morphine to keep him quiet. He was bad, and I gave him the morphine every time he would wake up. I got him this far, I was going to save him and wasn't about to let [his screams] kill us now. Finally, I got him out of there. Sadly, I think he was killed by an airdrop. The aerial drop came through, mortar ammunition, and it hit the aid station. I'm pretty sure he was killed by the falling box.

JACK BURN
511TH PARACHUTE INFANTRY REGIMENT,
11TH AIRBORNE DIVISION

The movie Saving Private Ryan *was built around a fictional extraction mission to locate and safely return Private James Ryan after three of his brothers were killed in action. The movie was based partially on the story of 101st Airborne Division trooper Fritz Niland, who lost three brothers during the war. Niland's mother received all three War Department telegrams announcing the death of her sons on the same day. To avoid another loss, and according to Army policy, Niland was snatched from the front line. The real story did not have the drama of the movie; Niland was uneventfully escorted from the front to the beach by the 101st's chaplain, Father Sampson. A similar, and previously untold story is related here by Jack Burn.*

It rained all the time in the hills of Leyte while we were there. Mud was all over the place. But that day it didn't rain. Jack Barker was a platoon leader, and they called him "Jack Rabbit" Barker because he never walked, he always double-timed it everywhere he went. As I recall, he had a sister who was killed, who was a nurse, and a brother in the Air Corps that was killed in Europe. His parents asked for their only surviving kin to return home. I believe the War Department had a policy on this.

Anyway, they organized a small patrol, and our job was to escort Barker to the beach. We were walking down a path from the mountains that led to the beach. There were about ten of us in the party, and I think most of the guys were Marine artillery observers. I was the scout and out front. On the way down to the beach, we went around a corner, and there were about six Japs on the trail cooking potatoes; they saw me and ran. It was kill or be killed. The firefight didn't last more than thirty minutes, and we killed all of them.

It took us the entire day to get down to the beach. When we got there, the officers had a liquor ration, and one of the officers gave me his, and Barker and I sat and had a drink. He told me how much he didn't want to leave us since we were his brothers.

EDWIN SORENSON
511TH PARACHUTE INFANTRY REGIMENT, 11TH AIRBORNE DIVISION

As the 11th Airborne Division slowly advanced west toward Ormoc, they were confronted by elements of the Japanese 26th Division entrenched along a series of steep ridges that were separated by gorges several hundred feet deep. The final push began on December 20, but the 511th's lead battalion was stopped by the terrain and dug-in Japanese. Then, in the early morning hours of December 22, the men of D Company made a crucial breakthrough that led to the ultimate link-up between the 187th Glider Infantry Regiment and the 32nd Infantry Regiment at Albuera, near Ormoc.

One of our sayings was, "I don't give a rat's ass." That's how it all started. It started in the States. You've heard the story. This is a ridge that was narrower than the top of a bed. Another company tried to take it day after day as I understand it. They were trying it in daylight, and they were getting shot up. They couldn't take it.

It came D Company's turn, and the company commander said, "We are going to hit them just before daylight and take the ridge." The firing heated up, and we kept going. Then the race was on. There was a charge. I was seventy-five or one hundred yards behind [the charge]. One of the fellows started yelling, *"Rat's ass! Rat's ass!"* [He gathered six of his men together and ordered a simultaneous toss of grenades, yelling *"Rat's ass!"* which also doubled as the signal to hit the ground.]

We caught the Japanese waking up. After we broke through, we were at a dogtrot; everybody kept moving forward. You'd see a Japanese, and if you weren't sure if he was dead, you'd shoot his head. There were hundreds of them. There were Japanese there that were alive, and you shot them. There was no place to take them, and you're too busy. If you go by, they're going to shoot you. I don't remember the count, but somebody said the official count was two hundred and something.

My understanding is that there was even a mini-hospital, and everybody was killed. The hospital was tiny. The wounded were laying on a few palm fronds, and we killed anybody that moved.

WILLIAM WALTER
511TH PARACHUTE INFANTRY REGIMENT, 11TH AIRBORNE DIVISION

William Walter recalls his war on Leyte.

Leyte was the worst ordeal of my life. You can't imagine. We went over thirty days up the mountains. It must have rained every day, and if it wasn't raining, the water was dripping off the trees. You were never dry. You'd lay in a water-filled hole or a slit trench. You were like a pig in a pen, laying in the mud.

We weren't getting fed since we were supplied only by airdrops. They used to drop rations to us, but we were so isolated on the top of this mountain ridge that they couldn't find us. Out of about thirty-three days, they fed us eleven days. We all lost pounds and pounds. We had jungle ulcers on our skin, impetigo. I had dysentery so bad! Actually, the elements were more of an enemy than the Japanese. After a while, we were eating anything. We were digging up roots, looking through our musette bags [small knapsacks] to find any old cracker—anything.

Between the weather and not getting fed and sleeping in the hole and getting sick, the emotions swell up in you. I remember one of our guys found a cracker in his bag, and I looked at him and said, "Give me a piece!" He said, "No." I went to take it from him, I was so hungry! That's one of the emotions you experience in war: pain, hunger, heartbreak, love, hate, and fear. All the emotions—you're kind of living on the edge. Everything is on a serrated raw edge. You're more alive than any point in your life since you experience every emotion.

The fellow I was with for those thirty-three days was a bonding that only death can separate, and that's what happened . . . he got killed.

I was in the hospital so bad with dysentery, and I couldn't go with him on a patrol. My friend, who was also our platoon leader, went out, and a sniper shot him. At the time, I was in the hospital and didn't even know it. The company clerk, who checked on people's dispositions, came into the field hospital and said, "Well, your boy got it." When he told me Bob Steele got it, I cried. It was tearing my heart out. I couldn't help it. I still feel it. He was such a soldier. He got the DSC [Distinguished Service Cross], and they were going to give him a battlefield commission because he was so good. When I lost him, I lost a lot. [cries] That part of the war I didn't like, if you know what I mean. We get together like at this reunion, we don't discuss that very much. We bring up the funny things. It's the stuff you don't want to think about.

There's a camaraderie; it's hard to explain. You've never been closer to anybody but your wife than you were with your army buddies. There was a bonding there that is hard to realize. Underneath, we were close as hell. That's why when you lose somebody, it really hits you hard.

I vividly remember when we were on Starvation Hill, the artillery shells were flying, and my buddy had his leg blown off. I had been home on a furlough with him, met his wife, and even went to the hospital when his wife delivered their little boy, and him and I went out and drank some beers to celebrate. There he was with his leg off. I went up to see him the next morning, and he had bled to death.

Sometimes when I hear "Taps," it gets me. I shiver. It hits home. I think about the best friends, the ones left behind. That what's "Taps" represents, the loss of somebody. This is the hidden war—the things that are rooted in your soul that grab you.

JACK HERZIG
503RD PARACHUTE INFANTRY REGIMENT

On December 15, 1944, Colonel George Jones' independent 503rd Regimental Combat Team and the 19th Regimental Combat Team waded ashore on the island of Mindoro. MacArthur wanted the island as a base for air operations in the invasion of Luzon. Mindoro was weakly defended, and within ten days an airstrip was operational, with several more under construction. However, a Japanese radio station located in the northern portion of the island continued to provide early warning for enemy antiaircraft batteries, fighter planes, and flak boats based on Luzon. Since the radio station was located in the fairly large Philippine town of Paluan, it was not feasible to destroy it by air attack or naval bombardment. Accordingly, B Company of the 503rd Regimental Combat Team, reinforced by a machine-gun section, was chosen to land some distance south of the town, then hike up to attack and destroy the radio station, along with its complement of about eighty Japanese soldiers. In the following e-history, Sergeant Jack Herzig reveals the essence of small-unit combat in the Pacific.

As we hiked up toward the enemy station, my 1st Platoon was in the lead. Moving down the trail, we encountered a Filipino youth who tipped us off about a Japanese patrol that was heading our way. As we had done before in New Guinea and Noemfoor, we set up an ambush with Jim Pascarelli, the BAR man of the first squad, as the base for fire and to his left the BAR gunner from the second squad, "Press" Ferguson. Ted Hoggatt, Bill Prendergast, "Junior" Malo, and Bill Harris took up positions covering the trail with their rifles. Sergeant Don Blum and I, both carrying Thompson submachine guns, moved off to the right as far as we could to kill any of the enemy who might not be cut down by the BAR and rifle fire. I arranged that we would all open fire when Pascarelli, who had the best field of fire, did. We heard the enemy coming. The first in line was a very large soldier, wearing a white loose shirt, who turned out to be a Japanese sergeant. Pascarelli's first burst took down the first four or five of the enemy, Ferguson's BAR jammed, and the rest of the enemy party fell under our fire.

Don Blum and I went in to be sure that there were no survivors who could pose a danger to us. We both happened to see the soldier with a captured Garand rifle as he had Don in his sights and pulled the trigger. For some reason, the rifle did not fire, and I was able to dispatch the enemy soldier in the next few seconds. As fate would have it, both Don Blum and "Press" Ferguson were to be killed the next day as we assaulted the radio station.

When we were getting ready to continue our march and talking about how fortunate we were that the Filipino youth had been able to give us information about the Japanese patrol, a captain, who clearly was not part of the 503rd, came up to me and said that I should have detained the young fellow. We were all rather high-spirited about what had happened, so we were not surprised when Ted Hoggatt said, "We were busy killing Japs. Where the fuck were you, sir?" Our Captain Smith evidently chose not to hear that and the "foreign" captain backed off. Someone said later that he was CIC [Counter Intelligence Corps], which did not mean a thing to us.

By nightfall, we had arrived at the outskirts of the settlement of Paluan, which was in two neighborhoods about three to four hundred yards apart. It was located at the apex of a very large bay, opening to the west, with a population close to a thousand living in three or four rows of "houses" built of local materials like bamboo. The Japanese had taken over the "new" school and the "old" school in the middle of the north section of the settlement, which were in a line end-to-end at a right angle to and about one hundred yards from the beach. They faced out onto a former playground that had been turned into a parade ground, and there was a new, small two-story building in which the radio was located. That building also had a watchtower on the top where a lookout had an excellent view seaward to sound an alarm in case of sighting any landing force.

We met about midnight to develop our plan, which had my platoon entering the eastern part of the area two squads abreast and setting up close to the schools in which the enemy was sleeping. The light machine-gun section took a position close enough to be protected by our left flank. We were set up so that we and the machine guns would have raking fire over the parade ground. The 3rd Platoon was to set up to our right facing south onto the parade ground and schools, and the 2nd Platoon was to our south facing north but in cover so that they would not accidentally be hit by fire from our 3rd Platoon. We were situated like a horseshoe with the schools, the radio building, the parade ground, and the Japanese in our center, and the open side being the shore. The local people had told us that the Japanese garrison formed into ranks every morning at sunrise to say prayers to the emperor on the parade ground. That was when our machine-gun section and the 1st and 3rd Platoons would destroy the enemy. The Japanese had placed an ammunition dump several hundred yards north of the schools that was guarded by four soldiers. This target was given to our guerrillas to whom we had given adequate weapons.

Captain Smith set up company headquarters a few yards behind my platoon, and our 60 mm mortar platoon took cover a hundred yards behind us. The same old brilliant moon that caused us problems when we landed was still up there making the area very bright, but we managed to get in place in the deep shadows of the houses despite the lookout on top of the radio building. As daylight started to break, we heard sounds familiar to any soldier: that was of the Japanese first sergeant getting his troops up and out. To our great dismay, there was firing off to our right alerting the Japanese in the schools, who immediately took shelter under their buildings. The guerrillas had been seen by the Japanese guards at the ammo dump and had been fired upon, thereby alerting the entire Japa-

B Company .30 caliber machine gun in action in Paluan.
(courtesy of Jack Herzig)

nese force. Although we didn't have a specific target, we fired at the schools and the radio building for perhaps a minute. Ernie Larson, a rifleman in our first squad, stood up and took the classic position of a model target shooter. He squeezed off one shot, knocking the lookout over the side of his little box on top of the radio building, who then slid off the roof into a crumpled heap. "Just like Errol Flynn," laughed Ernie, as he took cover.

The Japanese soldiers had constructed dugouts under each of the school buildings that were reinforced by thick logs. They had also prepared a maze of trenches they would have used in case of a seaborne attack that they were now manning to escape our fire. These preparations presented us with a formidable defense by the enemy while we could only take cover behind the logs that were standing on end supporting the civilian houses. From under the schools, we started to take rifle fire, which we were able to suppress, but then we came under heavy fire from a machine gun with us in the 1st Platoon as the primary targets. Pascarelli spotted the machine gun and engaged in a kind of duel and was able to put it and its crew out of action.

However, that was too late for several troopers who had been wounded and Captain Smith, who had been shot in both legs. During what seemed to be a standoff, our 3rd Platoon, from houses that gave them the advantage of elevation, was able to pick off some of the defenders who were moving through the trenches. The 2nd Platoon cut off several attempts by the enemy trying to escape from the schools to move to the south. Sergeant Blum, Ferguson, and several other troopers, firing as they went, ran into the new school in an attempt to locate and destroy the enemy under the floor. Blum was killed, Ferguson wounded, and the other troopers forced out by heavy fire from under the floors. We had to get Ferguson out as soon as possible. "Ted" Kaczor, from our mortar platoon, who was a big strong guy, said he'd go in and get Ferguson, who was pretty large too, while Ted Hoggatt, John Serba, "Junior" Malo, Max Kulick, and I would cover for them. Off we went, firing to prevent enemy fire from the dugouts. Kaczor came rushing down the steps practically carrying the wounded Ferguson when from under the building rolled a hand grenade that went off at our feet, killing Ferguson but leaving the rest of us, including Kaczor, unharmed. I've seen a lot of action, but that memory of Kaczor hauling Ferguson down those steps while we were trying to protect them is one of the most vivid in my mind.

By midafternoon, I still hadn't seen any officer. Our platoon had lost some of our best people, but we were trying small-group forays and sniping where we thought we might have some effect. In a maneuver like that to get Ferguson, we stormed in and brought Don Blum's body out of the school with no opposition this time. However, our wounded, which now included Prendergast, also from our platoon, were not getting adequate treatment. The lieutenant from regimental headquarters assumed command and ordered that we withdraw to the other smaller, southern sector of the settlement. Some of us thought that we shouldn't leave what we had fought to take. We did move out and set up a secure area where, after local people shared their food with us, we were able to really sleep well for the first time in several nights. PT boats picked up our dead and wounded. Among the dead was that sergeant from regimental headquarters. My 1st Platoon had suffered the most casualties: Sergeant Blum, Ferguson, Prendergast, Hoggatt, Larson, and several others.

During the night, the Japanese had abandoned their positions, and the dozen or so survivors took off to the north. At daylight, we went back to the scene of the fighting where the local people had already started to bury the dead Japanese.

Our new commander gave me, with the remnants of my platoon, the assignment of pursuing the fleeing Japanese. So the eight of us picked up water, extra canteens, C rations, ammunition, and food from the rest of the company. With several local fellows to act as runners, we took off after the Japanese with no more instruction than that. Over the next several days, we learned that five of the Japanese had drowned in a boat trying to make Luzon, others were killed by Filipino guerrillas, and the rest evidently were lost in the jungle. About a week later, I got word that some of us were to be picked up by a Navy PBY seaplane, and several days later, the rest of us were also returned to our base in Mindoro.

Some say that our company never recovered from the raid when we landed on Corregidor several weeks later. The lieutenant who took over command of B Company was killed on the island of Negros in June 1945. Some of the old-timers of B Company said that it was not a totally bad thing. I was twenty-two years old then.

I met Ted Hoggatt in San Francisco in June 1945 as we were being sent home for discharge. I met Captain Smith at Fort Benning's Airborne School in 1951 when both of us were recalled to active duty for the Korean War. This time I was a lieutenant. Ted Kaczor was badly wounded on Corregidor in the attack on Water Tower Hill just a few feet from me, losing the use of his legs. He died within a few years. Max Kulick killed himself in 1950. So the war did not end for many of us in 1945.

Max had an older sister in New York City who had been in touch with my mother, also in New York, during and after the war. Seems that Max never was able to reconstruct his life after he was discharged.

Max Kulick, haunted by the war, took his own life
in 1950. (courtesy of Jack Herzig)

Maybe, like me, he had a well-meaning uncle who told him that he'd been out of uniform "three weeks now" and ought to "get going" as a civilian. Three weeks seemed like a short time to be back after three years in the furnace of the Pacific. Hell. He'd spent three weeks in a hospital in New Guinea shivering from the chills and sweats of a "fever of undetermined origin." Maybe he couldn't see the future peddling frozen food door to door off the back of a truck or being a "private investigator" for the Great Northern Detective Agency in Hackensack, New Jersey. He couldn't see the future after trying to tough out several miserable days on the Ford light-truck assembly line in Fort Lee, New Jersey, or being a cub reporter for the *Jersey Journal* in Union City, New Jersey. Maybe he couldn't find a replacement for a home to return to since his sister's life had changed over three years. Or perhaps, as the end of the unemployment program for former GIs ran out after a year, he couldn't find any replacement for the security of the company of fellow human beings who had shared the dangers of a shooting war and had even taught him to play double pinochle. And maybe the faces and places in his extensive collection of hundreds of pictures that he had taken during his service possessed more reality and promise than his present life. So he journeyed back to Australia, which was more real and promising than his life in the big city. So it made sense to Max to go back to the place that had offered such positive feelings. My wife, Aiko, and I were doing some research for the Department of Justice and found Max's name on a ship's manifest when he returned to the United States in 1949 from Australia. Even that trip didn't work for Max. Death offered more promise and less pain than life. So he ended the pain. He was just as much of a casualty of war as was Sergeant Donald Blum.

MILES GALE
511TH PARACHUTE INFANTRY REGIMENT, 11TH AIRBORNE DIVISION

Miles Gale remembers his last day on Leyte.

I try to forget the war, but I can't. After the division broke through and linked up with other units on the other side of the island [near Ormoc], we came down from the mountains and went to our base camp near the beach. I remember sitting in this warm water with my arm in a sling. The water was up to my chest, and that ocean was nice and warm and clean. The water would lap against my body. I scrubbed between my toes. The skin from being in all that mud and water would fall off in large strips. But to sit in that warm water . . . what a good feeling. There was a whole bunch of guys doing the same thing I did. After that, I went back to my cot and went to sleep. It was so nice to know you were safe.

Luzon

> We have shared the incommunicable experience of war.
> In our youths, our hearts were touched with fire.
>
> — OLIVER WENDELL HOLMES

A MASSIVE NAVAL BOMBARDMENT on January 9, 1945, announced the arrival of a day Americans and Filipinos had awaited for three years: the Allies were ready to fight the Japanese on Luzon, the main island of the Philippines.

Victory would not come cheaply; the bombardment killed more Filipinos than Japanese.[1] Still, the Americans were back in force in their former territory, and the Japanese commander who had grudgingly sent tens of thousands of troops for the failed defense of Leyte saw his goal only as slowing and damaging the Allies. The only question was when, not if, the Americans would succeed.

With only 275,000 troops and limited firepower and air support, General Tomoyuki Yamashita did not try to stop the invasion of Luzon at the beaches. He instead applied a defense designed to tie down as many U.S. divisions as possible. He positioned the bulk of his army, 152,000 men known as the Shobu Group, on high ground in northern Luzon and had them dig in and wait for MacArthur to come to him. Defending Bataan and Clark Field were thirty thousand men known as the Kembu Group, while the Shimbu Group, eighty thousand strong, held Manila and southern Luzon.[2]

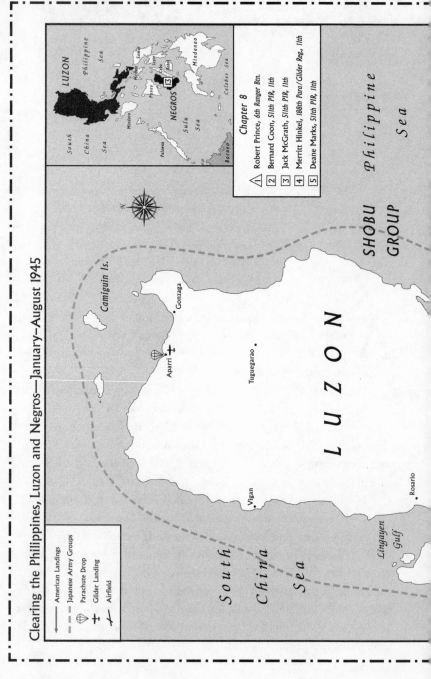

Clearing the Philippines, Luzon and Negros—January–August 1945

Legend:
- American Landings
- Japanese Army Groups
- Parachute Drop
- Glider Landing
- Airfield

Chapter 8

△ Robert Prince, 6th Ranger Bn.
2 Bernard Coon, 511th PIR, 11th
3 Jack McGrath, 511th PIR, 11th
4 Merritt Hinkel, 188th Para/Glider Reg., 11th
5 Deane Marks, 511th PIR, 11th

LUZON

NEGROS

Philippine Sea

South China Sea

Celebes Sea

Sulu Sea

Palawan

Borneo

Mindoro

Samar

Leyte

Cebu

Panay

Bohol

Mindanao

13

Camiguin Is.

Gonzaga

Aparri

Tuguegarao

Vigan

Rosario

Lingayen Gulf

L U Z O N

SHOBU GROUP

Philippine Sea

South China Sea

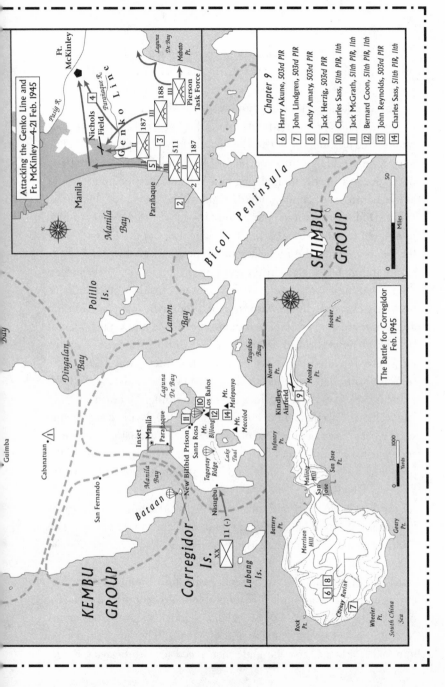

Attacking the Genko Line and Ft. McKinley—4-21 Feb. 1945

Pasig R.

Ft. McKinley

Laguna De Bay

Mabato Pt.

Nichols Field

Paranaque R.

G e n k o   L i n e

4

188

Pierson Task Force

187

3

511

187

5

2

2

Manila

Paranaque

Manila Bay

N

Chapter 9

6 Harry Akune, 503rd PIR

7 John Lindgren, 503rd PIR

8 Andy Amaty, 503rd PIR

9 Jack Herzig, 503rd PIR

10 Charles Sass, 511th PIR, 11th

11 Jack McGrath, 511th PIR, 11th

12 Bernard Coon, 511th PIR, 11th

13 John Reynolds, 503rd PIR

14 Charles Sass, 511th PIR, 11th

Bicol Peninsula

SHIMBU GROUP

0   50
Miles

The Battle for Corregidor Feb. 1945

Hooker Pt.

North Pt.

Monkey Pt.

Kindley Airfield

9

Infantry Pt.

Malinta Hill

San Jose Pt.

San Jose

Battery Pt.

Morrison Hill

Cheney Ravine

6 8

7

Wheeler Pt.

Geary Pt.

Rock Pt.

South China Sea

N

0   1000
Yards

Guimba

Cabanatuan

Dingalan Bay

Polillo Is.

Lamon Bay

Bay

San Fernando

Bataan

Manila Bay

Inset

Manila

New Bilibid Prison

Paranaque

Tagaytay Ridge

Nasugbu

Laguna De Bay

Santa Rosa

Los Baños

Mt. Bijiang

Mt. Malepunyo

Mt. Macolod

Lake Taal

10

11

12

14

Tayabas Bay

KEMBU GROUP

Corregidor Is.

11 (-)

Lubang Is.

Against minimal resistance, the Allies landed at Lingayen Gulf, using the same beaches the Japanese had landed on in 1941. The Sixth Army established a beachhead and cautiously began its drive south toward Manila, more than one hundred miles off.

As his forces drove on Manila, MacArthur ordered a series of daring raids to free prisoners of war and civilians held by the Japanese. On January 30, more than a hundred members of the 6th Ranger Battalion, over a dozen specially trained long-range reconnaissance troops known as the Alamo Scouts, and hundreds of guerrillas raided the Cabanatuan camp. Dodging Japanese patrols and tank forces, the raiders traveled more than twenty-five miles behind enemy lines to the camp. Led by the Alamo Scouts, the Rangers took up positions on two sides of the camp and attacked early in the evening of January 30. One platoon eliminated the guards, while another poured a fusillade into the Japanese barracks, and a third group crashed through the main gate. Within an hour, more than 200 Japanese guards were dead and 513 prisoners— living skeletons who had endured more than thirty months of captivity—were liberated. The Rangers lost two men, and seven were seriously wounded. Covered by the guerrillas, the raiders and POWs made it back to Sixth Army lines the next morning. MacArthur would later remark, "No incident of the campaign in the Pacific has given me such satisfaction as the release of the POWs at Cabanatuan. The mission was brilliantly successful." The raid caught the attention of the press and the American people, and several raiders were sent home for a Victory Bond tour.[3]

As the Cabanatuan raid was unfolding, two Eighth Army divisions landed at Bataan on January 29 and south of Manila on January 31. The southern assault was intended as a diversion and an alternative force to seize Manila.

The 11th Airborne Division executed the third landing, aimed at securing Manila with a coordinated amphibious-airborne assault.[4] On January 31, the 11th Airborne's two glider regiments stormed ashore at Nasugbu, about seventy miles south of Manila. The Japanese offered minimal resistance, and the glidermen raced toward Tagaytay Ridge, about thirty miles east of Nichols Field, Fort McKinley, and Manila.[5] On February 3 and 4, the 511th Parachute Infantry Regiment plus an artillery battalion jumped on the ridge, executing the airborne phase of the operation and linking up with the glider troops on February 4.[6]

The airborne troops pushed north toward the Parañaque River to a few miles south of Manila. Before them stretched the Genko Line, a belt of bunkers, machine guns, and artillery anchored by Nichols Field and Fort McKinley. This was the heart of Yamashita's defenses in the Manila area. To punch a hole in the Genko Line, the 511th crossed the Parañaque under heavy fire. Pillboxes and bunkers were cleaned out using rifles, grenades, and flamethrowers. After suffering heavy casualties, the paratroopers were able to pierce the line.[7] Finally, on February 12, after a massive artillery and aerial bombardment, the 188th Glider Infantry Regiment (GIR) and an attached battalion of the 187th GIR took the key Japanese strong points at Nichols Field.[8]

The men of the 511th now turned their attention to Fort McKinley, whose big guns had been pounding the 11th Airborne since the first week of February. Using the same infantry tactics that they used to crack the Genko Line, the paratroopers attacked the fort. Recognizing the hopelessness of the situation, the Japanese commander, Rear Admiral Sanji Iwabuchi, ordered the garrison to detonate McKinley's ammunition and pull out on the night of February 17–18.[9] With the fort in Allied hands, the encirclement of Manila was complete.

Nonetheless, the battle for Manila was both long and bloody. The Japanese were surrounded but bitter house-to-house fighting was required to clear the capital of the Philippines. As many as 100,000 Filipino civilians were slaughtered by the Japanese or killed by indirect fire.[10]

The bloody battle up Luzon, and for the rest of the Philippines, would continue.

ROBERT PRINCE
6TH RANGER BATTALION

After landing on the beaches at Lingayen Gulf, Sixth Army began the long drive south toward Manila. By the end of January, it had fought its way to the outskirts of the city. Thirty miles behind Japanese lines lay the POW compound at Cabanatuan. Fears mounted that the Japanese would slaughter the prisoners, so a daring raid was devised to free the men. Robert Prince, who commanded the lead assault company, recalls the raid.

I'll be frank with you. We didn't have a lot of action before the raid. Other parts of our battalion had some action on Suluan Island before Leyte. We landed on the second day of the Luzon landings. They didn't have a mission for us on the first day so we landed on the second day. We were guarding the Sixth Army headquarters and being used in small units for various missions. They sent one of the companies to a small island in the Lingayen Gulf. It turned out that there were no Japanese out there. While they were gone, the next mission came up: Cabanatuan. They called me in and said, "Colonel Mucci wants you to put your company on alert because we got a mission." He was over at Sixth Army headquarters, and he came back and told us what they expected of us and said, "I want your company and one platoon from F Company [a little over a hundred men] and some radio and medical people from headquarters." He had an eye for PR and had a couple of Signal Corps people from Sixth Army join us. He said, "I want all volunteers." So I addressed the company and said, "I'm going to turn around, and every man that wants to volunteer take one step forward." I turned around, and they were all in the same row. I thought none of them stepped forward when actually they all stepped forward.

I can't remember the timing details, but we decided no helmets because we wanted to move without noise and without extra weight. We had probably two days' rations, plenty of ammunition, and extra medical equipment—not so much for us but for the prisoners. We didn't normally have bazookas, but they gave us some of those to block this main road. We needed the bazookas just in case we were attacked by tanks.

Robert Prince, assault commander for the Cabanatuan raid. (U.S. Army)

They took us by truck to a town called Guimba. There we met Major Lapham, who had been in the guerrillas since Bataan. He took us to the guerrillas—several hundred who were armed with nothing more than rifles, and some didn't even have those. They were to set up roadblocks. They were in on the planning, and one of them was to block the road toward Cabanatuan, which was four miles to the camp, and one of them was to block the road on the other side to Cabu where there was a Japanese battalion-sized force. They moved out, and the ones that were in position near Cabu were in a beautiful enfilading position and practically wiped out that battalion.

We started in the late afternoon or early evening for this twenty-five- or thirty-mile march. Crossing a road, you'd have to go in spurts because the Japanese traffic was going up and down the road. Then it was dark, and we'd go through these little barrios, as people would call them. People would come out and greet us, and they'd offer us pieces of fruit or something. It was sort of a gala. You were going into a situation where the civilian population was 100 percent anti-Japanese and pro-American. If there had been pro-Japanese in there, they would have executed them right away. So you had a sense of security.

Outside of the main roads there were no roads. We were traveling through rice paddies. It was the dry season, so you got about a four-inch dike around every little paddy. We went back there in a jeep a year later, and it's pretty tough driving even in any season because you're going over one bump after another.

We got to another little barrio and spent the night there. The next day, the plan was we'd attack. But the Alamo Scouts went out and found out that there was a sizable Japanese unit that was bivouacked near the camp, so we delayed the operation twenty-four hours. We rested that day and took the info the Scouts gave us on the camp and improvised our plan. The thing that has astounded lots of people since then is that we had no time for rehearsal. I've talked to latter-day experts, and they just can't believe we didn't have any rehearsal. But there was no time for a rehearsal. That's why they sent us in, because there was no time and they were afraid they'd murder those men like it happened on Palawan. The Japanese poured gasoline on the men and burned them alive; it was horrible.

Anyway, we spent the day revising our plan, and about 5:00 or 5:30 the next evening, we started out toward the camp. We crossed a river, waist deep. We were under full cover until we got to the far side of the river. When you come over that bank, you're in full view of the camp. You had a couple hundred yards of open field to crawl across. Then we would be protected by an embankment next to the side of the road. We were crawling with our guns cradled. We didn't make any noise.

I had the platoon from F Company crawling up a dry creek bed. They had the furthest to go. They would be the first to open fire on the camp. We hoped to go around 7:30 P.M. Mucci or the G-2 at Sixth Army had the foresight to get the Air Corps involved, and this was a major part of this operation. You heard John Cook today talk about the P-61 night fighter; this pilot was supposed to divert the guards, and he did a masterful job. He'd cut the engines every once in a while, and these guys [Japanese guards] would look up, and he'd rev it up again. It was a great show . . . the ultimate diversion.

We were in place at 7:30 P.M., and it was at about 7:40 P.M. when the first shot was fired. It was on the F Company guys in back. One of the guards in the towers spotted them.

I was right in front near the main gate. When the firing started, the guard in the tower in front of us shot the gun out of the hand of a guy who was supposed to get him. The fellow with him killed the guard and shot the lock off the gate, and away we went. It was utter noise—lots of small-arms fire. I was standing right in front to direct traffic and see what had to be done. We had something come at us. If they were mortars or rifle grenades, I don't know what they were, and we had two or three explosions. It wounded a few men. Captain Fisher was hit, and one of the men said, "Call a doctor. This man's been hit." And he said, "I am the doctor." His medical sergeant came up to him, and he was shot and it destroyed his liver. He lived to the next morning.

By that time, our guys had finished off the guards and were bringing out POWs. I held a hurried discussion with some of the men who felt we had all of the POWs. I remember going into each hut or building with my .45 cocked. It was dark. I called out, "Is there anybody in here?" There were no replies. Only one man was left behind. He was deaf and fell asleep and didn't know we were there. Fortunately, he was later rescued by the guerrillas.

We were carrying some of them [POWs], but a lot of them walked. I'd say it took fifteen or twenty minutes to get them moving. Some of the men were skinny, in varying degrees of poor health.

I fired a red flare, which was a signal to the guerrilla forces that we left the camp. You could hear the firing because it wasn't far from the camp. Eventually, they were to fall back from their positions and form a rear guard. So we walked back down to the river and crossed the river. I then fired a second flare that indicated that we crossed the river. We went a mile or two to another small town. We asked for carabao carts [drawn by water buffalo], and the Filipinos volunteered, and about twenty-five showed up. Each one carried about three guys. I got up on the last carabao cart and rode with one of the medical doctors, Lieutenant Musselman from Nebraska. Here, after three years in a prison camp, he volunteered to stay with Captain Fisher and try to help him. Sadly, Fisher died the next day.

We walked back twenty-five miles. That's about thirteen or fourteen hours. About 3:00 A.M. we got to the main road and positioned bazookas on either side of the road as we crossed it. I'm not sure when the head of the column got back out. We arrived back at Guimba, and the reception committee included General MacArthur. I missed it since I was at the back of the column that was still moving in.

BERNARD COON
511TH PARACHUTE INFANTRY REGIMENT, 11TH AIRBORNE DIVISION

The third prong of MacArthur's plan to secure Manila began on January 31. Two glider regiments from the 11th Airborne stormed ashore at Nasugbu, linking up with the 511th Parachute Infantry Regiment, which jumped on Tagaytay Ridge on February 3. The 11th Airborne pushed north toward Parañaque, a suburb of Manila, and ran into Japan's strongest defensive positions, the Genko Line. Bernie Coon recalls the fighting on the way to Parañaque.

The 511th dropping on Tagaytay Ridge, February 3, 1945. (courtesy of Miles Gale)

We didn't hit any resistance after the jump. We were on our way to Parañaque; that was our destination. On the way, a machine gun opened up. I jumped over a wall to get out of its way, and on the other side were five dead Japs with no clothes, and they had been gutted. Their intestines were spread out all over the place. The Filipino guerrillas took their clothes and gutted them. That was my first experience with the dead. I said, "The hell with the machine gun" and jumped back over the wall!

I try to forget it. When I saw that movie, *Saving Private Ryan*, I used four handkerchiefs while I was watching. It was so real. One scene in the movie reminded me of when our medic got shot through both femurs and was bleeding. We had no instruments—we lost them on the jump— and we couldn't do anything for him. He turned to me and asked, "Am I going to die?" and I said, "Yes, you are." He said, "Let's talk about something else." [chokes up] We started talking about baseball, and he slowly bled to death. The movie reminded me of that. I had to go through his pockets and pull out pictures of his family. It was horrible.

Worse than that was in church. The stone walls were three feet thick, and I was talking to four other men. I was about to turn toward one of them, when we heard shells getting closer, so I turned to grab my helmet. Just as I was about to turn, a shell hit the door case and burst into the room and took the lieutenant's head off. I landed on my stomach and slid across the floor. The concussion was so bad that I couldn't hear anything for three days after that. For the next several days, we used the church as an aid station.

Later we got a call from the other side of the church. A fellow was sleeping near the fireplace, and a shell had come down the chimney. It hit him so hard that his innards were hanging out his mouth. I said, "He doesn't need us." The whole room was full of plaster and dust. You couldn't see, so we were holding hands to find our way.

When Manila was burning, they [the Japanese] set the town on fire, and all these refugees were coming out. We treated over a hundred in one day. One lady, her foot was missing, but she was walking. I don't know how she could do it; the pain must have been terrible. Some of them [the townspeople] were burned because they [the Japanese] had put them in their houses and tied the doors shut and set the house on fire. The atrocities were terrible. We had a women who had forty-two bayonet stabs in her body; they just kept sticking in about an inch all over her. I had a little nine-year-old boy—they tore his arm right out of the socket. He kept saying, "Give me a gun, and I'll go back and kill them all." Then I had a little baby, it wasn't even nine months old; they had thrown it up in the air and caught it on a bayonet. Now that stuff isn't necessary in a war.

JACK McGRATH
511TH PARACHUTE INFANTRY REGIMENT, 11TH AIRBORNE DIVISION

Jack McGrath, a medic, recalls the action around Parañaque and the 11th Airborne's thrust into the Genko Line.

We had our machine gun set up on our end of the Parañaque Bridge when we heard this damn jeep coming for miles. He kept coming and coming. Finally we saw the son of a bitch was going to cross the bridge. I got up and went out to meet him to tell him to turn around. They just went right by me. I yelled, "Turn around!" But they went right by me.

They zoomed by, and it was General Swing, our division commander. They went a couple of seconds past us, and the Japs cut down on them and killed the chief of staff who was riding with him. He came roaring back and said, "Why didn't you stop me? Why didn't you stop me?" We were telling him to "Shut up, you bastard!" He woke up the Japs, and they cut down on us, so we were all mad. We took the wounded over to where the headquarters was. They kept shouting, "Medic!" I figured they had their own medic, but I went over anyways. As I went into this Filipino house, one of our medics says, "Go on, Mac; the son of a bitch is dead." Swing is standing right there. Oh, man, I could see it hurt him, like the way his chief of staff was referred to as a son of a bitch in such a casual manner. You think they would have stopped. What did he think I was doing out there? Asking him the score of a baseball game?

Charred pillbox on the Genko Line. (courtesy of Miles Gale)

As a medic, you see a lot. A friend of mine was a medic, and he got shot through one side and out the other. He was laying in the mud, and we were holding a poncho over him, and Doctor Nester took his guts out and put them in a mess kit and sewed his holes up, sprinkled him full of sulfa powder, and he lived. We had another shot in the head, and they did a brain operation on him, and he lived until we tried carrying him out. We killed him carrying him out. We didn't have real litters, so we had to make them out of branches and fatigues.

We moved toward Nichols Field. We had to take a tough position. We knew we were going have casualties, and lo and behold, this tank destroyer shows up to ask directions. Well, we were going to take that tank destroyer away from him. Here was the perfect opportunity to blast the Japanese with a big gun like that. We thought that was wonderful, and he [the tank destroyer commander] got a little leery and thought we were going to take his tank destroyer from him. I was in favor of it, and he said, "Look, I'll give you three rounds." And he blew the Japanese all to hell.

We just walked through it [the line]. It could have been a lot worse since it seemed like every Jap had a knee mortar or a machine gun.

Shortly after that, they were calling for a medic. Sergeant Futch was lying there, and he had big gaping holes in his body—one below the throat, another at the solar plexus, and a third just above the pubic bone. Blood around him was three-quarters of an inch deep. I knelt in the blood and opened Futch's jump jacket and pants. Blood turns dark and solidifies real fast on hot concrete. It was on a sidewalk. Then some captain says, "Look, let's get the hell out of here because they have more coming!" We were in favor of that. He then looked down and saw Futch on the ground and asked how he was. I said, "He's dead." At that moment, he made a death gurgle. That's when they let out a noise when their muscles relax. The captain looked at me like I didn't know what I was talking about and said, "Take that man to the aid station!" I threw him over my shoulder in a fireman's carry. His blood ran down my back and into my boots and "squish, squish" every step I'd take. I got to the station and a friend of mine asked me, "Why did you bring him back? He's dead." I said, "I know, but I was ordered to." We checked him again, and he was indeed dead. So I went to the river to wash myself off. I was really bloody. I looked like I was in a butcher's shop. It rots in the sun. You smell like death.

We dug in for the night, and lo and behold comes this Filipino with this gal and she's for sale—or, I should say, rent. I'd never had a girl and didn't want to die without knowing, so I asked him what the price was, and we agreed on half my rations and half my money. We went into this little house. She was forced into it because of the war. We started doing it, and all of the sudden it sounded like a freight train . . . whammo! They shot some shells through the roof at the apex. Splinters and building supports came down on us. With all the dust, you could barely breathe in there, and she went crazy, screaming. I got her calmed down and started again. When shells pass where you see flashes of light, they were close to my head, and this time she went crazy—I mean absolutely crazy. After we tumbled out of the house, the machine-gun crew hooted and hollered. The pimp asked me if we were going to be there the next day. I said, "I doubt it." But we agreed if I was, it would be the other half of my remaining money and rations. But we moved out.

MERRITT HINKEL
188TH PARA/GLIDER INFANTRY REGIMENT, 11TH AIRBORNE DIVISION

Fort McKinley was the final hurdle in the Genko Line. Its capture completed the encirclement of Manila, as Merritt Hinkel recalls.

The war has flashed back in my dreams. But I've been living with jungle rot for all these years. I've had it all over my body since 1944. It hasn't left. The great Veterans Administration, even though they have records showing I had it, kept saying you never had it in the service.

Have you ever had goosebumps? Let them weep, and then the itch starts. I couldn't even work at times. [After the war] I became a vacuum cleaner salesman, and my hands were so bad I'd wear surgical gloves. This was when they were cotton. Bad idea. That's when all the pus and ooze would seep right on through. Can you imagine someone taking his handkerchief out in front of your wife, wiping his face so it wouldn't fall on his suit and his hands, his hands with surgical gloves on looking like that? Wouldn't you be jumping up and down to buy from him? They were jumping up and down to get me out of their house! It was on my back, my face, and at one time I was totally covered.

As we were approaching Fort McKinley, I saw a group of Japanese with light machine guns, and if they got set up, they would have slaughtered us because they had a great field of fire. But we came up behind them. The next thing I knew, I was on my back. He [a Japanese soldier] was standing over me, and his bayonet was stuck in the ground next to me. I'm trying to push his rifle out of his hands. I thought of releasing it and shooting. But the next thing I knew, this man collapsed like he fainted. His face was looking at me. Just above his eyes, which were wide open, almost dead center on his forehead was a little brown dot where a bullet went in. I rolled over to take a shot at the other guys, and Al said I pulled off eight rounds one at a time. I got my rifle spring mixed up with a guy from Chicago, and this caused the rifle to fire a single shot at a time.

I finished off what I had. Al was asking me repeatedly, "Hink, are you okay? Hink, are you okay?" I heard every word of it, but I couldn't answer him. I was scared shitless and just blocked everything out. My war was that ten or fifteen yards in front of me; that's your life. You try to live it.

I rolled over and fired eight more shots. I got up and they're yelling, "Bend over! Get down!" I ran about a hundred yards, dashed faster than Jesse [Owens], and got back to our guys.

Another person I'd like to mention was Lieutenant Bush. He was a man, a soldier's soldier. He always put us first. His family needs to know what happened. I remember [during one of our patrols] there was an explosion, and everybody hits the deck.

Again we were on a patrol. You look at him [Bush], and here he is standing up. We said, "Lieutenant, get down!" He said, "You guys stay here, and I'll see if it's safe." I said, "Lieutenant, that's our job, not yours."

On Nichols Field or near Fort McKinley when several of our guys were hit, the guys said, "We'll go get them." I think there were two men out there. Bush said, "No, they are my men. Just cover me." They were in a ditch or draw, and Bush went over the top to rescue the men. And this guy [a Japanese soldier] jumped up and before anybody could do anything, he shot and killed Bush. He wouldn't let any of the men do it; he had to get his men. This man deserves recognition—everything his family can get.

DEANE MARKS
511TH PARACHUTE INFANTRY REGIMENT, 11TH AIRBORNE DIVISION

*In the following e-history, Marks provides a snapshot of the infantryman's war as the 11th Airborne finally closed in on Manila.**

---

* Deane Marks passed away in 1999, shortly after providing this e-history.

The reality of war cannot be even imagined by anyone who has not been there. You see none of this in the movies. Only from a poor sucker infantryman can you learn what it is like, and the infantryman will very seldom talk about it.

Porteous, Guetzko, Westbrook, and myself were asked to get a stretcher and pick up First Sergeant Edgar L. Wilson's body. We hoofed it across the road towards the beach. We knew exactly where he was, because E-511th had been flanked by us the day before when they withdrew and left our squad in the polo field. The sun was up, and it was hot and muggy. When we arrived over by the beach area, we came upon a large ornamental concrete and tile patio. By the side of the patio, there was an ornamental tile and concrete walk, which looked down on the beach. The homes in this area were huge, sumptuous homes of the affluent of Manila. At the north end of the patio, there was a stairwell, which went down six or seven steps, took a turn left, and then went down another three or four steps to the beach. In the past, this route provided access for swimming and sunning on the beach. Wilson's body was laying face down on the landing. We had a difficult time getting the litter under his body, because it had swollen to twice its normal size and his uniform acted as a rigid envelope. His skin had already turned black from the sun, and his helmet strap had cut through his chin and cheeks. As we wrestled his body on the litter, the skin broke and gas and fluids flowed out. Someone threw up, and that made the other three of us do the same. We picked up the litter, with Westbrook and Porteous leading the way, followed by Guetzko and myself. As we moved up the stairwell, body fluids ran down the litter on Guetzko and myself.

As we carried Wilson's body back to the road, curious Filipinos looked at us in awe. One of them said, "Weelsohn"; that's how they pronounced "Wilson." Earlier, they had checked his dog tags. His wedding ring was still in place, but there was no watch or wallet. Speaking of the wedding ring, his finger had swollen to twice its normal size and the skin was cut. We made no attempt to remove it. We left that to the Grave Registration troops. I believe Wilson's body is still in the American Cemetery in Manila. They did not ship bodies back in those days.

Clearing the Philippines: Corregidor, Luzon, and Negros

All wars are boyish, and are fought by boys.

—HERMAN MELVILLE

THE TINY ISLAND OF CORREGIDOR lies several miles from Manila. Only a few miles long, it's a flyspeck compared to many of the other islands that make up the Philippine archipelago. Today, the jungle has reconquered it, obscuring broken concrete, smashed bunkers, and rusting pieces of twisted metal. On one edge of Corregidor sits the weathered Pacific War Memorial. A plaque reads:

Sleep, my sons . . .
Sleep in the silent depths of the sea,
Or in your bed of hallowed sod,
Until you hear at dawn
The low, clear reveille of God.

The plaque is a window into the painful events that overtook the island more than half a century ago.

Corregidor, also known as the Rock, is one of four fortresses built for the defense of Manila and its harbor. In 1942 it was America's last bastion in the Philippines and the scene of Lieutenant General Jonathan Wainwright's surrender of U.S. forces. Nearly three years later, General Douglas MacArthur's forces prepared to recapture the island.

MacArthur's plan involved a combined amphibious and parachute assault, one of the riskiest military maneuvers since both parts of the attack are highly vulnerable and require careful timing. Compounding the difficulty, Colonel George Jones' 503rd Regimental Combat Team would have to jump on the island's parade ground and golf course, each only a few hundred yards long and flanked with cliffs that dropped straight into the sea.

MacArthur's intelligence estimated that 850 Japanese troops defended Corregidor. Intelligence was wrong. Six thousand troops, many elite marines, were hunkered down in Corregidor's concrete bunkers and elaborate underground tunnels.[1]

In the early morning hours of February 16, Jones' paratroopers began dropping on the island, catching the Japanese by surprise, while about a thousand infantrymen, largely from the 3rd Battalion of the 34th Regimental Combat Team, stormed ashore.

The paratroopers and infantrymen, designated Rock Force, soon became immersed in a campaign of small-unit assaults. Squad- and platoon-size groups of men blasted and burned the Japanese out of pillboxes and underground defenses using flamethrowers, grenades, and pointblank howitzer fire, the brutal techniques Allied troops had found effective in earlier Pacific campaigns. The fighting was especially ferocious in the first days.[2]

The Japanese were hobbled by the destruction of their communications and the death of their commander in the first day of the assault; they lacked the leadership to launch anything but small-scale attacks. In an effort to regain the initiative, several hundred Japanese soldiers and marines attacked in a banzai charge against the 503rd in the predawn hours of February 19. A face-to-face melee erupted, and several positions were overrun, but the paratroopers held and repulsed the Japanese.

The battle for Corregidor lasted about eight more days, culminating with a massive explosion. Just past 11:00 A.M. on February 26, the Japanese detonated several tons of explosives and munitions cached in an underground arsenal at Monkey Point. The entire island shook; concrete, dirt, boulders, and body parts rained down from the sky, resulting in nearly two hundred paratrooper casualties, including fifty-two killed. Only a couple of dozen Japanese survived the battle.

Official closure came on March 2, 1945, when a flag-raising ceremony memorialized the completion of the battle.

Even before the battle for Corregidor ended, MacArthur planned another prison raid to free missionaries and civilians held at Los Baños. The raid, like the one at Cabanatuan, was flawlessly executed by elements of the 11th Airborne Division. John Ringler's B Company of the 511th Parachute Infantry Regiment dropped at 7:00 A.M. February 23, landing northwest of the camp. Converging overland was the Soule Task Force, consisting of the 1st Battalion of the 188th, the 511th Recon Platoon, a tank destroyer company, and attached Filipino guerrillas. A parachute battalion, supported by a pack howitzer company, crossed a large body of water known as Laguna de Bay in fifty-nine amphibious tractors.

Shortly after landing, the paratroopers neutralized more than two hundred Japanese guards and began organizing the internees for the return journey. Had the raid been delayed, it is probable that the Japanese would have executed them. Eventually, more than twenty-one hundred internees and their liberators were loaded into the amphibious tractors and transported to safety.

With the major objectives of Manila, Bataan, and Corregidor in MacArthur's hands, Swing's paratroopers were assigned to help the Sixth Army clear the southern part of Luzon, the Philippines' main island. Japanese defensive positions stretched from Laguna de Bay to Lake Taal, manned by the fifty thousand men who composed General Tomoyuki Yamashita's still formidable Shimbu Group. The 11th pierced the heart of Japanese defenses woven into the mountains of southern Luzon. Battles for mountaintop strongholds such as Bijiang, Malepunyo, and Macolod were burned in the memories of those who cleared them.

Macolod was particularly insidious. Here, Filipino slave laborers were forced to hollow out underground installations and help install artillery and automatic weapons that were positioned with interlocking fields of fire, maximizing their killing power. Once the work was completed, the laborers were ruthlessly murdered to ensure the secrecy of the mountain stronghold.

The Allies' progress was slow and bloody, but with the fall of Macolod and Malepunyo, large-scale enemy resistance in southern Luzon collapsed, and the 11th focused on mopping-up operations. The division prepared for its final campaign in the northern Philippines.[3]

Since May, Yamashita's Shobu Group had been withdrawing to planned defenses in northern Luzon. Led by the 37th Infantry Division, the Sixth Army continued advancing north as the Japanese melted into the countryside. With the hope of "annihilation of the enemy forces fleeing north," over one thousand men (Gypsy Task Force) of the 11th Airborne were directed to make America's last major parachute and glider assault of the war. Connolly Task Force, led by elements of the 6th Ranger Battalion, spearheaded the drive on Aparri from the ground, entering the area unopposed. The operation was a bust: the Japanese were moving in another direction. Two days later, Gypsy Task Force superfluously dropped on Aparri. The 11th would close out the campaign mopping up Japanese resistance in northern Luzon.[4]

Following the bloody battle for Corregidor, the 503rd Regimental Combat Team was transferred back to Mindoro. The paratroopers were scheduled to jump and reinforce the 40th Infantry Division's attack on northern Negros, an island several hundred miles south of Luzon, but the jump was canceled. Jones' regimental combat team was instead flown to the nearby island of Panay and moved to Negros by sea.

Armed with a large cache of automatic weapons (mainly from destroyed Japanese aircraft), the Japanese on Negros manned strong defensive lines, determined to wage a bitter battle of attrition. For the next five months, the 503rd engaged fierce Japanese resistance in the mountains of Negros.[5] Slowly and deliberately, Lieutenant General Takeshi Kono, the Japanese commander, held each line until it was about to be overrun and then retreated inland to another prepared defensive position. In June, the 40th Infantry was deployed to Mindanao, leaving the 503rd to battle the Japanese alone. Only at the end of the war did more than 6,150 Japanese soldiers come down from the mountains of Negros and surrender, bringing the battle for the Philippines to a close.[6]

HARRY AKUNE

503RD PARACHUTE INFANTRY REGIMENT

Without formal parachutist training, little equipment, and only fifteen rounds of ammunition, linguist Harry Akune, a Japanese American, was among the first Americans to land amid the splintered tree stumps, rubble, and enemy fire on the heavily defended island fortress of Corregidor. Akune was the only Japanese American to participate in one of World War II's most difficult parachute assaults.

I was waiting for Captain Donovan to go to the airfield. He was the S-2 [intelligence officer] and had a jeep with my equipment in it. So I was waiting around, and I came back, and the jeep was gone. I tried to find him, but the only thing I could assume is that he left without me. Trucks with troopers on them were moving to the airfield, so I jumped on one and got to the airfield.

I had an Air Corps officer guide me through the planes that were loaded and ready to take off. I went by and finally found this captain, and he was in full gear. I went up to ask him where my gear was. The only thing I had on were overalls and a fatigue hat. He points to the corner and says, "There." I see just a parachute, and I asked him, "Where's the rest of the stuff?" He said, "On the jeep." I said, "Where's it at?" He responded, "I don't know." I got my parachute and sat down next to the captain. When we were airborne, the door was open on the plane, so I was yelling over to the captain—he had a side arm and a rifle—so I asked him, "Captain, do you think that you can give me one of your weapons so I can protect myself?" He said, "If I get down there and I'm not using both, you can have one." I didn't know where we were going to land. But after I said that, another trooper across the way, true to a paratrooper, turned around, got concerned for me, and asked the crew chief, "Hey, chief, do you have a weapon on this plane? One guy doesn't have one." He went back to the aft of the C-47 and came back with a Tommy gun with a cylindrical ammo drum like Dillinger used. Anyway, he brought it back, and I never used anything like that before and didn't even know to carry it when I jumped. The trooper said, "I'll take it, and you can take mine." That's how I got a carbine with one clip—no food, water, helmet, anything.

So I went out the door. The first thing I lost was the fatigue hat since the prop blast blew it off. Here I go out the door, and I made all kinds of mistakes. This was my second jump. On my first jump, I was given a five-minute instruction.

As I was floating down, I didn't know how to judge distance height. I thought I was going to go into the ocean. So I frantically pulled on my back riser [risers attach the harness to the parachute], and I looked down and here was this jagged tree, sticking up like a spear right under me. I remember thinking, "God, I'm going to get impaled." I pulled the front and tried to pass the tree. The chute started turning, and I'm not sure what's happening. Luckily, I saw the tree go by, and I said to myself, "I made it." My foot touched, and I rolled on my back. I rolled downhill and slid down on my back all the way down that hill. Luckily, the parachute was holding my head up when I slid down about 150 feet. Nobody was around me. I knew instantly that I wasn't supposed to be there, so I cautiously started moving up toward Topside. I started going up. I was on a really steep hill. On the jump, I hurt my foot. As I'm limping up the hill, I see maybe a half a dozen rifles lined up at me. I thought to myself, "How much more trouble am I going to get into?" So I raised my hands and walked up to them. One of the guys recognized me—he remembered me limping around after my first jump. He was a sergeant and a demolition man. He cussed me out. He said, "You son of a bitch, don't do that again!"

I never did see the sergeant after that, but I wanted to thank him. Years later, I went to a reunion with some of his men and asked where

Dramatic photo showing a 503rd trooper exiting a C-47 on Corregidor.
The trooper's legs are on the left. (U.S. Army)

he was. They told me he was killed a few days later in Corregidor. I felt terrible.

I joined them and moved on. I found a helmet. The helmet was so big it was bouncing up and down on my head as I walked. I was getting a lot of small-arms fire, and I found cover in this lighthouse. I kept going with them, and we cleared an area.

I got to the command post. I went over to a barracks alone. I was trying to find documents [for intelligence purposes]. As I was rummaging through things, I got a big surprise. I turned over a box, and a Japanese soldier was looking wide-eyed at me. I thought I had it, but as I poked at him, I realized he was dead.

Documents started coming in. I was under a shelter half with a flashlight reading the documents at night. I got up, and everybody was gone. I was all by myself. I was afraid to move since they might think that I was the enemy. I crawled to a corner and waited to avoid friendly fire.

[On Corregidor] I went on several patrols with the S-2. I knew guys like Emery Graham, so I'd go out with him on one of the patrols. On one of the patrols, I found one message that was pretty critical. We expected 850 [Japanese] on the island, and there was a messenger carrying a message to other officers indicating that the commanding officer was killed and his rank was important. He was a naval captain, and they usually command at least five thousand men. The message gave Colonel Jones a feel for what he was up against. That one bit of information led to our strategy when dealing with Japanese. I continued to send anything I found of tactical importance on the prisoners.

Over the course of the next several days, we captured more prisoners. One prisoner was pretty weak and didn't want to talk. I finally told this guy, "If you don't talk . . ." At that moment, a Tommy gun went off . . . *brrrrr*. "You know what we do with guys like you?!" He assumed that we shot them after the Tommy gun went off. Boy, that guy straightened up. At first he was so damn weak. Then he became soldierly. I remember we were on the second floor and had to get to the ground level, so he smartly walked down that stairway. I told him to make a right turn and another right turn. I then told him to sit down, and he practically collapsed. I went down to try to give him some water or something. When I was trying to get the stuff, this sailor appeared pulling on the prisoner's ear saying, "I promised my kids some Jap ears. I'm going to cut your ears off!" I figured no matter who they are, they shouldn't be abused when they give up. I went over to him and said, "If you want some Jap ears, there's a lot of live ones out there. Leave this guy alone!"

We captured another prisoner that tried to swim to Bataan. We brought him into the CP. This guy got noisy and was yelling so I told him,

"Shut up!" Then I turned to look at the captain, and I heard a shuffle and the next thing I know, I was flat on my face. The prisoner had a stranglehold on me. The guard couldn't fire, so he started hitting the prisoner with the butt of a Tommy gun. All the other guys jumped in, started kicking. Someone hit him with a bottle. I'm trying to avoid their blows. At first, I knew he tried to take me with him. But gradually as life started to ebb, I could just feel that he was clinging to me as if clinging for life. I had his blood all over me, and eventually they took him out and shot him. Sometimes I feel guilty that I didn't stop it.

I was looking for a fresh uniform. I had his blood on me for almost a week. Finally, Emery Graham said, "We have an outpost near a water tank." I went over there and got on top of it where I could see the entire island. I was in an exposed position, standing bare-naked, but I didn't give a damn. I wanted to get that blood off.

Another Japanese prisoner came in, and he'd been shot through the penis and scrotum. It looked like a blown-up wiener. He was hurting, so I gave him first aid. There was a 503rd trooper sitting next to him, hurt and waiting for medical attention. He got a cigarette out and was going to smoke it when he saw this prisoner and the agony he was in. He turned around and gave him one. To me, here they were enemies minutes before. It was life or death; offering the light was such a beautiful gesture. I said to myself at the time, "I'm proud to be an American because of people like him."

JOHN LINDGREN
503rd Parachute Infantry Regiment

With their commanding officer on Corregidor killed the first day, uncoordinated pockets of Japanese were on the defensive. In an effort to regain the initiative, several hundred Japanese soldiers and marines launched a massive banzai attack in the predawn hours of February 19, overrunning several positions, including John Lindgren's mortar platoon. He relives the experience here.

It started with voices and some shots. It was late at night and very dark. You couldn't see anything. But it wasn't the voices—it was the feet. You could hear them marching, running around—that was really what scared me.

Fear stays with you. I'm sure you had moments in your life that really frightened you, and you remember it. That night, I didn't give much hope for getting through it. At the outset, we were in a very dangerous position because we were in a shell hole with the mortar platoon on the road called Cheney Trail. Most of the platoon and the mortars were in there. Our position in the middle of the road, the Cheney Trail, was the road they were attacking through.

They were swarming all over the place because they were coming up the road. We had to get out of there, or we were dead. I stayed in the shell hole to make sure everyone was out. I was the platoon leader. I told them to get out of there, and I remember someone said, "What about the mortar?" I said, "Screw the mortar, and get out as fast as you can!" They took the mortar with them even though I told them to forget it. Anyway, Leshinski had been dozing off, and he had taken his boots off, which is not a real good idea. I was there with him, and it was really getting bad with all these voices around. Clump . . . clump . . . clump . . . feet moving all around. Leshinski is there, and he insists on putting his boots on, and I said, "Jesus, just forget that, and get the hell out of here!" He didn't do it; he just wouldn't do it, so I said, "Leshinski, I'm getting out of here. I'm not going to wait for you to put your boots on!" Any rate, he didn't listen to me, so I took off. I was just really upset that he wanted to do this. He was stubborn. He refused to do it, and it cost him his life. I won't say he would have done any better had he gone back to the bunker, but at least he would have had a shot at it. Out there, he was a goner. It was just a question of time. So I crawled out of there and left Leshinski.

For some reason or another, the platoon [less than twenty men at that time], when they fell back in the company area, what we call the bunker, they went to the right, as you look westward toward the sea. They went to the right rear when they were moving, and for some reason or another, I got pushed off to the left.

So I came up to the bunker, and I'm shouting and yelling to take it easy, don't shoot, it's me . . . blah blah blah. I get back to the bunker, and there's a ramp there and a little wall. When I got back, there were three men: company commander Lieutenant Joseph Turinsky, Lieutenant Henry Buchanan, and our bugler, or the mail orderly. I've forgotten what his title was; I think it was the mail orderly, Corporal Joe Foley. Those three were there. I hadn't been there three minutes, and Turinsky was firing over there and all of the sudden just fell back. A shot knocked him down. He didn't say anything. He was dead. Then there were three of us left. Foley is firing, and he gets hit, so Buchanan says, "I'm going to take Foley to the company medic." He asked for my grenades. We jumped with two, and I very foolishly gave him my grenades. I shouldn't have. He took Foley and never came back. So I'm there all by myself. It was so lonely. You're just longing to see someone to talk to, and there's all this shooting going on around you. I was thinking if they get through there, they're gonna raise hell. I had a carbine. I could hear the Japanese soldiers crawling all over the place. I could hear them talking.

I could hear them talking, and, oh, I would have given a month's pay for a couple of grenades. I must have been there for a good two hours myself, and then I heard someone yelling in front in English. It was one of our people, a lieutenant by the name of James Gifford, and Gifford was coming down from the 1st Platoon position carrying one of his people [Sanchez], dragging him. He came up to my side of the bunker, and Sanchez leaves his BAR. He took Sanchez to the other side of the bunker where the medics were. I thought, "Boy, that son of a bitch is not coming back. He's gonna leave me here."

While I was waiting for Gifford to come back, I'm sitting there and there's a little path at the side of the bunker coming from the Cheney Trail. I look up and I see a Jap with a spear in his hand coming up the walkway, not really coming after me. It didn't appear that way. He was just coming up that way with this spear. No one shot at him. So I pulled the trigger on the BAR. It fires one round. It was dirty and jammed. I don't know if I hit him. In the morning, I went out that way, and I didn't see anyone there. But the thing is, the company had been cleaning up the battlefield kind of, and they were taking and throwing the bodies over the cliff.

A combat patrol on Corregidor. (courtesy of Jack Herzig)

At any rate, Gifford came back and, boy, I felt like a million dollars when he was there because I had someone to talk to, someone to plan what the hell we were doing. It brightened up the whole picture.

We stayed there, and I was using Sanchez's BAR. There were only two places where you could fire: you could either fire over the parapet or go outside the parapet to the right of it where Foley was. What I did, I kept switching. I'd fire over the parapet, but it was hard to see anything. Then they started firing the flares from the ships. When the thing went up, it was a brilliant white light; it was incredible. You could see just about every stone and pebble and everything else. I guess it might have helped us in that when they went up, everyone froze and didn't start moving around, but that was about it.

I remember a flare went off, and I was perspiring or something. I wiped my face and looked at my hand when the flare went off, and there was blood all over it. The blood came from grenade fragments in my head. If I had my helmet on, probably nothing would have happened. I'd lost that damn helmet. I felt all right. I didn't even know I'd been hit until I saw the blood. I was focused on the bunker and that little pathway up there to make sure no one got through. I was very keyed up. I wanted to protect my side of the bunker. That is what I was mainly interested in. I felt all right except I was very thirsty. We jumped with two canteens of water, and we didn't get anything to replace that water for three days.

Once dawn came, Gifford and I went into this little room in the bunker. The doorway—anyone who was over five foot five never could get through. I'm sure it was built by the Japanese. We sat there, and by then we figured we were out of danger. We just watched the outside of the doorway in this little room. We smoked a cigarette; that was really, really nice. Finally Doc Bradford, our surgeon, he had some medics with him, and he went right to work. The medics came, and they had those stainless steel basins that probably hold a couple of gallons of water and it was full of water. I looked at that thing and took my damn canteen cup out and dipped it in there, and, Jesus, the medic was horrified. He said, "That's for the badly wounded men." I never did get my drink.

I went back to Corregidor on the fiftieth anniversary and stayed on the island for about three weeks. One thing that bothered me very much was how young these guys were. I was the oldest guy in the platoon by far. I was twenty-three. These guys were seventeen, eighteen—high school kids. That's why I really went back. I just wanted to try and really remember them. I wanted to have the experience as close to what we had that night as I could. I spent the night in that room alone. I relived that night and thought about the names of these guys. I just wanted to see if I could sit there and remember them—not so much what we did but the people that died there.

ANDY AMATY
503RD PARACHUTE INFANTRY REGIMENT

Andy Amaty, in the 503rd command post, recalls his role in the attack on the night of February 19 and subsequent fighting on the Rock.

I was the communications sergeant. The night of the big attack, I was on the 300 radio. It was a backpack thing. I said to the fellow on the destroyer, "Send up more flares!" We called them star shells. They sent up one and then came back to me: "We are going to have to stop shooting star shells." They don't know where I am. So I said, "What the hell do you mean you can't send up any more?! I don't give a shit who I am talking to. Put the captain on." He said, "The old man wants to save them for tomorrow." I said, "Put him on this goddamn radio!" I said it with such authority. He did know who he was talking to. I said to him, "If you don't fire those shells, there isn't going to be a fucking tomorrow!" They started firing the shells.

When I came back from a patrol [after the attack], I saw Sergeant Donald Campbell. Donald had tears in his eyes. I didn't notice anybody missing at that time. Before I left, I told Campbell to watch over one of the replacement troops who didn't even look eighteen. I told him to keep him out of harm's way. This replacement was only about seventeen years old. He was true cannon fodder. He was constantly trying to get into the action. They were dangerous to themselves because they thought they weren't going to get killed. That's a nice attitude, but then they forget what the enemy's bullets can do. They don't ask how old you are.

I saw his tears and asked him, "What's the matter?" He said, "Youngy [the replacement] got killed." You could have hit me with a club, that's how bad I felt. I said, "What the hell do you mean he got killed? My order was for you to keep him in here!" Then he said he got shot down here in front of the cave. I wanted to know how it happened. He said,

The aftermath of the explosion at Monkey Point, which leveled the hill
and the area around it. The overturned hulk in the center of the photo is the
M4 Sherman tank attached to the 503rd. (courtesy of Jack Herzig)

"The lieutenant ordered it." That's all I had to hear, so I went down to
him. You can't be afraid to say something when you know you are right.
Frig the enemy and frig anyone else, I'm going to have my say and put
this son of a bitch in his place so he don't kill somebody else. So when I
got to him, I chewed his ass out. I told him to his face, "You murdered
that kid!" It makes you bitter over the years. If a man was worth his salt,
he would apologize. It happened but he ignored it, and he has never
shown up at a reunion.

JACK HERZIG
503RD INFANTRY REGIMENT

Jack Herzig recalls the fighting around Malinta Hill, a high point on the eastern part of Corregidor, and the explosion at Monkey Point that killed many of the men in his battalion.

I have experienced some events that remain so clear in my mind's eye that they could have happened yesterday.

I traded my Thompson for an M1 rifle and a bag of rifle grenades. The grenades came in handy as we used them to clear out the caves around Malinta Hill along with help from "our" M4 Sherman tank that was attached to us for this mission.

As we were securing that area, we had gotten some rifle fire from what turned out to be the rear shaft of the tunnel buried under Monkey Point in which the main remaining Japanese force had taken shelter. Later, we found out the tunnel was quite large, with a concrete interior that had been built by our Navy to serve as a radio reception station. In it had been stationed some forty U.S. Navy communication specialists who were collecting high-level Japanese diplomatic coded messages for some time prior to the attack on Pearl Harbor in one of the most guarded secrets of the war. These specialists were so valuable that every one of them had been evacuated by submarine so that they would not fall into the hands of the Japanese. We had sealed the emergency exit which was in the B Company area. About 8:00 A.M. the following morning, the tank was assisting A Company to destroy or seal the main entrance to this very large tunnel on which we were standing. My ankle was giving me fits, and I was standing alongside a telephone pole. I had leaned my M1 against the pole and was eating from my canteen cup a combination of dry cereal with powdered milk and sugar to which we added water. Lieutenant Winston Samuels, who had just joined us before we landed on Mindoro, and I were watching the M4 tank firing into the main entrance to the tunnel. Part of the battalion command section was gathered on the west side of the same slope, just below us. Samuels said, "This is the strangest modern war. No quarter is asked or expected." He took a few steps away from me, and then the earth erupted in a huge explosion set off by the Japanese in the tunnel practically under our feet. Everything seemed to happen at once, but I could never recall the sound of the blast. Samuels was swept out of my vision by a large boulder that bounced off the ground alongside of him. I fell against the pole with it between me and the largest area of the explosion. I thought that I should try to get my knees separated since one rock would smash both of them. Then somebody fell against me who was hit by a rock; I felt the blow and heard him grunt from the impact. I don't know who it was, and it never occurred to me to find out.

Flames burst out of the doorway of the shaft behind me, so I knew that there would be no danger of an attack from that area. As I slowly stood up, there seemed to be only a few guys who also stood up. Everything and everybody was covered with a shower of dirt and rocks. The green ponchos of the battalion HQ were no longer green—many were red. The tank was thrown several hundred feet. Troopers were trying to help guys more injured than they were. Some just disappeared in the huge blast. Some were moaning, unable to move. Some were still, never to move again. I took one look at Jim Halloran, whom I had introduced to his sweetheart, and I knew he was in that category. I held my rifle and thought this would be a hell of a time for the Japanese to launch an attack, but it turned out that almost all of them perished in the Monkey Point tunnel. Things get mixed up after that: I don't remember the 3rd Battalion arriving, I don't remember leaving the area or anything until the next day. For a long time after that, everybody flinched at any loud noise.

CHARLES SASS
511TH PARACHUTE INFANTRY REGIMENT, 11TH AIRBORNE DIVISION

While the 503rd RCT wore out the Japanese on Corregidor, other operations were being planned. Charles Sass recalls the spectacular raid on Los Baños, about twenty-five miles south of Manila, which led to the liberation of over two thousand missionaries and civilians.

As we approached the drop zone, I could see daylight beautifully from the edge of the big mountain which was just to the east. And it was pitch black below. That's kind of an odd thing, but maybe you've seen it? It's just at dusk when everything at the bottom is dark and everything above is bright. It took on a certain unreality. I knew one thing; I wasn't too sure I wanted to go down there. I almost wanted to keep heading for the daylight.

I remember the stand-up, hook-up very much according to drill. And we did the jump very well. The pilots of course got us there beautifully. The drop zone was terribly small, and only one guy got hurt as far as I know. He hit a railroad track and knocked himself out. We were told to be careful of a ring of rifle pits that were dug specifically for antiairborne or anti-something—I don't know. And there it was, son of a gun, and I'm going to land right in the middle. Nobody was in it, but I remember reaching in my pocket for a grenade to destroy this thing. I remember hitting the ground with my hands in my pockets. That's unheard of! [laughing]

I landed, and six or eight guys said, "Follow me." It was that sort of thing. One platoon had the north end of Los Baños and one went through the middle, and we went, a dozen of us, through a ravine. It seems like it took a while, but I was told it was only a few minutes to hit the south end. I was up front, and what I knew was that a Jap tank was coming. I called for a bazooka, and so did the officer in charge [John Ringler]. [The bazooka men] came running up and said, "Those are our people!" We took off right into the south end of the camp. Each of us took one of the barracks.

My most vivid memory is bursting through a barracks door and seeing these people. I swear it choked me up, and I see them to this day. They were a miserable bunch, stunned by what I don't know but I assume by my coming through the door. [As I entered], this Japanese soldier went out the other door; he took a shot at me. Thankfully he missed, but it was frightening to me to have these people almost crawling off their bunks into the corridor, which is one reason I couldn't shoot back at this guy. Forgive the term, *worms*, but that's what struck me. They're looking, and there was a dullness in their faces. It was momentary. I saw some of them pick up that we were their liberators. That was a very vivid picture—one of very few in fact.

One guy, as I recall, looked like Elie Wiesel, like that very famous picture of him—when he was a kid from Dachau looking up from his bed unbelieving. That's what it is like. A very blank stare, searching, very penetrating, eyes wide open. I think it was deeper than that . . . a very deep hurt. Something perhaps they can't explain. They're expecting something . . . death by the Japanese was almost certain. And here's a fracture in their expectations. It was like a slow-motion movie; everything happened very slow.

They started to move out. I was only in there about a half a minute. I was chasing this guy, and I hit the door head-on with my shoulder, and it went off the hinges. In that brief period, he was gone. I found out later the place was honey-combed with sewage pipes, and there were a lot of the Japanese hiding there. And good for him. I'm glad he escaped from me. His death is not on my conscience.

Prison is such an unreality. I worked in one for about a month. It's a totally different world. When we got them [missionaries and civilians] back to New Bilibid, they started opening up. The only person who was not subdued was a four or five year old. One little kid kept me up until dawn telling me about Christmas, which consisted of a can of Campbell soup, which they split among the members of the family. There was rapture. I assured her she was going to have all of the Campbell soup she would ever want.

There was also a Filipino girl who must have been nineteen or twenty, I guess, and for some time a lot of the villagers sat with her in the middle of a circle absolutely silent. At one point after some long time, everybody got up and moved in and embraced her and I guess took her home. I was told it was a welcoming back after her having been, maybe by necessity, a sinner in the camp. The explanation to me was that she was intimate with one of the guards. There was a great joy when he [her father] said, "This is enough of this. Let's take our daughter home."

JACK McGRATH
511TH PARACHUTE INFANTRY REGIMENT, 11TH AIRBORNE DIVISION

Jack McGrath remembers the 11th Airborne's push into southern Luzon.

We started at the New Bilibid Prison where they put us on trucks, and we caught up with the battalion at Santa Rosa. I don't know who took Santa Rosa, but if we took a town, the Japs would set fire to the next one. They didn't at Santa Rosa; there was very little damage to the town. We went in there, and there was a big yellow stucco building. It was a government building of some sort, and we went down the basement and the Filipinos, the guerrillas, had these—they called them *makapili*, traitors. They were abusing them like you couldn't believe. The blood was on the floor; you couldn't walk; your feet would slide like you were on ice. They were cutting their ears off and forcing them to eat them. They did all kinds of horrible things to them. Those people were extremely brave. I don't know if you know that, but they are . . . those people. Whether they were truly traitors or a neighbor getting back at somebody—we often wondered about that. They were fatalistic. They knew the jig was up, and they were going to die, but they died wonderfully. I remember they cut one prisoner's ear off, and they told him, "Eat it!" They then asked, "How'd it taste?" And he said, "It was good."

They then told us to stick around; they were going to have a big do-ings at the church on Sunday. We were pulling out, so one of our guys talked them into doing it that night. It was right by the church where they tortured about twenty people. I wasn't proud of it, but I witnessed it. We had a major who tried to stop it, but we booted him out of there.

We didn't give a shit. In war, you finally get to a point where you're an animal. I couldn't visualize the war ever ending. I thought this is what I would be doing all my life. Common sense would tell you that can't be, but that's the way I felt. They tortured those people, and for the finale they burned a woman alive at the stake. What she had done was marry a Japanese officer. I believe he was the one in charge of the massacre where they put the people in the church and doused it with gasoline and burned it. That was a bad smell. It was worse than rot . . . the smell of burning flesh.

BERNARD COON
511TH PARACHUTE INFANTRY REGIMENT, 11TH AIRBORNE DIVISION

By the middle of March, the 11th Airborne was spearheading the Sixth Army's drive into southern Luzon. Bernie Coon recalls a routine reconnaissance mission gone wrong.

It was a beautiful clear and bright day as we walked, uphill and down, through the thick underbrush and sugarcane fields. We just walked and walked. Finally we entered enemy territory, and all of the sudden mortar shells were bursting all over the place. I was over a little to the right from where the shells were landing. I felt quite safe, but our captain in charge of the patrol hollered, "Medic, medic!" I worked my way back to him. He said, "I didn't want you; it's for those two guys out there." These were the point men—scouts. I said, "They are both dead, but if it will help you any, I'll go out there," which I shouldn't have because we were trained to save ourselves to do the most good. I went out, but I didn't get out to them before I got hit. First, I got hit in the right arm, and it blew both bones out and I fell on my face because the explosion blew my helmet off. While I was lying on the ground, I got hit in the other shoulder.

My patrol got orders over the radio to pull back and leave the dead and wounded. They got orders to pull back because they had all kinds of artillery fire going up. So they all left, and I'm laying there on the ground. If you have never lain wounded in enemy territory and watched your fellow men pull back and leave you, then you cannot appreciate my feeling at this time. Now what to do? Here I am, bleeding very freely and helpless. Around me for companions are my buddies—dead. The war is over for them. Both arms are fractured and so numb I cannot move them. Because of the continued bleeding, I decided my end was rather near, so I spent several minutes in thought with my mother and family and prayed.

I passed out after a while—from loss of blood, I guess. When I woke up, these two Japs were crawling towards me with their camouflage branches sticking out all over. I was thinking, "This is the end." First thing they did, they threw me over on my back. I was on my stomach, and they tried to unfasten my belt that holds all of our equipment, but it had slipped up too far, and they couldn't get it unfastened. I was sure they could feel my heart beat because they were working on my chest. That didn't work, so they threw me back on my stomach—with two broken arms, don't forget. I kept my composure, didn't breathe. It was a case of play dead or die. I heard them pull their bayonets out, and I thought they caught on to me, but instead they cut my backpack off and then they took my wristwatch, went through my pockets, and then they left.

I awakened at dawn, dreaming that I was having a warm cup of coffee with my pals back at the aid station, only to find myself lying on a hill, cold and hungry, and very much alone. In the distance, I could hear the chattering of the Japs. I remember seeing four of our B-25s approaching. One ship just peeled off and seemed to dive right at me. I could see the flash from its four machine guns. I could hear the bullets thudding the ground, and then they dropped their bombs, and that raised me right off the ground. I think they were using me and those other dead troopers for markers. I never felt more alone. Overhead, a few vultures were sailing around. I decided that as soon as darkness came, I would try to get to my feet and head for camp. Night finally came, and it was spent trying to get up, but with no success.

I didn't get up that night, and I didn't get up the next day; I just couldn't get up. So the third morning, I got up and I could see them—the Japs—in front of me. They weren't very far away. They had dogs, and I thought, "Oh God, those dogs are going to come over here and start barking" . . . but they didn't. Flies were everywhere. I remember the flies laying eggs in my wounds and maggots formed. The only positive thing was maggots eat away dead tissue; thus, gangrene is prevented. There I lay—sunburned, thirsty, weak, full of maggots. Finally, by rolling down the hill, I came up in a sitting position. Then I pulled the bones back in my right arm. I could use my left hand a little bit. I just turned my back towards them and started walking. I walked for two days. I was up on my feet, but I could only go a few steps and then I'd have to sit down. I hallucinated a couple of times.

I came to a shack, sort of a bamboo house that was built up on the lake, and I thought, "Shall I go or shall I stay away?" I figured Japs might be there, but I thought, "I'm so thirsty I'm going to take a chance." On the way down, I'm sure I saw a Jap standing there with a rifle in his hand, but when I got there, it was a piece of wood leaning up against the building with a bottle laying across the bottom, which looked like a foot to me evidently. I sat down in the doorway of that shack, and then I laid down because it was getting dark. Come morning, I had a hell of a time getting up. I couldn't get back up on my feet for quite a while. I finally made it. There were two water buffaloes or carabaos tied to a tree. One of them was down on the ground, it was so weak from lack of water and stuff I guess. I thought, "If I could only untie them!" But I couldn't use my hands that much, and I couldn't use my right arm at all because that was completely nerve damaged, so I had no use of it. I think I found a big iron jug of water in that place. I kicked it over with my foot, and I cupped my hand and I got a little bit of water, and I took off again. So then I came across this dried creek bed, and it looked easier walking in there because there was nothing but a hard, cracked bottom. I kept telling myself, "I can't go on, I can't go any further." I sat down on this big boulder, and I happened to look down, and there was a puddle of water behind the boulder, so I got some more water. Then I was going up quite a big hill, and I heard voices so I hid in the bushes. It was a Jap patrol. When I came to, I was covered with ants. They had eaten the flesh off my chest quite a bit. I scrubbed against the bushes as much as I could to get those off. I was going up another hill, and I fell back once and hit my back on a tree, and I could feel the blood pouring down my back because my left scapula was gone and I had a hole blown through my shoulder. I could feel the blood running down my back. I finally got up the hill, and at the top there was a little bamboo platform, so I sat on it to rest, and that's when I looked over to my right and I saw this big boulder and it was shining. I went over to see what it was. It was a basin in the bottom of the rock that was full of water and full of mosquito larvae—loaded with them—but I drank it anyway.

I could see the smokestacks from the sugar mill where I started from in the first place. I went down the hill, and there was a farmer working his field, and I walked right in his house because he didn't come to me. He finally came in; he thought I was a robber or something. I tried to ask him for water. He didn't have any but he said, "Hospital." He pointed up the road. I went up the road, and I got to the perimeter where we were. It was just getting dark and I thought, "Okay, God. They're gonna shoot me because I didn't have any password." One of the soldiers came out when he saw me, and an officer came out with a bandage we were all issued. I said, "What are you going to do with that?" He said, "They didn't tell me how bad you were." I said, "I have to go up to the aid station." It was probably about a city block. "I can't walk any further so you have to get me an ambulance." He told them how to put me on a stretcher without bending me because I was in such pain. They took me to the aid station. I was full of maggots at this time. The first medic to come out poured alcohol in my wounds to kill the maggots. I didn't feel it. I was numb.

I fell asleep after they bound the wounds. The next day, a colonel arrived from General MacArthur's [staff] to interview me. They took me by ambulance to New Bilibid Prison. Throughout the entire experience, I felt God was with me, holding my hand, guiding me.

Two years and seven operations later, I got out of the hospital. I had a double bone graft in my arm. I lost four inches of bone in my right arm, so I have a short arm. Nothing worked on my arm, but finally I was able to wiggle my finger and slowly regained control of my arm.

JOHN REYNOLDS

503RD PARACHUTE INFANTRY REGIMENT

After clearing Corregidor, the 503rd was transferred to the island of Negros, where the Japanese waged another bloody battle of attrition. John Reynolds recalls a day of fighting.

My unit was advancing on a very narrow front with the road looking like an umbilical cord trailing behind us. Each day seemed to be a repeat of the previous day, but there is one day the memory of which is still implanted in my mind.

On April 20, 1945, the 1st Platoon, under Lieutenant Nickles, secured the hill and advanced to the next hill on the right front. The Japanese were stubbornly defending each hill. They were dug in in well-prepared defensive positions and had a variety of automatic weapons. They constructed interlocking fields of fire, making it nearly impossible to flank their positions.

Surprisingly, only mild resistance was encountered on the assault, but as soon as the hill was secured, the enemy countered with very intensive machine-gun and small-arms fire. A mortar shell killed Lieutenant Nickles, amputated T/4 [Technician Fourth Grade] Upchurch's leg, causing him to bleed to death, and slightly wounding Private McLaughlin. I remember McLaughlin rising; blood was running down his face, dazed from the mortar fire, yelling: "Nickles is dead, Nickles is dead."

A few minutes later, Private Huerter was lightly wounded by mortar fragments. Shortly thereafter, Lieutenant David, in command of the attached machine-gun platoon, was killed by an enemy sniper. About a half an hour later, the 2nd Platoon joined the 1st; one squad, under Sergeant Minor, aided in securing the ridge, and the other two squads acted as litter bearers. Upchurch was the first of our group of twenty-six replacements assigned to D Company to die. Lieutenant Nickles had been appointed as CO [company commander] of D Company just prior to the Negros mission, and some of us were told that he did not have to be with the 1st Platoon as we made our attack but wanted to go to understand the nature of the Japanese defenses.

That short half hour has impacted my life, even today, and it will continue to affect my thinking until the day I depart from this earth. At the beginning of the mortar attack, I was lying on my back, and I wanted to move to a more covered position, but I knew from my training that to get on my feet was to invite certain death. I could hear the cough of those knee mortars as they left the tubes just a short distance away, and I could see them as they arched over towards our position on the hillside. After what must have been only a minute but what seemed like ages, I couldn't watch any more and rolled over on my stomach, face down against the ground, and thought, "I'm going to get killed on my mother's birthday." I didn't, of course, but my life and approach to life has never been the same after this experience.

As I stated earlier, there are things that I try to remember and can't, but other events are as clear in my memory as if they happened yesterday. Two such events occurred later the very same day and early the next morning. I remember them clearly because their relationship was so ironic—and for the superstitious were quite understandable. Late in the afternoon, or early in the evening, three or four of us were going back a short distance to D Company CP to bring some rations. We had already reached the bottom of the hill, whose taking had cost us so dearly, when a corporal named Bokencamp, a long, lean, lank Texan, came running down the slope, and as he caught up with us, he said, "Wait for me. I don't mind dying, but I don't want to die alone." Early in the dark of the following morning, with the company on perimeter, his words would prove to be very prophetic. The Japanese succeeded in entering one of the forward trenches, killing Circo and Bokencamp.

It was a typical day on Negros during that phase of the fighting. The Japanese would kill ten men a day, and pretty soon that adds up to one hundred dead men.

CHARLES SASS
511TH PARACHUTE INFANTRY REGIMENT,
11TH AIRBORNE DIVISION

Charles Sass recalls his most vivid memories of the fighting in southern Luzon and the fall of the Japanese mountain fortress at Malepunyo that marked the collapse of large-scale Japanese resistance there.

My most vivid image of the war is something you wouldn't expect. It is having gone a half a mile down a railroad track into Japanese territory presuming there were people with me and there weren't. Turning back and seeing that landscape and that railroad is a subject for [Salvador Dalí]. I was absolutely above—in outer space, you might say. I just stood there and scratched my head. I can't imagine anything else I would have done.

Most of those little events were just that. Very few people actually fired a rifle or threw a grenade, and it was purely circumstance that I did those things.

Your relationship with the men you're around is closer than anything you can imagine. It's been described as love, but that's too strong of a word for me. But these men are all part of you—even the guys you don't like, and there are plenty of those. You depend on each other. There was no need for commands since we knew what to do and how to cover each other.

When we went up one of the mountains, we were, I swear, holding hands. We caught the Japanese inside the mountain with their pants down, and we cut them down; it was as simple as that. The mountain had been blasted, and I know they didn't expect us to follow the bombs as close, but we did. We cut them down in their entryways. Eventually, a flamethrower came up and detonated ammunition in the mountain, and this set off explosions inside the mountain. They kept going for days. Every time a big one would go off, the mountain would shake, and that was kind of scary.

One guy came to the cave entrance and set off a satchel charge and took out at least a dozen of our people. They were all wounded.

Then we got a radio call from one of the companies that said essentially, "We are in big trouble and been ambushed." So we took about half a dozen guys, which was all we could spare at the time, and went down the mountain. We connected with them and carried their people to the top. Some of them didn't make it.

I was carrying one of the men. He questioned me before we went on. He said, "Did we beat them?" I spent about one hundred yards telling him, "Ya, you beat them." He was gone when we got to the top. He was hit in the legs and elsewhere.

John Donaldson, my best friend, when we came back from this other mission, dug out a foxhole for me and lined it with his own poncho and he said, "Hey, buddy, it's going to be all right." He knew my feelings at the moment, which were pretty rotten.

One of our squads had been ambushed on the hill below us maybe a week before. There's an image. They went up the wrong hill and went into a Japanese strong point. They were trapped and had no way of getting out. We could see them vividly from the top of the hill.

I happened to be alongside the radio, and this sergeant called in and told us what he was going to do. I remember his words, "So and so is wounded; so and so is dead." He gave the whole report very cold and very calm. He said, "I'm going to kill the wounded and then myself." He was pretty cold about it. I don't know how many days it took to get up the spine of the mountain, but the burial party found remains of the squad and the sergeant's body.

I never opened up completely—perhaps more since I've talked to you. Big things you can swallow. It's the little things you have a hard time with, you start choking up. A good friend of mine borrowed my canteen and after part of a burst cut through the canteen, his closing words before he died was, "Make sure Sass gets his canteen back." I can't ever forget that.

CHAPTER TEN

Into the Jaws of Hell:
Iwo Jima

Uncommon valor was a common virtue.

—ADMIRAL CHESTER NIMITZ

BURIED SEVENTY-FIVE FEET UNDERGROUND in a war room in Iwo Jima ringed by a labyrinth of caves and tunnels, the island's commander, Lieutenant General Tadamichi Kuribayashi, carefully read the latest intelligence report. His eyes focused on the important sentence: "170 American ships moving northwestward from Saipan."[1] His troops were ready.

Actually, there were over 450 ships steaming toward Iwo Jima, including transports carrying the 3rd, 4th, and 5th Marine Divisions. Iwo would be the 5th's first and only combat assignment; at its core were many former parachutists and Raiders.

For eight months before their arrival, fifteen thousand Japanese had worked around the clock to hollow out Iwo Jima. Using mostly hand tools and at times gas masks to tolerate the putrid smell of sulfur, the Japanese created underground hospital wards, barracks, and storage rooms connected by an eleven-mile maze of tunnels. Aboveground, hundreds of pillboxes and bunkers ringed the island. Iwo Jima was arguably the most heavily fortified island in the history of warfare.

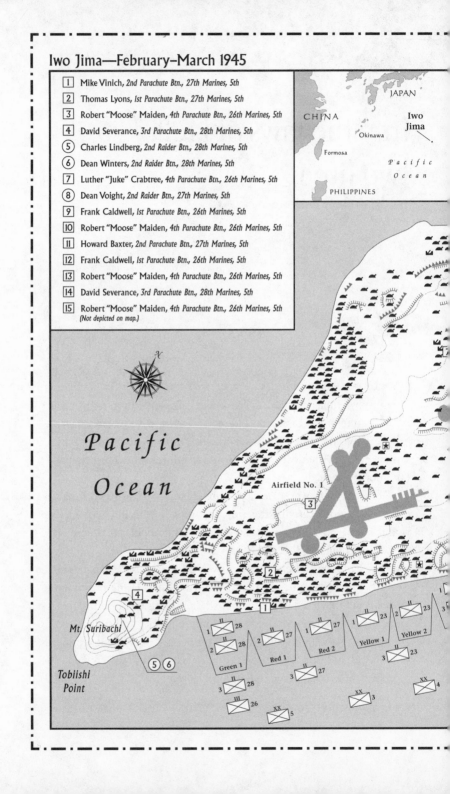

Iwo Jima—February–March 1945

1. Mike Vinich, *2nd Parachute Btn., 27th Marines, 5th*
2. Thomas Lyons, *1st Parachute Btn., 27th Marines, 5th*
3. Robert "Moose" Maiden, *4th Parachute Btn., 26th Marines, 5th*
4. David Severance, *3rd Parachute Btn., 28th Marines, 5th*
5. Charles Lindberg, *2nd Raider Btn., 28th Marines, 5th*
6. Dean Winters, *2nd Raider Btn., 28th Marines, 5th*
7. Luther "Juke" Crabtree, *4th Parachute Btn., 26th Marines, 5th*
8. Dean Voight, *2nd Raider Btn., 27th Marines, 5th*
9. Frank Caldwell, *1st Parachute Btn., 26th Marines, 5th*
10. Robert "Moose" Maiden, *4th Parachute Btn., 26th Marines, 5th*
11. Howard Baxter, *2nd Parachute Btn., 27th Marines, 5th*
12. Frank Caldwell, *1st Parachute Btn., 26th Marines, 5th*
13. Robert "Moose" Maiden, *4th Parachute Btn., 26th Marines, 5th*
14. David Severance, *3rd Parachute Btn., 28th Marines, 5th*
15. Robert "Moose" Maiden, *4th Parachute Btn., 26th Marines, 5th*
    (Not depicted on map.)

JAPAN

CHINA

Iwo Jima

Okinawa

Formosa

Pacific Ocean

PHILIPPINES

Pacific Ocean

Airfield No. 1

Mt. Suribachi

Tobiishi Point

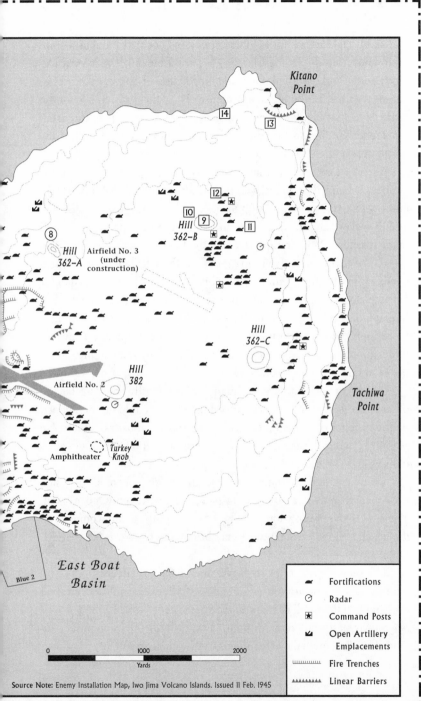

Kitano
Point

14   13

12

10
Hill   9
362-B   11

8

Hill   Airfield No. 3
362-A   (under
            construction)

Hill
362-C

Hill
362-C

Hill
382

Airfield No. 2

Turkey
Knob
Amphitheater

Tachiwa
Point

East Boat
Basin

Blue 2

	Fortifications
	Radar
	Command Posts
	Open Artillery Emplacements
	Fire Trenches
	Linear Barriers

0   1000   2000
Yards

Source Note: Enemy Installation Map, Iwo Jima Volcano Islands. Issued 11 Feb. 1945

Barely eight square miles in size, the island, located about nine hundred miles from the Home Islands, was part of Japan's "Inner Vital Defense Zone" and governed under the jurisdiction of Tokyo. Iwo had two airfields, with a third under construction. The Allies wanted Iwo for the airfields to base fighter escorts for B-29s heading for Japan and as an emergency landing area for the bombers. Japanese aircraft based on the island were a threat to the recently captured Marianas.

As dawn rose over the island on February 19, 1945, the weather was perfect—a balmy 68 degrees with practically unlimited visibility. At precisely 8:30 A.M., the control ship lowered its pennant, releasing the first assault waves. Around 9:00 A.M., the first wave of American Marines made it ashore. As the ramps dropped, the Japanese remained strangely silent. The 5th Marine Division landed on the left flank of the beachhead, while the 4th Marine Division hit the right. The beaches quickly became clogged with men and equipment.[2] Soft black sand and the steep fifteen-foot sand terrace immobilized many of the vehicles. Then, as more men continued to funnel onto the beaches, Japanese heavy artillery, mortars, rockets, and machine guns suddenly came to life, raking the exposed troops in a deadly crossfire.

It was part of Kuribayashi's plan. After carefully studying Japan's other island battles, he concluded that the enemy could not be stopped on the beaches or by counterattacking with fanatical banzai attacks. He planned a defense in depth and waged a war of attrition that would gradually wear down the landing forces.

The first part of his strategy was to let the beaches become congested with men to maximize the killing power of his weapons.[3] It worked. There were over twenty-four hundred American dead and wounded on the beaches alone, making Iwo Jima's beaches as bloody as Normandy's Omaha.

The second part of his strategy came as the Americans pushed inland. The miles of tunnels and countless pillboxes would ensure that every inch of the small island would be contested.

Slowly, at the cost of many men, the 5th Marine Division pushed inland. The division had two regiments in the initial assault force: the 28th

Marines, commanded by former Raider Colonel Harry Liversedge, and the 27th Marines, commanded by Colonel Thomas Wornham. The 26th Marines were in reserve and came ashore in the afternoon.

The 28th first cut across the narrow seven-hundred-yard neck of the pork chop–shaped island, severing it into two parts. The regiment was then tasked with taking Mount Suribachi, the dormant volcano that dominated the southern portion of the island, defended by about two thousand Japanese. Around its base and embedded throughout the mountain were over two hundred blockhouses and caves.

The assault on Suribachi began February 20, with the regiment's three battalions battling to clear the base of the mountain and sustaining heavy causalties in the process. By midafternoon on February 22, the main Japanese defenses had been breached. Kuribayashi had expected the mountain to hold out for two weeks.[4]

The next day, a forty-man E Company platoon, led by First Lieutenant Harold Schrier, was given the honor of scaling Suribachi and securing the crater. The patrol made the steep climb up the mountain and raised a small flag that Schrier had been presented from the 3rd Battalion commander, Lieutenant Colonel Chandler Johnson. Japanese emerged from several caves to contest the mountaintop but were dispatched by the patrol.[5] Around noon, a larger flag was brought up and the smaller flag lowered. As the larger flag was being raised, Associated Press photographer Joe Rosenthal snapped perhaps the most famous picture of World War II.

While the 28th Marines subdued Suribachi, the 5th Division's 26th and 27th Regiments continued their slow push toward the northern portion of the island. They were joined by the 4th Marine Division, moving up Iwo's eastern side. The 3rd Marine Division, which had been released from reserve, pushed up the center.

Objectives were measured in yards, and casualties were horrendous. After securing Airfield No. 2, the Marines ran into Japanese defensive positions behind it, built around a mutually supporting series of hills and ridges. In the western sector of the island, the 5th Division had to contend with Hills 362-A and 362-B. The middle of the island, dubbed the

"Meat Grinder," contained landforms such as a bald hill nicknamed the Turkey Knob and a depression known as the Amphitheater.

Each of these crags became a war in itself for the small groups of men who fought desperately for them. One of the bloodier battles was waged on Hill 362-B. On March 3, the 26th Marines had nearly three hundred casualties trying to take it. It was typical. Since the beginning of the drive north, only four thousand yards were gained—at a cost of about thirteen thousand Americans killed and wounded.[6] But slowly, Kuribayashi's main defenses were cracking. The Americans had gained control of approximately two-thirds of the island.

By the middle of March, the 5th Division drove within fifteen hundred yards of Kitano Point, the northernmost tip of the island. There, Kuribayashi concentrated the remains of his garrison. At this point, the battle had continued several weeks beyond the most optimistic American projections. On March 14, an itchy General Holland M. Smith declared victory and raised the colors. For the average Marine, however, the fighting would continue for several more weeks.

Repeated efforts were made to coax the island commander to surrender. He reported to Japanese forces on nearby Chichi Jima: "The enemy's front is 300 meters from us, and they are attacking by tank firing. They advised us to surrender by loudspeaker, but we only laughed at this childish trick." Shortly afterward, Kuribayashi was promoted to full general. On March 23, Kuribayashi sent his final message, "All officers and men of Chichi Jima—goodbye from Iwo." The 5th overran the last of the Japanese defenses on the evening of March 25, but in the early morning hours of March 26, the final tragedy would occur. About three hundred well-organized Japanese defenders headed for a rear area near Airfield No. 1, killing and wounding scores of surprised airmen and Marines. Shortly after the final Japanese raid on the rear area, the Marines began to pull off the island. Control was handed over to the Army's 147th Infantry Regiment. Mopping up continued, and on April 1, sixteen hundred additional Japanese would lose their lives and nearly nine hundred would be captured.

The battle for Iwo Jima was the costliest in Marine Corps history and

Marines storm ashore on Iwo Jima. (USMC)

the only time during the Pacific war that the enemy would inflict more casualties on an attacking force than it had suffered. The final American casualties were 24,053, including 6,140 dead.[7] Japanese losses totaled 19,977 killed, plus about 1,100 prisoners. General Erskine, 3rd Marine Division commander, summed up the campaign during a dedication of one of the massive cemeteries on the island: "Victory was never in doubt. . . . What was in doubt, in all our minds, was whether there would be any of us left to dedicate this cemetery."

MIKE VINICH
2ND PARACHUTE BATTALION, 27TH MARINES, 5TH MARINE DIVISION

Around 10:00 A.M. on February 19, Iwo Jima's beaches became engulfed in a mael-strom of machine-gun, mortar, and artillery fire. Trucks, tanks, and the dead piled up along the crowded shoreline. Sergeant Mike Vinich recalls arriving on the beaches during the height of Japanese fire.

I can't hardly even describe it to you . . . the misery and the difference between this and all of the other island fighting I'd experienced. Coming to Iwo was a different kind of fight.

We were just nearing the beach, and I looked up at the heavens. I was only twenty years old, and my birthday was on the twenty-eighth [of February] or the first [of March] since I was born on the twenty-ninth [of February], a leap year. I thought to myself, "God, am I ever going to make twenty-one?" The ramp went down, and honest to God, the bullets came in.

Many of the men were machine-gunned to death as they were exiting. I was pulling bodies of my men aside as I tried to make my way out. Blood was everywhere. It was very similar to the opening scene in *Saving Private Ryan*, but I think the fire was more concentrated on Iwo.

The ash terraces are what saved us. We dove up there and kind of crawled over, and the mortars, artillery, and machine-gun bullets were still coming in. They had us zeroed in from Suribachi. I was on a bit of a knoll when a machine gun cut loose and got me in both legs.[8] I fell down and broke my femur against this rock. My hands were spread out, my rifle was out of my hands, and all of the sudden . . . *chew* . . . *chew* . . . *chew* . . . the bullets went right across my hands. This woke me up! When you get hit, you are in such shock. I thought somebody hit me with a baseball bat; I didn't realize. If you ever go deer hunting or elk hunting and you shoot one of those animals, they are so shocked. That's the way we were when we were hit. It always came back to me when I went hunting. In fact, I really never went hunting that much after because I felt sorry for the animal because I went through the same trauma. But anyway, I was on a higher knoll, and the machine gunner got me through both legs, and when the bullets came where my hands were, I started rolling over to find cover. When I rolled down there, my BAR man was shot through the chest and was just gurgling. I couldn't help him at all. His eyes were turned back in his head, and he was just gurgling. On the other side of me was my other BAR man, and he was hit through the chest. It was dark before they eventually got me off the beach and into a barge and hoisted up into a ship. There were wounded and dying men all around—some hit in the chest, some in the neck. What they said in their dying breaths has haunted me all my life. They said two things: "Oh, God" and "Oh, Mom." It was so sad. There must have been forty of us lying in the gangway on stretchers waiting to go into surgery.

I let all of the bad wounds go ahead of me—the ones through the head, chest, and abdomen. I said, "Let them go; I'm coherent." I kept getting morphine from the corpsman, which alleviated the pain. Finally a doctor came up to me and said, "There's a thing called gangrene, and we don't want to get in that kind of mess. You better get on the gondola and get into sick bay." They finally put me on a stretcher and wheeled me up. I looked down, and there was two washtubs filled with arms and legs. I said to the doctor, "I hope mine are not going to end up there." He said, "Corpsman, get these washtubs out of here."

It was miserable. I've relived it many times. I reflect back on it when I'm in the company of other veterans, with other men who had similar experiences. In sleep, nightmares—it never leaves you.

THOMAS LYONS
1ST PARACHUTE BATTALION, 27TH MARINES, 5TH MARINE DIVISION

Thomas Lyons recalls the carnage on the beaches and the breakout toward Airfield No. 1.

It was pretty rough going in. When we hit the beach, it was, of course, black sand, and there was a steep embankment right out of the water. For the first several yards, the Japs couldn't even see you because we were down behind the embankment. One of the boats got hit after they were done unloading, killing everyone.

We got off the beach. As we were moving toward the runway, [one of the men] got completely emasculated. A shell exploded right in front of him, right under his feet. He was begging people to shoot him. His intestines were hanging out. He had small splinters all over. He begged people to shoot him. The chaplain told him he could make it, and he was hauling him back to the beach, but he didn't want to be saved and died on the beach. He had so many cuts they didn't have enough bandages to cover them all. He was a very close friend of mine.

I set up the guns ready to blow up a pillbox when a captain ran up and told me, "Don't shoot that pillbox because I want to use it for my headquarters." I said, "Well, there's Japs in there." And he said, "I'll get them out." About that time, they started shooting; they got part of my gun crew. I was looking at them through a pair of binoculars, and something knocked it out of my hand, and when I picked it up, the prism poured out like sugar. A bullet would have hit me right in the eye. But it was deflected by the prisms in the binoculars. We had to blow up the pillbox and moved toward Airfield No. 1.

ROBERT "MOOSE" MAIDEN
4TH PARACHUTE BATTALION, 26TH MARINES, 5TH MARINE DIVISION

Moose Maiden remembers the painful push past Airfield No. 1.[9]

We started moving up along the side of the first airstrip. The afternoon of D plus one, things were confusing, and we had a hard time maintaining contact.

Captain Fields kept trying to establish contact on the right and left and get things organized. Sergeant Inman, who was our machine-gun section leader, he deployed one of the squads there. It wasn't my squad; we were still with the 3rd Platoon. He said, "On this line, action, enemy direct front, commence firing." He was pointing up toward the airstrip. The first casualty that I saw was this kid Murphy from Boston. He was a gunner, and he took one right between the running lights. These guys weren't amateur marksmen; they were pretty good. After that, we were moving on around, following the platoon we were attached to. Then 320 mm spigot mortars [which fired a 675-pound shell] started coming in. It looked like a milk can flying through the air. It was quite an explosion, needless to say. As we were moving up, this buddy of mine in one of our rifle platoons and I got the word to move out, and I said, "Hey, Joe, come on, let's go. Let's move out." He was motionless, face down. I rolled him over, and there were no signs of blood or anything, and his eyes were sort of closed. I slapped him in the face a couple of times and said, "Hey, Joe, are you all right?" I couldn't see any bleeding, so it had to be a concussion. I lost four guys. Reardon got wounded, Davila got wounded, McKelvie got decapitated, and Parker was just dead. I went to the platoon leader and said, "I can't employ my machine-gun squad. I've taken four casualties; there's only three of us left in the squad." He said, "Well, do what you can, but we'll sure need that machine gun."

About that time, Captain Fields collared me and said, "Moose, get over to our left flank and see if we're tied in with the 27th Marines." I left the machine-gun squad with one of the men. I'm skedaddling over to the east side. You talk about the defecation striking the propeller. There was a lot of firing going on, and as I moved left, I was checking with the guys; we knew everybody pretty well. I was to make contact with the 27th Regiment. I'm snooping and pooping and running and hitting the deck and running, and I see this bunker straight ahead of me, a Japanese bunker. This voice says, "Get down out there! Stop running around out there! You're drawing fire!" What an understatement that was! I'm risking my butt to try and get tied in with the 27th. As it turned out, inside that Japanese bunker was the commander of the 2nd Battalion, 27th Marines. After I got inside, he chewed my butt out rather vociferously. I explained to him that my captain, Captain Tom Fields, told me to get over and make sure we were tied in on the left flank with the 27th. He said, "Well, that's been done. Now get your ass out of here." I returned and contacted Captain Fields and reported. He had been a track man at Maryland, All-American, and trying to follow him around in that sand . . . it's like I got a little four-wheeled Jeep and he's got a Thunderbird.

We got pretty well organized. We'd taken a few other casualties. The one I remember most was the next day when we were moving out, and our lead units got pretty well out, a couple hundred yards there, and then all the sudden tons of mortar and artillery fire. As we were moving forward, one of the 5th Division tanks hit a mine and lost his right tread, and he spun around a couple of times and the crew immediately abandoned. We had a platoon sergeant with us, and he jumped up on the back of that tank and got the .50 [caliber machine gun] going, and he was really peppering them out there to our front. He got shot off the tank and died right there on the spot.

Then we got word to hold up, and then we got word to pull back. Things were a little confusing, needless to say. Earlier, we were getting a lot of fire from around the edge of the first airfield. The Japanese had a trench line around there, and they were firing and throwing grenades. We'd say, "Hey grenade . . . grenade!" I don't know how many somersaults I did down that slope because I could see the grenades coming and falling. I remember my machine-gun and the mortar section leaders saying, "C'mon! Let's go up and get those dirty little bastards. C'mon! C'mon!" They both got seriously wounded by grenades. Lewis caught one almost in the midsection, and one of the other men got hit bad in the face. He spent years in the naval hospital after that. We were talking and I said, "Look out. Here comes more grenades!" I'm doing another backwards somersault, and he tries to field the grenade and throw it back, and it blew off his right hand. It was a pretty clean amputation and very little bleeding. I got out his battle dressing and tended to it. I'll never forget, he says, "I'm from Wisconsin. I'm right-handed. I like to hunt and fish." I got him fixed up and said, "Do you know where our aid station is?" He said, "No, I'm with the 3rd Battalion." I said, "Do you see that clump of trees down there?" "Yeah." "That's where our battalion aid station is. Do you think you can make it?" He said, "Yeah. Oh, do you want my Tommy gun?" He had a Tommy gun. On one of my backwards tumbles, I broke the stock on my carbine. It wasn't worth crap, so all I had was my .45 in my shoulder holster. I said, "Oh, you bet." I watched him go down toward the aid station, and I had my new prize award, this Thompson submachine gun.

DAVID SEVERANCE
3RD PARACHUTE BATTALION, 28TH MARINES, 5TH MARINE DIVISION

The 28th Marines were charged with the capture of Mount Suribachi, which dominates the southern part of the island. E Company commander David Severance recalls the attack on the mountain and the forty-man patrol he sent to the top.

We returned to our battalion, which was facing Suribachi, in the eastern sector. There were two battalions facing the mountain: the 2nd on the left and the 3rd on the right. My 1st Platoon was committed in the afternoon of the 20th and suffered some casualties. Just before dark, I moved my 1st Platoon out and put my 2nd and 3rd Platoons on the line ready to attack. In the morning of D-Day plus two, the plan was to have tank support in our attack at 8:00 A.M., but the tanks weren't rearmed or refueled, so we delayed H-hour to 8:15 A.M. They weren't ready, and we delayed it again until 8:25 A.M., and they weren't ready at 8:30 A.M., so they said, "Go without tanks," which we did. It was a big rush around an open area. We were apprehensive. We were charging downhill into fortified pillboxes and bunkers that stretched all the way across the base of Suribachi. The only cover we had were shell holes and bomb craters. It appeared that we would lose a lot of men because they had a series of pillboxes stretching all the way across the base of Suribachi.

About 10:30 A.M., the tanks finally showed up, which was a great help. Before that, we had to move in with fire support and flamethrowers. We made good headway, but we had a lot of casualties. Late in the afternoon, we moved around to the east side of the volcano and took up positions in the rocks there. The destroyer escorts fired all night up on the mountain. We didn't have anybody come into our area. There was some infiltration from Japanese units trying to get through and move north. The next morning, the Navy came in and started dropping 100-pound bombs on us. We had signal flares that we'd fire with a grenade launcher. I found out they had the grenade launcher, and I had the flares and didn't have any cartridges to fire them. I got on the regimental phone, got their regimental commander, and the communicator came up and asked who I was and I told him, and I said, "Redwing Six! This is Bayonet Easy Six! Friendly planes are bombing our position! Over!" He asked me to repeat, so I repeated it. There was a silence, and then he came back and told me I wasn't authorized to come up on the frequency. I was upset. My battalion commander was nearby asking what was happening and was able to stop the planes from bombing us. We didn't have any casualties.

The morning of the 23rd I got a call to send a platoon up the mountain. Just before that, the battalion commander sent a four-man fire team from Fox Company. They reached the top of the volcano without anyone taking a shot at them, so he decided to send a platoon up. We had suffered about 30 percent casualties by that time. I sent Lieutenant Schrier over to the CP where the battalion commander, Chandler Johnson, had a flag of the USS *Missoula* and told Schrier if he got to the top put the flag up, which he did without being shot at. I think everybody figured the Japanese were just waiting for a larger party before they opened fire. I'll never forget his words: "If they get to the top." He said "if." At the time, I thought I was sending those men to their deaths. We were standing by to extract them, so to speak. But nobody shot at them. Once the flag was up and Lowery took a picture of it, a couple of Japanese came out of a cave and threw some grenades. Lowery fell over the side of the mountain and slid probably twenty or thirty feet and broke his camera. The Japanese were shot immediately.

About that time, the secretary of the Navy and Lieutenant General Holland Smith just arrived on the beach, and the secretary of the Navy told the general "that flag up there means a Marine Corps for the next five hundred years." Apparently he also indicated he'd like to have the flag as a souvenir, and this word got back to Colonel Johnson, the battalion commander, and he said, "No, he can't have our flag. We put it up there. We're going to keep it." So he sent Lieutenant Tuttle down on the beach to get another flag. Tuttle told me just as he was leaving that the colonel said to get a larger flag. I don't know whether his intentions were to get a larger flag so it would be seen or whether he wanted a more prestigious flag for the secretary of the Navy. Tuttle went and got a larger flag—the flag that had been in the salvage depot in Pearl Harbor, but there's no indication it had been aboard any ship that was damaged. About that time, Tuttle got back to the battalion command post, and also about that time, I sent the detail with Sergeant Mike Strank carrying wire up the mountain. When they got to the top, they told Schrier they wanted to take the small flag down and put the other one up. They switched the two flags. There's a picture of them. Then Joe Rosenthal took the most famous picture.

CHARLES LINDBERG
2ND RAIDER BATTALION, 28TH MARINES, 5TH MARINE DIVISION

Charles Lindberg, the last surviving flag raiser, recalls clearing the base of Suribachi and the journey to the top.

Tomorrow is the anniversary [of the flag raisings]. I've gotten gifts and cards—surprisingly, even people that want my autograph. It brings back a lot of memories. I am the last survivor. When I talk about this, however, no names should have been used on the flag raisings because we didn't get up there by ourselves. It was the collective actions of a lot of people, and there were a lot of Raiders and paratroopers up there with us.

Iwo Jima was a massacre. I never expected anything like that. People

The first flag being lowered as the larger flag is raised in the background. (USMC)

were dying left and right. [Japanese] were in caves and bunkers. You had
to rout them out. I was a squad leader for an assault squad—demolitions,
bazookas, and flamethrowers; bunker busting, routing them out of caves
. . . explosives wherever we needed it. I was the flamethrower operator. It
was hazardous, but I liked it. Someone told me that I was crazy, but I
liked that weapon.

We cut Suribachi off from the rest of the island. That was the first
thing we did. The 28th was tasked with taking the mountain. It took us a
few days to get to the base of the mountain. Typically we'd sneak up
close, get an opening, and let them have it. It was an awful sight to burn
them alive. You fire bursts. A burst is all it takes. If you fired it all at once,

[the tank of napalm] would last six seconds. We could hear the screams. On a daily basis, I saw the aftereffects, which were grisly. You pull all the oxygen out of a cave when you shot a flame. They suffocate. [Near the base of the mountain] I know I burned out a bunker, and the smell of burnt flesh was lingering in the air and someone said, "They never had a more pleasant smell than burnt bodies." At that point, maybe I didn't have any feelings. You'd burn them because they'd do it to us. They have a tendency for torturing. I think they got some of our men in Guadalcanal, if I remember correctly. I was numb; just doing my job.

That morning we reported to Colonel Johnson, our commander of the battalion. He handed Lieutenant Schrier, also a Raider, a flag and said, "If you get to the top, raise it." We were a forty-man patrol. We started up that mountain, and surprisingly we went all the way to the top with no resistance—not a bit. We got up on the rim there, and we kind of put our men on the flanks. The first thing Schrier says is, "Get the flag up!" Two of our men found this long pipe up there. They brought it over, and we tied the flag to it, and we brought it up to the highest spot we could and we raised it.

Then everything broke loose down below. The troops started cheering; ships blew their whistles and horns. It's something you don't forget. It was one of the most exciting points in my life. That was something I'll never forget.

As this was happening, the Japanese started coming out of the caves up there, and we had to move against them. The first cave we kept them in. It had two ends to it. I took my flamethrower and went to the other side and threw a flame in. We were waiting for them to come out, but nobody came out, so we sealed it with explosives. Later we dug it open, and there were dozens of dead bodies in there.

That was just one cave. There were a lot more caves up there—some that we didn't get to but somebody else did. We had that mountain secure by about noon. At that time, my tanks were empty, and so was my other flamethrower operator's tanks, so we went back down and reloaded in case we had assaults that night . . . we'd be ready for them. In the meantime, Colonel Johnson wanted the flag replaced. A bunch of men came up and changed the flag [we raised], and Rosenthal took his picture, had his film developed, and nobody even knew there was another flag several hours before it. Once we planted the flag, it meant we took their eyes away from them. Suribachi was controlling the Japanese fire on that island.

We had about 30 percent losses to clear the mountain. Somebody told me only a few guys in our platoon got off that island without being hit.

DEAN WINTERS
2ND RAIDER BATTALION, 28TH MARINES, 5TH MARINE DIVISION

Dean Winters, a member of the forty-man patrol that scaled Suribachi, recalls dispatching the Japanese who emerged from caves after the flag was raised and the push toward the northern part of the island.

Lieutenant Schrier, a Raider, asked for volunteers to go up Suribachi. There were three of us just to help them carry stuff up the mountain. As a kid, I'd climb mountains, so it wasn't too hard on me. I carried a box of hand grenades. I loaded this stuff to carry up there and was there when the first flag went up. It was just a little flag, and it went up on a pole, and I was around the other side of the crater. I was really proud of the flag when it went up. I love the flag and this country. Whenever I see the flag desecrated, I get tears in my eyes and so angry.

Once the flag was up, a bunch of Japanese came out of a cave. They pulled a banzai charge. I shot one of the first ones out of the cave and took his helmet off. He had a flag inside his helmet. I looked at him, and he looked just like me. He was a kid, young. It was heroic coming out of there. [crying] I didn't think too much then, but I've thought about it ever since. His face is in my eyes. I see him when I go to sleep at night. We thought his mother would like to have it [the flag] back. It had his name on it, and signatures of his friends on it. It had a poem of some kind on it also. Several years ago, I gave it to the Mormon missionaries [in Japan] to see if they could find the mother and father of the man. Apparently they were in Hiroshima and were killed.

I went down the mountain after the second flag was raised. So I went back with my squad. They took a picture of us with the Japanese flag I captured.

We started up toward the north end of the island. They started shooting at us with mortars. After that was over, I went up to a little path that was there, and the Mole [a member of the platoon] was crouched behind a rock and I told him to get up there with his men. I kicked him in the butt. "You're supposed to be up there, not down here goofing off!" He was dead. I kissed his dirty little face, and I put him in the shade as much as possible, and I went on.

The next day we were attacked again, losing several men killed or wounded. Every hundred yards, there was another canyon where you had to dig the enemy out. One of our comrades was captured by the Japanese and pulled into a cave where they tortured him by splitting his finger webs up to his wrists. He was screaming uncontrollably. Our lieutenant got so angry he went in after him and was killed in the process.

There was hardly any of us left in the entire company. For me I was hit on March 14. My hip joint was shot all to pieces. Four Marines from the Marine Corps band were moving me to the rear, and one of the men was killed in the process. Since the war, I've been confined to a wheelchair and have tried to live a good life. However, I relive the war every day.

LUTHER "JUKE" CRABTREE
4TH PARACHUTE BATTALION, 26TH MARINES, 5TH MARINE DIVISION

Luther Crabtree painfully recalls tenderly removing his brother's body from the field of battle during the push north.

To push forward, we had to use flamethrower tanks, demolition, and flamethrowers from the assault squads. I was a member of the assault squad of Dog Company.

I was the demolition man. It was just one pillbox after another that we had to eliminate. Practically every day, but especially on the 26th of

February, about a week after we landed, Dog Company was pinned down, and the assault squad was called. I worked up on the left side of the pillbox that was holding up the advance. My flamethrower man, who was also from Columbus [Ohio], worked up on the right-hand side as I was working through the front lines; my brother was in the advance squad, and he was lying there. He had been shot through the head and was dead. My brother was hit in the temple, probably from rifle fire. It wasn't shrapnel. There was just a pool of blood as he lay there on his side. I worked on through and eliminated the pillbox, went up after the flamethrower man, and fired napalm in, and we eliminated the pillbox.

That evening the company commander, Tom Fields, laid down a smokescreen, and I went out along with three buddies of mine and brought my brother back for the evening and stayed with him that night. My brother was one of our top squad leaders in Dog Company; he was

Luther Crabtree visiting his brother's grave on Iwo Jima. (courtesy of Robert Maiden)

very popular. He was a corporal, same as I. I think everyone in the company—and I really sincerely mean this—liked Tiny so much that it was almost a joint belief that we should do that. That night I laid beside him, thought of the normal things and brought him home, my parents and all the things . . . yeah, I prayed. I prayed every minute on Iwo Jima. I prayed when I was in the foxhole. I prayed when I was out in front of the front lines. When it's your brother, I think it's a very different situation altogether. We were very close. In fact, most people thought we were twins. I always admired Tom Fields, our captain, for stopping the battle and putting down the smokescreen so that we could bring him back. That was one of the most difficult days of my life. It is something that continuously has been on my mind all the time. It's something you never forget. It worked out that I was able to go out and get him and bring him back. Then the only thing I could do was go back with the company and advance.

We advanced on up the other side of the island. As far as Iwo Jima is concerned, the most difficult part of the battle wasn't in the first few days. The greater proportion of the battle, the greater number of casualties, occurred in the last ten or fifteen days in the far north end of the island, where we ran into a tremendous influx of fire—every type of fire from caves and pillboxes. It was one after another. We had to advance fifty to one hundred yards out in front of the line. We had advanced to that point, and then our men got pinned down, and that's when the assault squad—my bazooka man and loader and flamethrower man and myself, worked through the lines and eliminated the pillbox cave that was holding them up.

I didn't have any anger throughout that entire battle; I was numb. As I look back on that, I think I was so well trained that I just did my job. In battle you almost act instinctively. The paramarines had such great training, and of course the Raiders, that I think everybody just reacted just as they were trained to react.

DEAN VOIGHT

2ND RAIDER BATTALION, 27TH MARINES, 5TH MARINE DIVISION

The 5th Division's push north continued to be measured in yards and bodies. Every small terrain feature became a major obstacle. Here Dean Voight remembers the 27th Marines' attack on a ridge that guarded the approach to Hill 362-A.

Iwo Jima was as close to hell as you could get. I can't even begin to describe it to you. It was always hot—active gunfire all the time and explosions going off. People getting killed right and left.

There weren't very many left in my platoon. Walsh had taken a squad up to attack some Nips who were dug in along a ridge near 362-A; I was in the area at the time. I had been putting somebody's rifle together, for one of the beginners. It got sand in it, and he cleaned it. The platoon was making a flank job on this hillside, and when I looked up, I saw a Nip with a potato masher, which is a hand grenade, and he was heaving it. As he heaved it, I picked up the rifle and I fired at him and he went down. [Gunnery Sergeant] William G. Walsh jumped on the grenade to protect the squad. He got the Congressional Medal of Honor for that. He was my platoon sergeant, and I was acting sergeant at the time. When he was killed, I had to take over the platoon, and at that time I think there were about twelve of us left. I had to form my last platoon out of machine gunners, beginners—people that hadn't seen action before—to make a whole new platoon. Wherever other people were left over, I got them so I would have a fighting platoon.

They then issued me machine gunners and mortar men. All the platoons that had a few left, they jammed them into mine to form another platoon. We of course had to continue on with the battle. We came up on this hill, and there were Nips buried in caves around the other side of the hill. By that time, Frank O'Reilly was back in charge of the platoon, and he wanted me to locate fire for tanks [targets for tanks to fire at]. The tank came up, and I got on the telephone with a fifty-yard cable on it, and behind it I was telling them where to fire, giving the quadrants to fire.

At that time, they had hit a delayed-action mine; they didn't get hit by the mine, but I did. It blew me up in the air, and I still had the phone in my hand when I hit the ground. I saw them stop the tank, and they were getting out of the bottom. I did a little cursing, and I told them, "Get back in the tank. The mine got me; it didn't get you!" I was still directing fire.

It just happened that the same guy that was in charge of the tank, ten years later, right here in this town where I live now, I was out golfing with him and found out he was the tank operator! We were talking about the war when we were golfing, and I made the statement about him and his goddamn tanks and he says, "Was that you that called me a bastard and told me to get back in the tank?" I said, "That was me." He said, "Well, I'll be damned, after all these years!" Luckily, I wasn't wounded. It did do some damage to me, but I never knew about it until many years later. I went to the hospital because I was having trouble in the liver area, and they opened me up and discovered I had a concussion there. All it did was create blood clots, blood pooling, all around my liver.

We re-formed again, and I had a couple other guys added to my platoon when I got wounded. I got shot in the rear end and groin. That finally took me out.

FRANK CALDWELL
1ST PARACHUTE BATTALION, 26TH MARINES, 5TH MARINE DIVISION

On the morning of D plus 13, March 4, the Americans were in control of about two-thirds of Iwo Jima. They had taken it at a staggering cost of nearly thirteen thousand killed and wounded. The day before, the 26th Marines launched an assault on Hill 362-B, a key strong point in Kuribayashi's main line of defense. The attack produced hundreds of casualties and five Medals of Honor. F Company alone lost forty-seven men. Here Frank Caldwell recalls the assault on 362-B.

I landed with Fox Company, 2nd Battalion, 26th Marines and was Fox Company commander for over a year. I left with myself and 44 Marines out of over 250 that we came in with. All my lieutenants and first ser-geants were killed.[10] I landed with these men, and I had about a hundred replacements. We left the island on the 26th of March. I felt relieved to get the hell off the island, but I felt pretty bad for the fact that we had a lot of wounded and over one hundred killed. I had to spend the rest of the day in the hull of the ship writing letters of condolence to their next of kin. Three pages per casualty in longhand, in triplicate. We didn't use typewriters. We had to tell the next of kin how we knew this fellow. Some of them I had to lie a little bit because I didn't know everybody or how they got killed.

While we were fighting, [replacements] would come up at night, and we would have to brief them very quickly and familiarize them with things. Most of these replacements had been clerks and this and that, and a lot of them didn't know what end the bullet came out of. We had to re-ally get them up to speed. You want to call somebody cannon fodder, that was it. We would do the best we could. One thing I did was to put some black tape across our helmets, and they would know then they were Fox Company's men. That helped a lot because they didn't know who their boss was or who they could go to, particularly at night. That helped a hell of a lot. This was the only outfit on Iwo Jima that had black tape going across their helmets. It kept the morale high. They didn't panic.

The saddest thing that I had happen to me, I was talking to my Lieu-tenant Clark, who was an old boy from Mississippi. We came over on the boat together. He always called me Skipper. We talked every night. All the time we'd be in touch on the telephone. [A few days before the attack on Hill 362-B] the Japanese closed in on him. He called me and said, "Skipper, they're coming in." I could hear the blasts in the background. He was dead. He wasn't more than forty feet away from my position. They were throwing grenades, and they were firing weapons; they got every-body in there. All these men were platoon leaders that I had been with for over a year. A year is a long time in World War II.

We had made a classic charge across this incomplete airfield near 362-B. It was very high and rugged. There were a lot of canyons near it. We were going across that. This was early in the morning somewhere around the 3rd of March, and this is where we lost a hell of a lot of people. We were firing at cliffs, but I couldn't get the company from our 3rd Battalion [George Company] to come abreast of it; they were on my left. I could see them way over to the left, way back behind my left flank.

After Hill 362-B was secure, our own artillery came down too close, hitting us. But they still said, "No, that's not our artillery; that's the Japanese artillery." I said, "Bullshit! I know which way that stuff's coming." It tore up one of our guys, mutilated him. [My men] took his innards and so forth and his skull and all that stuff and put it on a stretcher, and one of my sergeants marched right back to the [battalion commander], ran across that airfield, and said, "This is what your goddamn artillery has done to us!" It was too close to the end of the island for it to be Japanese. It was a friendly-fire incident. We had had some previous friendly-fire incidents early on with the damn tanks coming up behind us firing away. They just mowed us down. They didn't tell us they were coming—nobody told us they were coming—and it got a lot of people shot in the back or smashed under their treads. That was early on—about D plus 4 or D plus 5. I had to make something up in the letters home for those people. I couldn't say he was killed by [friendly fire]. I did the best I could. I had to write a lot of letters.

ROBERT MAIDEN
4TH PARACHUTE BATTALION, 26TH MARINES, 5TH MARINE DIVISION

Robert Maiden recalls the fighting around Hill 362.

Moving forward, we encountered a minefield which the engineers cleared a path across and laid a white tape on it. One of the kids that was in my machine-gun squad was Lonnie Corrazine from Texas. The word was, "Okay, you're the next now. Double time across, stay on the white tape. If you should receive fire, hit the deck on the tape." Well, as luck would have it, Corrazine fell off the tape. He must have hit what was, I would say, the equivalent of a 250-pound aerial bomb booby trap. All I saw after the explosion was the upper half of his body about twenty feet in the air.

Later, we got word his mother couldn't believe that her son was dead. She kept writing Captain Fields for months after the war that she couldn't believe that Lonnie had died. How can you tactfully tell a mother without getting too gross in description of the details?

We got up to Hill 362, near the unfinished Airfield No. 3. A buck sergeant had the mortar section. This one afternoon, we got this replacement lieutenant. The sun was getting ready to go down, and we were digging in for the night and checking passwords and ammunition and everything, and this lieutenant wanted to look over the parapet to look out in front and everybody said, "That's not a very good idea, Lieutenant." He did it anyhow, and this sniper nailed him. The bullet went through the right lens of the binoculars and came out the palm of his right hand. The impact blackened both his eyes. He let out a scream and fell down. Somebody said, "You dumb shit, we told you!" He was evacuated.

Thus commenced the battle for Hill 362, the seizure of it. I've never seen such ugly terrain in my life. There were gullies and caves and trails and overhanging rock shale, and you just had to go very slowly and methodically and check out everything as you moved forward. We didn't move very far that first day. We got about 150 yards and the company commander said, "This is lousy terrain to try and defend. Let's pull back to where we were." We did, and it was a better defensive position. The next morning, we started out. This corporal who was in the company office—he was a clerk and he had been with the 4th Parachute Battalion—had an expert rifle badge. I missed expert by one, so I was a sharpshooter. We're with him, and we're moving along this sort of a trail through this little gully, and all the sudden the Japanese came out of a cave to our right front and they saw us and I yelled, "Get them!" And I opened up with that Tommy gun. One of our men, the expert rifleman, he had an M1, and I heard the eight shots go off and the clip flying off, and those three Japs were still running. I sat down and started laughing. He said, "What's so f-ing funny?" And I said, "The expert rifleman. Cheese and crackers . . . you had the perfect opportunity, you fired eight rounds. Those guys are going to be shooting at us tomorrow." Oh, he was pissed. We finally captured the hill and continued moving forward.

HOWARD BAXTER
2ND PARACHUTE BATTALION, 27TH MARINE REGIMENT, 5TH MARINE DIVISION

Howard Baxter recalls the fighting on Iwo.

I've had many, many vivid memories of Iwo Jima. All the vegetation was gone on the island because of the shelling. You'd dig a foxhole, and you couldn't sit in it because all the sulfuric steam would just about burn your britches off. If you wanted an idea what hell might look like, Iwo Jima came the closest to it. It was the bloodiest I'd ever been in. A close second was the Chosin Reservoir [Korea]—hellfire and brimstone.

About the third day, we lost our squad leader, who had been in the 2nd Parachute Battalion and had knocked out a sniper for us on Choiseul [the Choiseul raid]. He was the best boxer in the outfit. We came under a tremendous artillery barrage, huge shells breaking all over. They could just about drive you nuts. I was kind of flat on the ground. It was pure sand. I flattened myself on it. I looked over, and the squad leader jumped in a shell hole and lit a cigarette. The next thing I knew, a shell landed in his hole and blew him to smithereens; there wasn't anything left of him.

We were the worst hit. Our companies were reinforced, but out of our platoon of forty-six or forty-seven men, I was one of two men left at the end of the battle. In my company, I was one of twenty-seven men out of two hundred-and-something left. That will give you an idea of what I'm talking about.

Something you learn in combat, you don't get too close to people. It hurts too much. You don't want to go through that. You shut down your emotional system. We lost three platoon leaders. The third replacement officer came in. We'd lost a lot of men, and our morale was low. You reach a point and you'd say, "The hell with this. I'm not going to get out of my foxhole."

That changed when Ira Goldberg, a new lieutenant who'd never been in combat, came in as our third platoon leader as a replacement. He was a very quiet man, a learned man, well educated. He never shouted or lost his temper. He was only with us four or five days. He instilled morale in the platoon the short time he was with us. Whenever we had to start advancing again, he didn't shout or yell at us. His coolness under fire, leadership, he was the kind of Marine we wished we could have been. He led us by example. A few days later, he got cut in half by a machine gun. After the war, his brother wrote a letter to the association [postwar veteran association] asking if anybody knew him. I wrote back and explained how he died.

I saw some on the beach—men that just froze. I can remember people flipping out. We were under tremendous artillery barrages. The shells were just breaking in, and big hunks of shrapnel were falling all over the place. I had a piece of shrapnel about the size of a small refrigerator that landed along the side of my shell hole. It was molten red hot—just sizzling. It just missed the whole frame of my body by about six inches. It burned itself in the sand. It was steaming, and you could almost see through it, it was so hot.

During a barrage, this guy I had gone through parachute school with was from an Indian reservation and about 6'4" and 200-some-odd pounds. He turned into a screaming maniac. He lost one of his best buddies who had been blown to bits right in front of him. He was going to march right into the enemy, and it took about four guys to hold him down. They finally got him back to the sick bay.

One of my most vivid memories is going up to this pillbox. A great portion of it had been destroyed by the bombardment, but the Japanese piled pieces on concrete near the entrance. I was ordered to charge the pillbox. As a PFC [private first class], I had the squad and formed a half-circle around the base of the pillbox and charged it all by myself with my BAR blazing at the concrete that they had built up around the entrance.

I blasted the entrance, and I'm sure a lot of bullets ricocheted inside of the pillbox.

All of a sudden, all hell breaks loose. They had a hole on the top of the pillbox, and they are firing mortars straight up and they would land right outside of the pillbox, and we had several guys killed or wounded. We were just doing our duty. Our platoon sergeant pulled us back and broke down and cried. He lost one of his best friends. He reached a point and had a good bawl for about five minutes, and then he was all right. I couldn't do that. I felt if I let myself go, I'd be gone. I just jammed it down inside. I think a lot of us did.

FRANK CALDWELL

1st Parachute Battalion, 26th Marines, 5th Marine Division

On March 14, another flag raising took place to signify the official U.S. occupation of Iwo Jima. For most Marines, the declaration was premature; two weeks of hard fighting remained. Many of the Japanese refused to surrender and were buried or burned alive in their caves by tanks, satchel charges, and flamethrowers.

Tanks were, at this particular stage of action, the key to our victory. [But] we could not get them up on that rough terrain, and we couldn't budge. We couldn't even lift our heads. Fortunately, it was the luck of the Irish. Somebody in the 5th Division had come up with a design to armor the bulldozers. They just took a plain old bulldozer and put armor sheeting around the driver's position. This engineer platoon leader came up and said, "Do you got a use for this bulldozer?" I said, "You're damn right I have!" So I put the bulldozer to work. The first thing I know, he was fooling around, leveling off the terrain up there, and he went out a little bit beyond the front line. I said, "Get these tanks up here." I called the tanks. I had a whole platoon of tanks. I got that bulldozer operating, and I called the engineers to come up and do a little mine clearing. I called on the artillery to give us artillery support.

We went on out there, and the tanks were right behind [the bulldozers], and the infantry of my company was on the flanks, and some of my infantry jumped in the tanks and fired the machine guns to site the targets. Then the most vivid memory I have while we were doing all this was one of these tanks was a flamethrower tank—a Zippo Sherman—and it ran up near this cave and out comes a bunch of Japanese. One was an officer and he had his sword pulled, and he charged the tank at maximum range. The range of the flamethrower was about seventy-five feet. This tank guy didn't do a damn thing—he just sat there. That officer was pissed off; he charged this tank out of desperation. He had his sword up high, and he came into that tank, and the tank gave him a blast with the flamethrower, hit the officer right in the crotch, and he jumped up high—still had his sword up high—and then he fell forward flaming, jamming his sword in the ground.

We went barreling on, and the first thing you know, we were moving right along there, and that particular night I had a swarm of reporters come up to see me. One was from the old *Herald Tribune* in New York. He was some hotshot New Yorker, and he introduced himself. We were getting a lot of incoming and he said, "You know, I'm used to this stuff. I made the Anzio landing with the Army, and we caught hell up there. Give me some names." He wanted to get some names of people. He thought this was going to be a kind of deal where he could just sit down and interview people. What happened was we were getting some incoming and one of my PFCs—his face was badly hit—was being pulled out on a stretcher; he died en route. He passed right by us there. This reporter says, "Now who is that?" I said, "His name is Murphy." He said, "What's he done?" I said, "He was a platoon leader of the 1st Platoon of Fox Company." [Platoons were normally led by a lieutenant, but the severe losses on Iwo often forced PFCs into the role.] Then it started hitting a little bit more. I turned to talk a little bit more to this guy, and he had left the hole. I could see his tail running way back. He just had had a little too much.

One night we were digging in, as we always have to set up our position and a few things like that and get our machine guns in, our mortars set, and clear the area, make it secure. We'd see something like a hole or something, and we'd throw something in it to make sure there wasn't anybody alive in there like a Jap who may give us some trouble at night. We strung barbed wire around there a little bit. Right next to us, there was a little cliff about six feet tall; weathered down and up against that cliff was a pile of rocks with a hole in the top. I said, "Throw light phosphorus in there." We went on about our way and getting this laid in and that laid in and our CP set up, and all of a sudden these rocks parted, and out comes a Japanese soldier just reeking with smoke. His uniform was on fire. Tears were coming out of his eyes. I could even see that, I was so close to him. He had one of those Japanese grenades in his hand. He was in the process of throwing that as a last resort right amongst us. He got it away, but we dodged it, and we proceeded to mow him down. We quickly searched him because lots of times they were booby-trapped. I took his helmet off and found a picture in the top of his helmet of his family back in Tokyo or somewhere in Japan. He was standing erect with his helmet under his arm, wife and six children — cute-looking little children. Even after all we went through, all these tough Marines started to tear up a little bit . . . they choked up seeing that.

ROBERT MAIDEN
4TH PARACHUTE BATTALION, 26TH MARINES, 5TH MARINE DIVISION

The remains of General Kuribayashi's garrison defended the extreme northern tip of the island. Robert Maiden recalls the final push.

We could smell saltwater coming from the breeze off Kitano Point. We moved ahead, and there's this huge pit. We went down on foot, very cautiously, down to the bottom of the pit, and it was almost as big as a baseball diamond. We could see three big caves. You could have driven a 6x6 [large truck] with the top up into all three of them. They brought the intelligence guys forward and tried to get the Japanese to surrender. You could hear voices but they weren't responding to the surrender. They got no response whatsoever. At that point in time, the 5th Division had lost practically all their tanks, and Lieutenant Colonel Collins—he was the tank battalion commander—he came up with three tanks they borrowed from the 3rd Division. He wanted to make damn sure nothing happened to those tanks because they were on loan. Like a dummy, I volunteered, since I'd been down there, so I rode down in the lead tank in the gunner's position next to the driver. There were two gun tanks and a flamethrower tank, and the gun tanks fired two 75 mm rounds into each cave and dust spilled out. No results—so they backed out a little ways, and the flamethrower tank went up until he expended all of his fuel. He gave them a hot shot in each of the three caves. We thought, "Jesus, who could live through that?" Little did we know that they had three- and four-tier caves down below ground level. The tanks backed up, and I got out.

That night, we got hit pretty hard. There were a lot of grenades. I remember one of the [men] in the 60 mm mortar position he caught one, a bullet, right under the rim of his helmet, and he died. I was holding him. I said, "Bill, Bill, you'll be all right." It was dark, and I couldn't see that good. He died in my arms. Then things quieted down, and not thirty minutes later, we got some more grenades in.

[Next day] we were working on a cliff, and there was a cave down below, and they were shooting out of it. Crabtree and his demolition guys were lowering satchel charges down into it, and there was one kid down below us. He was the last kid in the company to get killed. He panicked and I said, "Andy!" He looked up. I said, "You're okay. Just stay down. We'll blow the cave. You'll be okay." Well, he panicked for some reason, got up to run, and they nailed him. The next day they pulled us back, because we were down to less than thirty guys in the entire company. They took us down, and we got to shower with warm ocean water. It was like somebody pouring orange juice on you, but it felt so good.

DAVID SEVERANCE
3RD PARACHUTE BATTALION, 28TH MARINES,
5TH MARINE DIVISION

Captain David Severance recalls the closing days of the battle.

My company was the extreme left flank of the whole line but we didn't have enough people to reach the beach. It was just a push. We pushed for two or three days. We took a lot of casualties, and because of the casualties, they pulled us out for a couple of days. Then we went back on the line, and we stayed there until March 26. I cut the size of my company down to two platoons. We originally went in with 230 men and 7 officers. I got about 67 to 70 replacements. I had a total of about 310. I had no replacement officers. They sent me a lieutenant; he lasted about fifteen minutes. He was running alongside of me, and somebody took a shot between my legs and hit him. They hauled him out. That was the only replacement officer I had.

In the meantime, I had two officers, and both of them were killed, so I had no officers. I had a first sergeant, a gunnery sergeant, and two small platoons.

We had objectives that were assigned by somebody. A battalion had a certain geographical objective. We pushed, tried to reach it—sometimes we did . . . usually we didn't. You'd push against an enemy you couldn't see. We'd find various caves and whatnot, pour fire into those, and blow them up and move on a little bit further. There was pretty much constant fire all the time. We had a lot of mortar fire. Every day there'd be some [casualties], some days worse than others. It begins to take a toll on you. It's hard to describe. You'd get so tired; it's just one day after another just waiting to get to the far end of the island. We knew that as soon as we covered all the real estate, they were gonna pull us out. It was just a matter of pushing, trying to get up to the north end.

About four or five days before the end, they gave me about fifty pioneer troops—all privates and one lieutenant—and I was sent out in front of the lines on a patrol at night to contact a battalion that was attacking across our front. A gorge was the last real estate we had to recover. They had a battalion that was gonna go down this gorge across our front right to left, and I was supposed to be there to contact their flank. We got up on the edge of the gorge, and there was a ravine running along our left flank, and we suddenly heard a bunch of Japanese down there, and I couldn't get in touch with my battalion. At about that time, I was trying to figure out what the hell I was gonna do because I couldn't attack with fifty recruits that had never fired a rifle. As I was figuring out what the heck to do, a messenger came up through the dark and said the patrol was supposed to be pulled back.

Dave Bowman in the mortars was killed on one of the last days. The pioneer platoon was relieving us, and he was in charge of one of the small platoons. He went up to show the lieutenant who was relieving him where the various positions were, and he got shot in the head. He was waiting for word that his wife was having a baby. It seems to me that he got the word just before he was killed. His wife, I think, had a boy. I'd also just received word that my wife had a baby born dead. It all came in the same mail. That got to me. I found a quiet place and cried.

ROBERT "MOOSE" MAIDEN
4TH PARACHUTE BATTALION, 26TH MARINES, 5TH MARINE DIVISION

Moose Maiden recalls his friends who didn't return.

They had guys from each company in the honor guard, and Chaplain Gittelsohn said some words that I've always been moved by:

> Here before us lie the bodies of comrades and friends. Men who until yesterday or last week laughed with us, joked with us, trained with us. . . . Some of us have buried our closest friends here. We saw these men killed before our very eyes. Any one of us may have died in their places. Indeed some of us are alive and breathing at this very moment only because men who lie here

beneath us had the courage and strength to give their lives for ours. . . ."

. . . Here lie officers and men, Negroes and whites, rich men and poor—together . . . theirs is the highest and purest democracy. We shall not foolishly suppose, as did the last generation of America's fighting men, that victory on the battlefield will automatically guarantee the triumph of democracy at home. This war, with all its frightful heartache and suffering, is but the beginning of our generation's struggle for democracy.

They raised the flag and then ordered it to half-mast. Everybody broke up, and just sort of wandered through the cemetery looking at crosses to locate members and buddies they knew. There were a lot that I knew. Serving so closely, united so to speak, part of a team—there's a love that's hard to explain. I cried. It was pretty touching to think you were among the living, and all my close friends were no longer around. I still reflect on that day.

CHAPTER ELEVEN

The Last Battle: Okinawa

It's a good thing how the Lord helps one block out unpleasant memories.
I don't think one can vividly remember those feelings and still have his sanity.

—A MARINE GRAVELY WOUNDED ON SUGAR LOAF HILL[1]

OKINAWA WAS THE LAST ISLAND in the chain that led to Japan and the last major battle of World War II. Located about 400 miles from the Japanese home island of Kyushu, it was an ideal staging area for the invasion of Japan. Okinawa's ports and harbors could shelter the Allied fleet and leave plenty of room for supply depots. Its large airfields provided an unsinkable aircraft carrier within striking distance of the Japanese homeland.

The Japanese knew an invasion of Okinawa was inevitable and in seven months of intensive preparation turned the island into a fortress. Strong points and defensive lines were dug in the hills and valleys of the highly defensible southern portion of the island. Here, Lieutenant General Mitsuru Ushijima assembled the bulk of his Thirty-second Army, over 100,000 strong, and the heaviest Japanese concentrations of mortars and artillery of the war. Ushijima's plan was simple: buy time and inflict casualties. His men would be sacrificed so that more time could be spent strengthening the Home Island defenses. Meanwhile, poorly trained kamikazes would attempt to ruin Admiral Raymond Spruance's Fifth Fleet as it supported the invasion of Okinawa.

Code-named Iceberg, the Normandy-sized assault on Okinawa was made by the Tenth Army, led by General Simon Bolivar Buckner. The initial assault consisted of two Army divisions and the 1st and 6th Marine Divisions. It began on April 1, 1945. The old Raiders, mostly integrated in the 4th Marines (of the 6th Marine Division), landed on Red 1, Red 2, and Red 3 beaches, on the left flank of the beachhead. The Japanese did not resist the landings. As at Iwo Jima, they held their fire, concentrating their forces in the southern portion of Okinawa, where they would make a fanatical last stand.[2]

Cheered by the relatively uneventful landing, the Marines wondered how long their luck would last as they headed straight for Yontan Airfield, securing it the same day. On April 2, resistance stiffened. Typical of the combat in the area, elements of the 3rd Battalion, 4th Marines were caught in a ravine that was ringed by Japanese defenders and had to fight their way out. For the next several days, the 4th advanced inland on Tenth Army's left flank.[3]

Meanwhile, Japanese kamikazes savaged the Fifth Fleet. By the end of the campaign, they had sunk 36 ships and damaged 368. Japan's famed superbattleship, the 69,100-ton *Yamato*, and its five-ship escort made a final, suicidal sortie but was sunk by U.S. carrier-based planes before it could reach Okinawa.[4]

Naval support to the U.S. troops attacking Okinawa remained strong, but up-close naval bombardment could do little against the Japanese in deep caves; only the men on the ground could drive them out. Advancing up the east side of the island, the 4th captured its objectives several days ahead of schedule. It then turned its attention to clearing the Motobu Peninsula. Here, the Japanese held a series of circular coral ridges, part of the 1,200-foot Mount Yae Take.

Yae Take was defended by approximately two thousand seasoned troops from the Japanese 44th Independent Mixed Brigade. A coordinated attack on Yae Take by the 4th Marines and 29th Marines began on April 14 against stiff resistance. The Japanese were dug in around Yae

Okinawa—April–June 1945

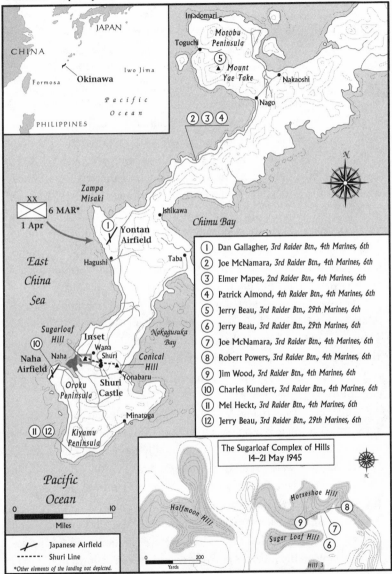

JAPAN

CHINA

Iwo Jima

Formosa   **Okinawa**

Pacific
Ocean

PHILIPPINES

Imadomari

Toguchi   *Motobu*
            Peninsula
            ⑤
            ▲ *Mount*
            Yae Take   Nakaoshi

            Nago

②③④

Zampa
Misaki

XX
6 MAR*
1 Apr

①   *Yontan*
     Airfield

Ishikawa   *Chimu Bay*

East
China
Sea

Hagushi

Taba

N

Sugarloaf
Hill
⑩   **Inset**
         Wana
Naha   Shuri
Airfield Naha   *Conical*
                          Hill
                      Yonabaru
Oroku   **Shuri**
Peninsula **Castle**

Nakagusuka
Bay

Minatoga

⑪ ⑫   *Kiyamu*
       Peninsula

Pacific
Ocean

① Dan Gallagher, *3rd Raider Btn., 4th Marines, 6th*
② Joe McNamara, *3rd Raider Btn., 4th Marines, 6th*
③ Elmer Mapes, *2nd Raider Btn., 4th Marines, 6th*
④ Patrick Almond, *4th Raider Btn., 4th Marines, 6th*
⑤ Jerry Beau, *3rd Raider Btn., 29th Marines, 6th*
⑥ Jerry Beau, *3rd Raider Btn., 29th Marines, 6th*
⑦ Joe McNamara, *3rd Raider Btn., 4th Marines, 6th*
⑧ Robert Powers, *3rd Raider Btn., 4th Marines, 6th*
⑨ Jim Wood, *3rd Raider Btn., 4th Marines, 6th*
⑩ Charles Kundert, *3rd Raider Btn., 4th Marines, 6th*
⑪ Mel Heckt, *3rd Raider Btn., 4th Marines, 6th*
⑫ Jerry Beau, *3rd Raider Btn., 29th Marines, 6th*

0   10
Miles

↘ Japanese Airfield
------ Shuri Line
Other elements of the landing not depicted.

The Sugarloaf Complex of Hills
14–21 May 1945

N

Horseshoe Hill   ⑧

Halfmoon Hill   ⑦
               Sugar Loaf Hill   ⑥

0   200
Yards

Hill 3

259

Take and stubbornly defended the mountain. After two days of battle, the crest of Yae Take was taken, and the Marines continued clearing the Motobu Peninsula.[5]

While the 6th Marine Division was securing northern Okinawa, the bulk of the Tenth Army was battling Ushijima's outer defenses in the southern portion of the island known as the Shuri Line. The line took its name from Shuri Castle, the ancient seat of power for Okinawa's kings. The castle anchored the line at one end, while every hill and ridge in a line extending from it was turned into a death trap. Shuri was a defensive masterpiece largely impervious to American bombardment. The hills were like ships buried underground, with galleries several levels deep connected by a network of tunnels; artillery and mortars were honeycombed into the rock. The Tenth Army inched forward, and stalemate set in. Then, on May 4, 1945, Ushijima launched his counteroffensive. The assault was timed to correspond with a massive dose of kamikazes and an amphibious attack, but it evaporated within twenty-four hours. Advancing out of their hardened defenses, the Japanese became "artillery meat." About five thousand lost their lives, weakening the Shuri Line.[6]

The Tenth Army ordered a four-division assault, including the 6th Marine Division, which moved south from their positions in the Motobu Peninsula. It was here that the elite troops made their greatest contribution. By May 12, the 6th was deployed in an area that was the scene of the bitterest and arguably some of the most decisive action of the campaign: Sugar Loaf Hill.

Sugar Loaf was a triangular system of several hills. Shaped like an arrowhead, it formed the point, while Half Moon and Horseshoe Hills made up the base. Each position was mutually supporting: troops attacking one portion were exposed to withering fire from the other hills. So well integrated were the defenses that taking one hill was meaningless; the Marines had to neutralize them all simultaneously.

The initial assault was made by elements of the 6th Division's 22nd Regiment on May 12. Over the next six days, battalions and companies melted away on the hills. Several rifle companies went down from 240 to a dozen men. The hill was won and lost several times. Finally, on May 18, the 2nd Battalion of the 29th took and held Sugar Loaf. With both the 29th and 22nd Regiments shot to pieces, the 4th Marines, the division's last reserve, was committed to holding Sugar Loaf and seizing the other hills. The Japanese furiously counterattacked but were repelled by the 4th Marines and artillery. Over the next two days, Half Moon and Horseshoe Hills were seized.[7]

With the Sugar Loaf complex finally subdued, other parts of the Shuri Line began to crumble. On the east coast, the 96th Infantry Division took Conical Hill (Sugar Loaf's eastern counterpart), and the 1st Marine Division smashed through the final defenses at Wana. With the prospect of being flanked from two sides, General Ushijima began a masterful withdrawal to his final line of defense in the Kiyamu Peninsula.

Meanwhile, the 4th Marines pushed westward into the port city of Naha, pressing on Ushijima's last defenses. The division's objective was the Naha airport, but rather than slugging through the Oroku Peninsula, the 6th Division launched the last opposed amphibious landing of World War II. Led by the 4th Marines, most of the division made a shore-to-shore landing on the tip of the peninsula on June 4. The Marines were greeted by their old adversary from Bairoko, and one of the last surviving *rikusentai* commanders, Rear Admiral Minoru Ota. Ota, with his five thousand men and automatic weapons removed mainly from wrecked aircraft, sowed the peninsula with mines and made the attack a ten-day nightmare for the Marines. Ota's final words to Ushijima before committing suicide were, "Enemy groups are now attacking our cave headquarters; the Naval Base Force is dying gloriously at this moment."[8]

After securing the Oroku, the 6th Division advanced south, linking up with the 1st Marine Division and the Army units. What was left of the Thirty-second Army made its final stand in the extreme southern tip of the island. After a bloody finale, which included the death of the Tenth Army commander, Lieutenant General Simon Buckner, by an artillery shell, organized resistance ended on June 22.

The battle was costly for all sides. More than 110,000 Japanese were killed defending the island. As many as 150,000 Okinawans, a third of the civilian population, also perished in the battle. American casualties were 49,151, including 12,520 killed or missing in action. The 4th Marines reported losses of 110 percent (by tallying replacement troop losses, it is possible to exceed 100 percent). Many Raiders made up the numbers. The battle was a bitter example of what an invasion of Japan would have entailed.[9]

It was not to be. The Pacific war ended with two large blasts. An atomic bomb was dropped on Hiroshima on August 6, and three days later another was dropped on Nagasaki. The Emperor sued for peace. On September 2, 1945, on the battleship *Missouri* in Tokyo Bay, representatives of the Japanese government officially surrendered.

The survivors then began their long journey home.

DAN GALLAGHER
3RD RAIDER BATTALION, 4TH MARINES, 6TH MARINE DIVISION

Around 8:30 A.M. on April 1, 1945, the 4th Marines landed on beaches designated Red 1, 2, and 3. The Marines quickly pushed inland, capturing Yontan Airfield. By the next day, opposition had stiffened.

After the landing, we walked across the Yontan Airfield. One of our planes bombed the airfield and blew up a plane inside one of the revetments. We got across there and were going up a rise. One of the guys in the platoon said, "Hey, Gallagher, they got your buddy." "Where?" "I saw him lying on the ground." The captain and I ran up to him and flipped him over and saw it was Red [John] Anderson. Christ, I felt like hell. He got it right square between the eyes. We squatted back down and got out of the way. A sniper was firing, but another fellow, I forgot his name, got up to Red and got his wallet out and gave it to me because he knew we were pretty good friends.[10]

The next morning, instead of a skirmish line we went in company files. Second Platoon was in front at the point. We were going up this little trail in a steep ravine, and I said to the captain, "There might be Japs up on the side over there." He said, "Ah, that's 1st Battalion." I said, "Bullshit!"

That's when the Japs started firing. Everybody opened up. I could look in front of that column of men, and they were dropping—dropping left and right. We dove for cover. I opened up; I had a carbine. I had a walkie-talkie radio, and the captain said, "Get on the radio and have them send us some help up here!" I ran the aerial [on the radio]. I said, "Love Five calling Love Six." I didn't get an answer, so I said, "I'll get out in the middle of one of these rice paddies and run the aerial up." Bam! A rifle shot hit me in the shoulder and spun me around. The company commander tried to patch me up. The runner tried to grab the radio and bam! he got shot right down the back. We left the radio there, and the captain wanted me to go back myself. I couldn't make it through the paddies, so I got in a muddy creek, but I didn't want to get too far down in the mud and get my shoulder dirty, so I was getting sniper fire while I was in there.

I came back to the captain, and at that time the machine-gun section was wiped out. The poor captain tried to get things organized and got shot right in the stomach and landed in the rice paddy and was there all day long. He was paralyzed. I could see him on his belly trying to drink water. I was hit pretty bad and having a hard time moving. It was getting dark, and I said we better start to bring back the wounded. I looked around, and someone is here and someone is there. All of a sudden, a machine gun opened up. That was the end of the rest of us. It spun me around, and my back was across a bush. I was paralyzed. I was scared shitless, and then I got hit in the ankle and across my back. I thought I was really fucked. Minutes after that, a corpsman came down and dragged me out of there. He gave me a shot of morphine, and I was shipped back to an aid station and eventually to a ship offshore.

JOE McNAMARA
3RD RAIDER BATTALION, 4TH MARINES, 6TH MARINE DIVISION

As many as 150,000 civilians perished on Okinawa. Some died by their own hand, while others were tragically caught in the crossfire. Joe McNamara remembers one such incident several days after the landing.

One night there was a bunch of firing. They passed the word, "Be alert. They're coming through the lines." The next morning, we found out it was the civilians that tried to come through the lines.

There they were out in this open field—all killed. Jesus Christ— dead children, women, old men. They said there were Japanese among them, forcing them to go. We were putting out pamphlets every day telling them [Okinawan civilians] to stay on the main roads and not to try to come through our lines. There were a lot of them killed. It was horrifying to see dead babies, dead children. We didn't have anything to do with it. Another group accidentally did it. Just the thought of all those people . . .

You'd try to get them [the civilians] out of the caves also. As we were advancing, we knew they were in there and tried to get them out. If we couldn't, we didn't know if there were soldiers in there and tossed in hand grenades. In a cave, you don't know who's in there or what they're doing. It took us a few days to cross the island, and we started north.

ELMER MAPES
2ND RAIDER BATTALION, 4TH MARINES, 6TH MARINE DIVISION

Elmer Mapes also remembers an incident involving civilians.

We had just set up our defense for the night, and of course they, the Al- lies, had informed the people of Okinawa, "Don't try and go through our lines at night." But the Japs [soldiers] would get with the Okinawan people and try and go through our lines. They even put on civilian clothes to infiltrate through us or escape; they used the civilians as human shields.

Things were quiet for a while when all of a sudden just everything started—machine guns, rifles. You could hear screams. I wasn't right next to it. I was in a foxhole twenty yards away or so.

After everything quieted down, there was a solitary baby crying—just a little tiny baby, no other sound. The baby was crying in the night.

Marines provide a drink of water to an Okinawan baby boy. (USMC)

Everybody was dead except this poor little baby there. The mother was probably dead.

In the morning, by the time I got to the point, I didn't even know what happened to the kid . . . I often wondered. Just all through the night that baby was crying. I suppose they [the men out front] were told not to go out there because it could have been a fake, a trap. It was a sad day and typical of most of our days on the island.

PATRICK ALMOND
4TH RAIDER BATTALION, 4TH MARINES, 6TH MARINE DIVISION

Patrick Almond, who was near Elmer Mapes, recalls the night that civilians tried to cross through his lines and the drive north to Mount Yae Take.

The third or fourth day after we landed . . . it was late at night. Oh, my God, that was pure slaughter. [sigh] I will hate the Japanese for that reason if for none other. I was in the group when they pushed the first bunch of civilians on us. We were set up on a road, and the Japs came down with the civilians in front of them. We were ordered not to let them pass. The order came down, "Do not let them through!" There is no telling how many Japanese soldiers were killed wearing kimonos with split-toed shoes and a rifle sticking out under the kimono.

They were screaming and crying. There was a little baby strapped to a woman's back crying all night. You don't go out and try to save the baby at night.

The next morning, we walked right through the dead Japs and civilians. We saw all the dead women and children. There were thirty-some-odd civilians and about ten soldiers. We found the baby. It fell in a crater in the road that was half filled with water on the woman's back. She happened to fall just right to preserve the baby and save it from the fire. We all marveled at her, and someone gave her some candy. I'm not sure what happened to the kid. But what the Japanese tried to do disgusted me.

We continued to push north and did get a bit of fighting near Mount Yae Take. We advanced through open fields, and when we got on Mount Yae Take, and looked back, we wondered how any of us got there. The sides of the mountain were open, and they [the Japanese] had clear fields of fire and didn't utilize them.

It was nothing spectacular, just crawling forward. The only thing I really vividly remember was this particular sniper. He killed three or four of my men. We located him by the sound of the bolt on his rifle. They flushed him out with a grenade. He was a twelve-year-old boy. His magazine spring was broken, so he was only able to slowly fire one shot at a time. He was a damn good shot. [sigh] The range was only fifty feet. The Japanese had left him there, and he did what they left him to do. We shot him right there.

JERRY BEAU
3RD RAIDER BATTALION, 29TH MARINES,
6TH MARINE DIVISION*

The Marines continued their push into northern Okinawa. The heart of the Japanese defenses there lay on the Motobu Peninsula in a series of circular coral ridges that made up Mount Yae Take. The coordinated attack on Yae Take by the 4th Marines and 29th Marines kicked off on April 14. It took several days of hard fighting before the mountain fortress was subdued.

Every Fourth of July, I fly the flag. I'm proud of it. I think I'm the only guy on the block that does it anymore. I also fly the Marine Corps colors. I actually had someone drop by the house the other day to say how much he appreciated it.

Memorial Day is also special. I pay about ten dollars for the priest to say mass for those that didn't return. We got to be pretty close to each other. Some people may not understand that, but I think about those men. Unless they were in World War II, Korea, or Vietnam, people have no idea what transpires in war.

I had a Jap jump on my back with a hand grenade. The 4th Marines were attacking from the west side, and we were coming from the east side, compressing. It was raining. We had a lot of rain in April, and damn it, it was cold at night, too. The word came in that our planes had spotted what they thought were a number of Japs in a valley about a mile and a half from where we were at the time. I had the honor of taking a patrol down.

It was mountainous country up there, and the trail went up a steep cliff to my left; it went about 45 degrees. The path widened. Some places would branch out five to ten to fifteen feet and drop off.

As we were moving forward, a Jap had dug in the side of the mountain and camouflaged himself. I always had sinus trouble. I should have

---

* Most Raiders were part of the 4th Marine Regiment, but some were detailed to other regiments within the Corps to help meet the high demand for battle-tested replacements. Jerry Beau was one such Raider who helped form the cadre for a battalion in the 29th Marines.

smelled the guy, but I didn't. I just passed him, and then I heard him hit the grenade, and he reached and got his left arm around my neck while he was sticking the grenade into my jacket. We had practiced this stuff quite a bit. I did the usual thing—took one step forward and crouched—and he went right over my head and he landed. I hit the deck and rolled. When the grenade went off, he was facing me. I was probably eight feet away or so, and when I rolled, I had my carbine on my left forearm, and the center part of the grenade that has the fuse, which is copper, the grenade exploded and [the fuse] hit that stock instead of my arm. There were two miracles there. That thing could have taken my arm off or, worse, killed me. I had all kinds of stuff on my left side. It took a minute or two, and then I looked back at the radio man, and we had these click signals instead of talking because the Japs were nearby. I said, "Jeez, how long have I been here?" He said, "Oh, less than a minute. You're all red." "It must be my high blood pressure." I said, "Baker, did you report?" And he said, "Yes." "Well, you should go on." He said, "Let me check around." I checked back, and my getaway man was watching the back and the side of the mountain. The reason I picked him for my runner was because he was an expert rifleman and used to do a lot of sniping.

It took me a couple of minutes, and I went over to the Jap and checked him out, and he was dying. He had a massive gapping hole in his chest. I took his wallet and whatever papers he had on him for intelligence purposes. I still got his wallet right here. After looking at him, I kind of felt sorry for the guy. He did his job, and he was gonna take me along with him. We caught one or two prisoners, and that whole group that was on that side of the mountain had the orders not to kill themselves, but if they were gonna kill themselves, take a Marine with them. That's what he was doing. He didn't have a rifle or anything, just his two hand grenades. I couldn't speak to him, of course, but I looked him in the eye and whatnot. Brave young guy, I'll tell you that.

By the first week in May, the 6th Marine Division was deployed near Sugar Loaf Hill and suffered through some of the bitterest action of the campaign and the war.

The first unit to attack the hill was the 22nd Marines, followed by the 29th. Jerry Beau recalls the action.

We charged up there early in the morning. Have you ever seen *Gunga Din* when he saw that view of the soldiers assaulting down on an open plain? That was how I felt; it was like the Charge of the Light Brigade.

They all had dugouts. We blew whistles and charged up there, across an open area about 400 yards wide, a valley floor sloping up to the hill. That was us going across the valley—fire and movement by squads and platoons and so on. It was really nice to see, but they still beat the hell out of us with mortars and artillery and machine-gun fire. We lost quite a few men.

You could hear them digging at night. In fact, when we charged up there, they had those little trenches that were about three and a half feet where they could crawl from one place to another. In those trenches, about every fifty feet, they had a hole going down into the hill. When we did finally charge up there, they all disappeared into the hill. They had good protection. The top of the hill had a cone—it was like an extinct volcano—and they had dug that out to the very top, and when we got up there, they started throwing grenades out of that. There were two guys in there. We tried to get up there, but we were covered from all angles by other Japanese machine guns and riflemen, so we couldn't take that little thing. We called back to the antitank guns and said, "Can you range in on that hill?" They threw two or three through there, and that sort of cured the thing. When we did get in there, we threw a fifteen-pound block of TNT down to the bottom and white phosphorus grenades and so on.

On May 19, K Company, 4th Marines relieved us. Stormy Sexton had the company, and some of my old boys were still there—those that lived for that long. The Japs counterattacked, and I think the company earned three Navy Crosses and a couple of Silver Stars; they took quite a beating.

We had the dead up there until they began to stink. I even accidentally sat on one of the bodies of our men while I was eating. This was the worst combat I'd seen in the war as far as mass killing goes.

JOE McNAMARA
3RD RAIDER BATTALION, 4TH MARINES, 6TH MARINE DIVISION

On May 18, after numerous failed assaults, the 29th Marines took and held Sugar Loaf Hill. The next day, the 4th Marines were called out of division reserve and tasked with relieving the 29th and clearing interconnected Horseshoe and Half Moon hills. Joe McNamara recalls the push on Horseshoe Hill and the effort to hold off a massive Japanese counterattack that night.

We're going along this trail, the guys from the 29th were coming down, and they looked like they'd been to hell. I'd never seen anybody that looked like these guys did, and they were all saying, "Take plenty of hand grenades with you." I thought, "Where the hell did these guys come from that they look like this?"

I was standing near the platoon leader, and we were getting directions on where we were gonna dig in that night. A runner came over from the company commander and he said, "There's a man wounded in a foxhole over there." The company commander wanted to get him out. I was standing next to the platoon leader, and the corpsman was standing there pretty close. One of my men said to the platoon leader, he shouted out, "I need two volunteers to get a wounded man out of a foxhole." I was standing right next to the corpsman who threw down his pack and said, "I'll go." And he took off. The platoon leader said, "Mac, you go with the corpsman." We got in the hole there—hell, they were shooting at us. There was another guy in there, and he wasn't hurt, and I told him to get out, we'd get his buddy out of there, so he took off. I unbuttoned this guy's blouse and could see that he was shot in the stomach—just a little round hole—and I leaned down to him and said, "Hey, Mac, are you alive?" And he moaned. I said, "Okay. We got to get him out of here." People were firing at us all the time we were in there, so the corpsman reached to get a hold of his shoulders, and I got a hold of his feet, and all of a sudden this one shot came in and the corpsmen fell back and said, "Mac, I'm hit." I could see he was shot in the throat. I ducked down. Finally, I raised

A bullet-torn helmet found on Sugar Loaf containing
an Easter card labeled "to my son." (USMC)

my head up and I shouted to where Albert Lasch was, and I said, "Lasch, I need help. I got two wounded men here. I need help." All of a sudden, they were throwing smoke grenades down there and phosphorus grenades, and stretchers came in and we got them out of there. We got back to where Albert was, and I got down on the ground. I was exhausted. I was just sobbing to myself thinking, "God almighty, this has really hit the fan, and we just got here." A little while later, another corpsmen came over to me. He patted my shoulder and said, "Mac, I'm sorry to tell you this but they both died." I said, "Oh, goddamn."

I shouted to Albert to hold up, and I told him that all of 2nd Platoon wasn't behind us. I said, "Do you want me to go back and get them?" Golden came up to me, he was in the 2nd Platoon, he said, "I'll go back and get them, Mac." I said, "Okay." So he left, and in ten to fifteen minutes, a stream of guys started coming, so we got up and started back up [the hill]. A guy came up to me and he said, "Golden was killed. An artillery shell came in and ate him up." I thought, "My God, if I went back there, maybe I'd been the one beat up."

That night we had several counterattacks. This place has been won and lost about twelve times. When I got up there, there was a couple holes filled with dead Marines and their heavy machine guns. I just walked along and saw this. Some guys were out in the boondocks looking around, and they came across some Japanese, so they came back and the 3rd Battalion went out there after them. Well, we walked into a little ambush; about a half a dozen guys were wounded. The platoon leader was wounded. The company commander, Stormy Sexton, ordered the platoon sergeant to take over. I was made the gunnery sergeant.

The first night we had counterattacks. The acting platoon sergeant was knocked out by a mortar shell. It landed on his head. I had gone back to get hand grenades from the K Company CP. There was a company there that was going to send up a platoon in our area. I said, "I know the way up there," so I led them up there, and I dropped off a squad at the 2nd Platoon, and I dropped a squad off at my platoon, and then I took another squad to the 1st Platoon. Well, this sergeant got into the foxhole there with the platoon sergeant and another noncom. There was a corpsman lying by their side. They were about five feet from me. All of a sudden, this mortar shell came in and landed right on the sergeant's head. It blew me partially out of my foxhole. There was blood all over my right arm. A Marine came up to me and said, "Joe, you're wounded." I said, "Just a second. Let me see where." I reached inside my jacket and felt along my arm and said, "Well, I'm not wounded." When I looked around, I saw this sergeant in the same position when I last saw him, but he didn't have a head. Pieces of his brain and blood were what were on my arm. There was a corpsman lying on the top of the foxhole who was chopped up by the shell fragments; he was just a bundle of rags. Good God, he was torn up.

I took over the platoon the rest of the night. The Japanese were coun-

Members of the 6th Marine Division near Sugar Loaf Hill a couple of days after it was secured. Shells are still exploding in the background. (USMC)

terattacking. All of a sudden, there were grenades coming in and this and that. The guys were throwing hand grenades. The shells were coming over. It seemed like you could just reach up and catch one, plus the bat-tlewagons [Allied ships] that were sitting offshore were throwing up star shells. It was crazy for a couple of hours.

I wanted to do a good job that night. I had the platoon, what was left of it, and when we dug in, I counted seventeen of us. Every half hour I moved up and down our lines to see that everybody was awake 'cause I really didn't think we were gonna make it through the night. I really thought this place had been lost so many times I didn't think we were gonna hold it, but we did.

ROBERT POWERS
3RD RAIDER BATTALION, 4TH MARINES,
6TH MARINE DIVISION

In the early morning hours of May 20, Robert Powers was ordered to reconnoiter part of Horseshoe Hill. At 8:00 A.M., the 4th Marines attacked, advancing two hundred yards. That night K Company dug in on Horseshoe, and the Japanese counterattacked in battalion strength (about seven hundred men), as Powers, awarded the Navy Cross for that night, vividly remembers.

Our company commander, Stormy Sexton, a regular one-on-one guy, asked me to take a recon patrol out because we just moved in late the evening before and it was starting to get dark when we moved in there. So I went out with three guys. We were all pretty close friends. We went forward, and we got up to this rim. I and one of the other men looked over the rim of this depression. It was kind of like a punch bowl, and, Holy Toledo, we saw three platoons [over one hundred] Japs down there. There was one NCO, and he was trying to get them marshaled and giving them orders and all that. They spotted us up on the rim and opened fire, killing two of my men. One was a good friend of mine, and the top of his head disappeared. The second man got hit in the chest and died. The last man was conscious, so I scooped him up in a fireman's carry and I started back.

On the way back, a Jap crawled out of a spider hole and tried to throw a grenade at us. It fell short. Actually, it was a dud. We dispatched him. I reported what I saw. They ordered us to move forward, and we had some mortar support near the ridge where we spotted them. We knew they were all over. Everything was honeycombed with caves and tunnels.

That afternoon, we took a lot of casualties from snipers and more mortar fire. They were picking our guys off. The day before, we knew they were going to attack us. It was won and lost so many times. There was a lot of trepidation. At any rate, we knew they were going to counter-attack that night. All day long, it was kind of an attrition thing.

I don't remember what time it was. We had 100 percent watch, two men to a foxhole. On a 100 percent watch, no one sleeps. They [the Japanese] came storming up to the top of that ridge and overran us. They punched through the lines throwing grenades and bayoneting. I just did what I was trained to do. When they hit, our 60 mm mortars threw up flares. It was utter pandemonium. They were mixing with our troops. They were in our foxholes, and we were just beating them back as best we could. At the time, we had a light machine gun, and they threw grenades in there and killed two of my new men. They were bayoneting those men, so I jumped in the hole and took care of them. This was hand-to-hand, but I shot them with my rifle. Everybody was fighting for the position and for their lives. We had less than half the platoon left.

I was the senior NCO at the time. Two of the squad leaders were killed. I did what I was trained to do; there was nothing heroic about it. The next morning, it was quiet, it was somber. You're beat. You're happy to be alive. But it was a terrible feeling seeing all of the dead. I remember coming home and saying, "Why did I come back and they didn't?" It's a terrible feeling. You don't feel macho; you're glad to be alive."

This past reunion I met one of my men—a great Marine who lives in the Ozark Mountains. Some people might think of him as a hillbilly. When I saw him, I hugged that guy like he was my brother. There's a bond when you go through it.

JIM WOOD
3RD RAIDER BATTALION, 4TH MARINES, 6TH MARINE DIVISION

Jim Wood, a sergeant in Charles Kundert's platoon, vividly recalls his night on the Sugar Loaf complex.

Our officer was a former sergeant. He moved up through the ranks. His name was Miller, and he was our lieutenant. He kept sticking his head over the knoll. You don't ever do that! The Japs, hundreds of them, were shooting, and he kept kind of looking over, and I said, "Lieutenant Miller, keep your head down." He looked at me—I'll never forget it—

and said, "Goddamn it, Wood, keep your mouth shut!" I said, "Okay." He took eight steps and came in, and the bullet hit him on one side of the temple and came out the other. Blew half his head off. It killed him dead as a doornail. His runner cracked up, so I had to slap him to wake him up. He just started screaming and fell down beside Lieutenant Miller, and I ran over and got him between my legs and slapped him in the face and said, "Hey, we're still fighting, man!" After I slapped him, I'd say about five or six times in the face, it shook him up. He was okay after that but was crying because it was his lieutenant, and he was his runner and he had done everything with him. At that time, there's only about fifteen or sixteen of us left, and my squad was in reserve that day. Then we got two more lieutenants after the next push.

We didn't go up Sugar Loaf Hill. We were right beside it. We went over the knoll about 8:00 A.M. My squad was in reserve. Well, about thirty-five or forty minutes, they came back and said, "Okay, we'll bring your squad down there." So I said, "Okay, guys, everybody better keep going. Anybody fails to go down this knoll I'm going to shoot you in the back. You're not gonna run!" We turned around, and all went down. About thirty minutes before that, another platoon was to the right of us, and two of the guys ran back. They didn't go down, so my guys saw that and I said, "None of you pull that, what they did twenty minutes ago. Two guys just cracked up and ran back. I'm gonna shoot you if you do." They all looked at me; they weren't going to do that. We all went down. We fought there, and as I indicated, out of the platoon of about thirty-nine men, about half were killed that night and over the next few days.[12]

CHARLES KUNDERT
3RD RAIDER BATTALION, 4TH MARINES, 6TH MARINE DIVISION

With the Sugar Loaf complex finally in 6th Marine Division hands by June 21, the 4th Marines pushed westward into the port city of Naha. On June 4, they made the last opposed American amphibious landing of World War II, on the Oroku Penin-

sula, and pushed south toward the final Japanese defenses in the extreme southern tip of the island.

We were on the edge of Naha. It was a standard fight through the city. You'd lose a few people every day, but what the hell? You'd get used to that.

You get used to death. You have to. You can't get carried away with that. That's the way it is. There's too many things that have to be done — things that have to be taken care of whether you want to or not. I think in my statistics that I kept, I Company had about 117 percent casualties, and K and L had a little more than that. That means we got replacements, so we had new bodies in there all the time, and you'd lose them too. The first ones were okay. At the end of Okinawa, it was really a sad state of affairs. Here I am, this nineteen-year-old kid, I was acting platoon sergeant, but it depends on who was around at the time. Some guys in there were thirty-nine years old. They could have been my father. One of them had six kids. I said, "Good God, what are they sending to us?" These guys were right out of boot camp. They went through boot camp training, maybe a little infantry training, but they certainly were not tried-and-true performers. It got to be a little on the nervous side. You'd try to help them stay alive. Sometimes it worked; sometimes it didn't work.

Most of the replacements would be dead the next day. One in particular, a nice nice young man from New Jersey, had just gotten word three or four days ago that his younger brother had been killed in Europe weeks before. So I said, "Come on, Alex, let's you and I go back and pick up a couple of crates of C rations. We got to keep the troops alive here." He went back with me, and we're getting sniped at. We're running along, and we jump in a damn hole together and I said, "Okay, let's go again, Al." Al didn't go. He got shot right through the heart. It missed me, hit him. Unfortunately, you get very much accustomed to these things. You don't want to get too close to them. Unfortunately, you always do . . . you can't help it.

You'd put them in the foxhole, and by the next day they were dead. I always thought if I kept them alive for three days, they were on their own and would be fine. I couldn't do much more than that.

The men were outstanding and did their duty. However, I had two in the platoon that weren't former Raiders. They were two buddies from Kentucky. These two were knocking gold out of the Japanese, and all that kind of stupidity. When things got tough, you couldn't find them. When the shooting really got heavy or the mortars got heavy all of a sudden, they were sick, complaining of stomachaches. But when it came time to collect gold teeth, they were great. I used to call them "mouth-fighters": talk a great war but when the shooting starts, you can't find them. We only had two of them. I finally told them to get the hell out of my platoon.

After pushing through Naha, we were briefed about the landing on the Oroku Peninsula. Our regimental commander gave us a short talk—more of the usual guff about "fine job, hate to have us go back again," best regiment bologna. Anyway, we landed at around 4:00 A.M., and my platoon followed B Company along the edge of Naha Airfield. I took out one patrol to investigate a revetment and some plane wreckage. We were fifty or sixty yards in front of them, when we were getting shots in the rear that were awful damn close.

I wheeled around and saw three Japs standing waist deep in water armed with rifles and potato masher grenades. They must have come out of their hiding spots after we passed them. I worked from left to right, seriously wounding the first two, just before the third nailed me. He had his rifle to his shoulder, and I had mine in the same position. I was firing at him, and he raised his rifle, and my damn rifle jammed. Fortunately, two of my men came around the flank and finished them off. The one I hit blew himself about nine feet in the air. We dug in on a ridge under some sniper fire and kept pushing south.[13]

MEL HECKT
3RD RAIDER BATTALION, 4TH MARINES, 6TH MARINE DIVISION

Although small pockets of Japanese still held out, on June 22, 1945, the island was finally officially declared secure. Yet fighting—and losses—continued, especially in the far southern portion of Okinawa. Mel Heckt recalls the death of his best friend, Edward Dunham, a day later. Dunham was posthumously awarded the Navy Cross.

The one that broke me up the most was after the island was secure. My friend, Ed Dunham, was shot in the head and killed. That was the time I sat down after I carried him down, and I really cried, bawled profusely. My voice was broken for almost ten minutes. We were very close friends. He was a rifleman, and I was a machine gunner, but we were oftentimes together.

The day began with Lieutenant James getting shot. The Japanese bullet knocked out three or four teeth, but didn't hit his cheek or lips. From that time on, Dunham sort of took charge of the company. We kept proceeding down south. When we got to that last ridge, we had to wait for the next day before we could get up. We found a way to get up, and Eddie was shouting orders for the rifle platoon. He was going to try and throw a satchel charge over the top of this ridge. All of the sudden, I didn't hear him yell or talk, and I knew something had happened to him. I ran up there, and I pulled him out. I felt Ed's pulse and thought for a minute that he was alive. But I was so worn out and panting that I probably felt my own pulse. I got a corpsman to help carry him out. I was quite broken up and gave the man hell for stumbling so much. We carried him down the ridge through a fire lane, and one of our men was pinned down. We got down to a safe area, and Doc Wells attempted to give him plasma but couldn't find his veins because he had lost so much blood.

I had a picture of his grave and a lot of pictures of him, and when I got discharged from Quantico, I stopped and saw my buddy's widow in Pennsylvania. Then I went to Wisconsin to see another man's mother, and then I went to a suburb of Detroit to see Eddie Dunham's parents. Everybody was just so nice and appreciative because I had pictures of their graves and pictures of them. I had copies made so they could all have copies.

It really didn't affect me for quite a few years. I always kept so busy going back to college and very active in my university, undergraduate and law school, and then going to work and being very busy there. It was a number of years later I began to become a little depressed on Memorial Day. A buddy of mine who was in the Marine Corps said, "Come on out to the cemetery on Memorial Day with me." I did. I've been going ever since. Now I don't feel badly on Memorial Day. I never had any nightmares or severe depression. I've been real lucky . . . lucky to come through it without a scratch.

JERRY BEAU
3RD RAIDER BATTALION, 29TH MARINES, 6TH MARINE DIVISION

Jerry Beau remembers the end of the battle.

At the end, you should have seen these dirty Marines who were rough, hadn't washed for weeks, smelled like hell, gently handing a woman or a

A Marine tenderly cares for an elderly woman. (courtesy of Frank Cannistraci)

little baby out of a cave. Oh, my God, they were so tender with them, you had to see it to understand it. The Japanese would put the civilians into the caves. They knew if we knew they were in there, we wouldn't blast them out.

I remember one incident where the children were accidentally wounded by shrapnel in the arm. They'd been wounded a couple of days before, and it was all infected. I vividly remember some of my men giving food to these people or carrying an ancient woman.

CHAPTER TWELVE

Home

We few, we happy few, we band of brothers;
For he to-day that sheds his blood with me
Shall be my brother.

—SHAKESPEARE, *HENRY V*

IN 1945 AND 1946, THE MEN RETURNED to hometowns across America. Most vets hung up their uniforms and melted back into society.

Victorious, America became a colossus of industrial strength and prosperity. The men threw themselves into peace. The qualities that had led veterans to volunteer for the Raiders, paratroopers, Rangers, and Marauders served them well in peacetime America. Many used the GI Bill to pay for college and home mortgages. Families were begun and careers built.

The war remains a defining part of their lives. Refracted through memories that are now nearly sixty years old, a part of them is still in the places they fought. They remember those who never returned. Some are still unable to talk about their experiences. Time and age have thinned their ranks. Every battalion or division has a newsletter that contains a roll of those who have passed, a list that grows longer with each month. The yearly reunions get smaller. But neither time nor age can diminish their love for one another.

JEROME MANDEL

503RD PARACHUTE INFANTRY REGIMENT

Jerome Mandel recalls the final days of World War II on Negros Island in the Philippines.

In 1945, I was a replacement second lieutenant platoon leader in the 503rd. I was about twenty-two years old when I arrived at Negros. It was raining like hell and muddy when I got there. I was assigned to B Company. They had their pup tents on a hill. There was only room for two people, but there were four of us in the tent. I was introduced around. It was a very cold and impersonal experience. The men didn't want to get to know me. It was a detached relationship since so many other platoon leaders were either killed or wounded. It was a blur. I remember it being wet, cold, and extremely miserable the whole time I was there.

Around the Fourth of July while visiting the town of San Carlos, we encountered a few Navy guys collecting souvenirs. These guys said, "Take care of yourself, kid, because this is going to be over soon." I thought, "How did you know?" In retrospect, this was an amazing revelation. And at the time I didn't believe it. We would return from time to time to San Carlos with souvenirs like samurai swords, pistols, and flags to trade with the Navy guys for booze.

We went out on a patrol, and that's when the last man in the 503rd was killed, a first lieutenant by the name of Turpin. He was an interesting man, and I had some limited discussions with him. It was a terrible experience when he was shot, and it was totally unnecessary. We were on a patrol looking down into this valley, and here was this hut. We didn't know who was in the hut, so he went down with two other men, and I'm on top of a hill with Captain Smith and several other people. This Japanese soldier, or whoever it was, leans out of the window and shoots him in the head, and he falls. Everybody opened fire on the hut. I remember yelling and really screaming, "Hold it! Hold it! He [Turpin] may still be alive." That place was annihilated. We were about five hundred yards away.

We finally went down there and picked him up. It was so unnecessary, especially since the word got around that this war was going to be
over soon.

Perhaps the worst thing that happened is that we had a man commit
suicide by laying down on one of his grenades. We called him Pop. It was
a sad, sad thing. He was the oldest enlisted man and had been overseas for .
about three years. He was married. If only he held out. He just had
enough. I didn't know how to handle it. I remember picking up his pos-
sessions, putting them in a box, and sending them home. They never
teach you this at OCS [Officer Candidate School]. The men were extremely upset and unsettled about the situation. I was told not to write the
letter to his wife. I was told that was done. Who did it, I don't know. I later
learned in a subsequent discussion that they never talked about an officer
getting shot in the back, a GI getting killed by friendly fire, or suicides. It
was always some great deed. I never found out what was in the letter.

On August 6, they dropped the first bomb. Shortly after [the second
was dropped], word reached us of Japan's surrender. It was really shocking that our intelligence didn't read the number of Japanese troops that
were opposing us. They were exhausted. I have pictures with these men
with elephantiasis coming down [to surrender] on stretchers and comfort
girls who were with them. It was horrifying. They weren't jumping off
cliffs like at Okinawa and things like that. These guys wanted to go home
just like we did.

I spent so much time dispelling it. When I got home, the only way I
could get rid of it was to go back to school and immerse myself in getting
a degree. So I went back for the final year of engineering school and got
my degree. They said keep going, continue to occupy your mind, so I
went to law school. Gradually, I started to get it behind me. If I would
have remained idle, this thing would have destroyed me. The death and
destruction, it was awful. How do you cure yourself from being involved
in such a chaotic mess?

I'll tell you candidly, I'm a tough cookie, but I have tears in my eyes
as I reflect on the guys that were left there . . . for what? For what? The
only definition of learning is when you change your way of doing things

in the future. If you change your ways, you've learned something. We haven't learned a goddamn thing. It's still going on.

HARRY AKUNE
503RD PARACHUTE INFANTRY REGIMENT

Harry Akune remembers the final days of the war and his reunion with his former enemies.

All these memories will last me a lifetime. When the war ended, I was attached to a group of Allied officers who were supposed to recover prisoners of war in Japan. I went in with the 11th Airborne, one of the first units to enter Japan.

I was on one of the first planes to touch down. I was in a C-54, which was a pretty big ship. A colonel was flying it, I guess because he wanted to say he was one of the first to go in. Atsugi airstrip was small, but he just brought it in beautifully. He slid right in. It was a beautiful piece of flying.

We had the field to ourselves and used one of the hangars. Allied POWs started walking in. They were told by their guards that the prison was open, and they could walk out and meet us. They were thin, looked like scarecrows. They stared at me with sunken eyes and had on torn clothes. They were really happy to be free. I remember they had all kinds of food for these men, but they were so frugal with their food they wouldn't leave one speck of it in a can even though they had a whole bunch of it there. It really impressed me that when they survived under those kinds of conditions, everything is so precious. My heart went out to them. They were really humble people. What impressed me is that they're suffering, but they became different people when they came out.

There was one story. I heard from two different prisoners at two different times. A Marine, I was talking to him, and I said, "What do you think of the Japanese soldiers?" "I don't like them because of the way they treated us." "What do you think of the Japanese people?" He said, "They are the salt of the earth." That surprised me. I don't quite get that and asked him what he meant. He said, "I'd be working out in the field in a vegetable patch, and this little old Japanese lady would come by and walk right by me and drop a hot sweet potato. Even with the guard looking at her, she'd just slip it to me. How can you hate people like that?"

When I got to Japan, I didn't plan on visiting my father, my brothers, or sisters. I ended up in Japan for a period because I lost my mother when I was thirteen. I was there until I was sixteen and came back. I hadn't seen them since 1936. By the time I saw them, it was 1945. I was hoping that I wouldn't meet them while the war was still on, brother against brother, or worse, fighting my father. I was hoping if I fought them that I wouldn't recognize them.

My brother was in the Japanese Navy training to be a kamikaze pilot. I planned on coming back without even contacting them or seeing them. They came from a very militaristic community in the southern tip of Kyushu. My father was a veteran of the Russo-Japanese War.

I was being reassigned to Tokyo and MacArthur's headquarters. Before I got reassigned from the POW recovery team, I had befriended a Japanese family who washed my clothes and stuff. They asked me where my parents were and if I made contact with them. I said, "No," being that I come from this particular militaristic area I didn't want any repercussions to fall on them. He said, "I think you should make contact because you never know if you're going to see them again." I declined. But he said, "Would you mind if I write a letter to them saying that I met you?" I left, and maybe a month later, I got this call from a bellhop where I was quartered. He said, "Lieutenant, your father is waiting for you in the lobby." I got off the elevator, and I looked and there's an old man full of coal dust (he was traveling on a train that had open windows). He was with my brother Frank (who was a kamikaze pilot). I asked them if they had a place to stay. I made arrangements with the mess hall and brought them food that my father hadn't seen since he was in America. Coincidentally, my other brother, who was stationed in Burma [in the U.S. Office of War Information], did propaganda work. Food was scarce, and he asked that we share it with the rest of the family still in Kyushu at Kadoshima. It took my brother and me three days to get there.

There was only one telephone in the town, and I'm using it to contact a Marine base to extend my pass since I only had three days. There were a lot of Japanese soldiers that had been discharged and they were amazed to see an American soldier, let alone a nonwhite American soldier (the occupation forces in this area of Japan were very limited). We also happened to be two guys these people went to school with when we were younger. We were curious objects to say the least. It was touch and go, and they're sullenly looking at us, giving us the cold shoulder. The thing that broke the ice was a man in the village that had seen his carrier go down in one of the major battles that marked the end of the Japanese Navy. He was lucky to be alive and said when that happened, "We knew we lost the war." The fact that a Japanese guy said this mellowed everybody.

We met my other brothers and sisters and almost started the war all over again. We were trying to place blame—who was at fault. My brother Frank revealed that he was on a train outside Hiroshima when the bomb was dropped. The windows on the train were blown out, and he saw the mushroom cloud and later went into Hiroshima and pulled bodies from the ruins. Shiro was too young and was just a messenger boy in the home guard. We were arguing back and forth. My brother Ken and I said, "Hey, Japan started invading everybody . . ." I was getting pretty loud, and my father stepped in and said, "The war is over." Since then, we never talked about it in that manner.

I knew that eventually we would have to invade Japan, and I knew the things that they would do: arm women and children with spears—everybody. I'm glad we didn't have to deal with it. It was a feeling of relief that we didn't have to invade, and sadness that we dropped atomic bombs. Ultimately, I think of the numbers that would have perished had we not used them; there would have been a tremendous slaughter. I'm relieved. Although many did suffer, it would have been a lot, a lot worse.

HOWARD BAXTER

2ND MARINE PARACHUTE BATTALION

Howard Baxter recalls his return home.

There's not a day that goes by that I don't think about the men who were killed, and I pray for them and their souls. But when you're in combat, you don't have time to grieve. You just don't have time. I've dwelled on it. I never even . . . [sigh] you just stuff it down. I just couldn't cry then. Some guys could, and they were better for it. I felt if I let myself go, I would have lost it.

It comes out in different ways. We all have a feeling of guilt of why I survived and other men time and time again got killed. Why? Why did I survive? I think there's an automatic reaction when somebody, even if it's your own best buddy, gets killed, that you think at least it's not you.

I never had a breakdown or anything like that, but I think it was harder on my two children. It was harder on my marriage. Fortunately, I've been married for fifty-seven years.

The first year I was home, if I went out to a restaurant, I would never order soup because if I ordered soup, I took the spoon and had a spoonful of soup, and I'd raise it to my lips and there would be no soup. I had tremors in my hand. That's how the emotions I stuffed inside would come out.

I had to quit my job at the animation studio in Hollywood because I couldn't sit still. I went out and got a job doing manual labor in order to work off the war. I really wanted to go out and work on a farm to help things grow, breathe fresh air.

CHARLES SASS
511TH PARACHUTE INFANTRY REGIMENT, 11TH AIRBORNE DIVISION

America was victorious, but many homecomings were bitter, as Charles Sass recalls.

My homecoming was a disaster. My family split when I was six, but I still lived now and then with my father in a small town in upstate New York. I came home, and there was a sign on the door that said: "The rent is paid for a month. Good luck." That was homecoming.

I took the next train south. [sigh] But before I left my best friend, who was my uncle, stayed alive to see me. He had terrible cancer, and he stayed alive long enough to visit with me for a few days, and then he died. He was my good buddy, and that was so great that I had a chance to see him before he passed away.

I went on the bum in New York City, which is a great city to be a bum. I was up there all of about a month. I would sleep in doorways and bus stations. I didn't have to do that, I had money, but I figured it was a good escape. There were a lot of us, and I wasn't alone. We found places to flop. There were six or eight veterans I hung around with in the middle of New York City. But we managed to find a little apartment that somebody vacated, and living there on the floors no one talked about the war. We were guys on the streets.

Eventually, I went on the GI Bill and entered college, majoring in a couple of things that had to do with communications. Illustration and design, even a little bit of architecture, and I put that all together and I came up with one devil of a career and have a great family.

DEAN WINTERS
2ND RAIDER BATTALION

Dean Winters lost the use of his legs during the war and recalls the long road to recovery.

I spent a lot of years in the hospital before I finally went home—about three years. I've had my share of nightmares, and I've had two flashbacks. One of them, I saw a Japanese ship in the harbor at San Diego. I saw the flag and I guess I went crazy and wanted to sink it. Then in Las Vegas, I was watching one of the main theater attractions. They had two pirate ships fighting—water was squirting up, explosions, and everything. I turned around—I was in my wheelchair—and there were a group of Japanese tourists. It brought the whole war back to 1945. I saw helmets on them, rifles, everything. I tried to run them over. My wife and people I was with wouldn't let me out of the hotel room.

For years I wouldn't talk about it. I've been going to the VA hospital for two days a week. I had a good psychologist. My wife means everything to me, and she's also been my therapy. They got me to talk about it. People didn't understand that it is so painful to discuss. As I'm talking to you right now, there are tears running down my face.

HARRY AKUNE
503RD PARACHUTE INFANTRY REGIMENT

Harry Akune reveals his homecoming.

When I finally came home, I couldn't go back to California. I felt like I was forced out. I didn't want to go where people didn't want me. I had a small gardening business; I lost all of that—all of the equipment, everything. But that wasn't much compared to other people I knew. So I went to live with a friend that was a sharecropper in Nebraska. Eventually I came back to California, had a family, and had a successful career.

Since the war, I've remained close to the men I served with. The 503rd is my family. When I found out my friend Emery Graham was dying, I had to see him. Emery had just come home from the hospital so he could die at home. When I heard that, I just took off and went to see him. A few years ago, the Army gave me an achievement medal for the intelligence work I did during the war. I wanted to give it to him to see his

Harry Akune *(right)*, his brother *(left)*, and their friends. (courtesy of Harry Akune)

smile. That's how much he meant to me. He seemed very happy when I gave it to him since he knew what it meant to me. He was at the ceremony when they gave it to me. He had a smile on his face before he died. I think he was buried with it.

I really felt very angry when I was first interned. I lost my freedom, and that was something. In the internment camps, you were restricted. But when I went into the Army, I had a reason why I wanted to go. It was, I guess, an experience in life that makes you think about different things. It's the condition I came out of. Even then, the fact that I couldn't leave the camp—it was like being in prison.

I really feel proud to be an American. Now I feel so free. To me, liberty and freedom are very, very important. Sometimes we take freedom for granted, but when you lose it, you really appreciate it.

Appendix

WWII ORDER OF BATTLE: U.S. AIRBORNE & RANGER UNITS

AIRBORNE AND 1ST SSF
EUROPEAN THEATER

DIVISION	INFANTRY REGIMENTS/BNs; PARACHUTE/GLIDER	ARTILLERY PARACHUTE/GLIDER BNS
13th	517[1] PIR / 190 GIR / 326 GIR 88 GIR; 515 PIR / 189[10] GIR	458 / 676; 460 / 677
17th	507 PIR / 193 GIR (550) 513 PIR / 194 GIR	464 / 680; 466 / 681
82nd	504 PIR / 325 GIR 505 (507)[2], 508[2] PIRs	376 / 319; 456 / 320
101st	502 PIR / 327 GIR 506 PIR / 401 GIR[9] 501[3] PIR	377; 463[8] / 321; 907
1st Airborne Task Force (created for invasion of southern France)	517 PRCT; 550[4] IAB 551 PIB[5]; 509 PIB	460 / 602; 463
Independent	509 PIB; 517 PRCT; 1st SSF[6] 550 IAB; 551 PIB[5]; 555PIB	

PACIFIC THEATER/CBI

DIVISION	INFANTRY REGIMENTS/BNs; PARACHUTE/GLIDER	ARTILLERY PARACHUTE/GLIDER BNS
11th	511 PIR; 187 GIR / PIR; 188 GIR / PIR	457 / 472; 674 / 674
Independent	542 PIB 503 RCT; 1st SSF[6]; 541 PIR[7]	

THE RANGERS

EUROPEAN THEATER OF OPERATIONS	
Darby's Rangers 1st, 3rd, and 4th Ranger Battalions	*Ranger Battalions:* 2nd and 5th

[1] The 517th PRCT entered the division in 1945.
[2] The 508th was officially listed as an attached unit to the 82nd Airborne. The 507th was attached to the 82nd in Normandy and became part of the 17th Airborne Division after *Market-Garden*.
[3] The 501st was officially listed as an attached unit to the 101st Airborne.
[4] The 550th Infantry Airborne Bat. was attached to the 1st ATF in southern France. This unit was the second airborne unit formed and trained initially in air-landing operations. Before southern France, about a hundred members were parachute-qualified. The unit fought with the 17th Airborne in Belgium and was nearly destroyed on January 4. Inactivated in March '45 and used to form the 3/194 GIR.
[5] Officially designated 1/551 PIR, but never received two additional round-out Bns.
[6] Most members of the 1st Special Service Force were airborne-qualified. The unit landed in the Aleutian Islands and was then transferred to the ETO.

(Continued on next page)

WWII ORDER OF BATTLE: U.S. AIRBORNE & RANGER UNITS

AIRBORNE AND 1ST SSF
EUROPEAN THEATER

DIVISION	AA BNs Cos	Eng BNs Cos	Sig Co	Ord Co	QM Co	Med Co	Prcht Maint Co
13th	153	129	513	713	409	222	13
17th	155	139	517	717	411	224	17
82nd	80	307	82	782	407	307	82
101st	81	326	101	801	426	326	101
1st Airborne Task Force (*created for invasion of southern France*) *Independent*	AT Co, 442 RCT	596; 887	512		334	676	D Co., 83d Chem Bn A Co., 2nd Chem Bn

PACIFIC THEATER/CBI

DIVISION	AA BNs Cos	Eng BNs Cos	Sig Co	Ord Co	QM Co	Med Co	Prcht Maint Co
11th	152; 675	127	511	711	408	221	11
Independent		879; 161					

THE RANGERS

PACIFIC THEATER OF OPERATIONS / CIB
6th Ranger Battalion
5307 (Provisional)

[7] The 541st remained Stateside for most of the war. Arrived in the Philippines in June '45. Inactivated August 10, '45, in Lipa, Luzon, Philippines. Assets used to form the 3rd Bns of the 187th and 188th GIR, which were subsequently redesignated "ParaGlider."

[8] The 463rd was originally the 456th. The unit was practically independent and only officially became part of the 101st Airborne at the end of the war.

[9] The 401st, like the 327th, was a two-battalion regiment. In March 1944 the 2nd Battalion of the 401st was sent to the 82nd Airborne. The 1st Bat., while officially remaining the 1st Bat. of the 401st during the first months of combat, actually functioned as the 3rd Bat. of the 327th, 101st Airborne Division. The unit was not officially the 3rd Bat. 327th until spring 1945.

[10] The 189th and 190th were inactivated and their men transferred to the 88th and 190th respectively. The 513th was also initially part of the 13th but was transferred to the 17th Airborne Division on March 10, 1944.

Notes

INTRODUCTION

1. Author's interview with John Mielke, 1st Raider Battalion; event occurred on Tulagi, 1942.

2. The Pacific was divided into two major areas. The larger was the Pacific Ocean Areas: North Pacific, Central, and South Pacific. These areas were under the overall command of Admiral Chester Nimitz. U.S. Army commander General Douglas MacArthur controlled the Southwest Pacific. In Asia, the China-Burma-India Theater was commanded by General Joseph Stilwell.

OVERVIEW: THE ELITE INFANTRY OF THE PACIFIC

1. Geoffrey Perret, *There's a War to Be Won: The United States Army in World War II* (New York: Random House, 1990), p. 167.

2. The Carlson reference is from Jon Hoffman's *From Makin to Bougainville: Marine Raiders in WWII* (Washington, D.C.: History & Museums Division, 1995). Edson is quoted in Joseph Alexander's *Edson's Raiders: The 1st Marine Raider Battalion in World War II* (Washington, D.C.: 1st Raider Association, 1995), p. 26.

3. Charles N. Hunter, *GALAHAD* (San Antonio, Tex.: Naylor, 1963), pp. 1–5; Charles Ogburn, *Marauders* (New York: Harper and Brothers, 1959), pp. 183–184.

4. After seeing a western movie featuring the famous Apache chief Geronimo, members of the test platoon bet Eberhardt that he would pass out while he stood in the door of the airplane before a parachute jump. Eberhardt retorted that he would yell "Geronimo!" so loud when he left the plane that even men on the ground could hear him as he made the jump. True to his word, Eberhardt successfully made the jump, and "Geronimo" was said to have been heard by the men on the ground.

5. Harris Mitchell, *The First Airborne Battalion: As Told by Its First Sergeant Major* (Rockville, Md.: Twinbrook Communications, 1996), p. 72.

6. James Huston, *Out of the Blue: U.S. Army Operations in World War II* (West Lafayette, Ind.: Purdue University Press, 1972), p. 118.

CHAPTER ONE: OPERATION SHOESTRING

1. "Joint Directive for Offensive Operations in SWPA" (July 2, 1942) provides insight on overall strategy. It's worth noting that the third task involved seizure of Rabaul itself and "adjacent positions."

2. The actual surrender document from Admiral Ghormley has disappeared, but the document is referenced in Merrill Twining's memoir: *No Bended Knee* (Novato, Calif.: Presidio Press, 1997), p. 97. Twining was a high-ranking officer on Vandegrift's staff who later achieved the rank of general and is considered an impeccable source.

3. The campaign for Guadalcanal was costly for both sides. The U.S. Navy alone suffered the loss of twenty-four ships, including two heavy carriers.

4. During the landings the 1st Marine Division did not include its 7th Regiment.

5. Tulagi details: "1st Raider Battalion After Action Report" (Sept. 1942); "Landing on Tulagi: Final Report, Phase II" (Sept. 1942), pp. 3–5.

6. "1st Parachute Battalion After Action Report," pp. 1–5.

7. 1st Parachute Battalion casualties are from Richard Frank's *Guadalcanal: The Definitive Account of the Landmark Battle* (New York: Penguin, 1992), pp. 78–79.

8. Details on the Makin surrender episode can be found in the official Marine Corps history of the Raiders by Lieutenant Colonel Jon Hoffman, *From Makin to Bougainville: Marine Raiders in WWII* (Washington, D.C.: History & Museums Division, 1995). Also see Oscar Peatross, *Bless 'Em All: The Raider Marines in World War II* (Irvine, Calif.: Review Publications, 1995), p. 81. General Peatross, a former Raider who participated in the Makin raid, also extensively interviewed the participants and corroborated the account. Also see George Smith, *Carlson's Raid: The Daring Assault on Makin* (Novato, Calif.: Presidio Press, 2001), pp. 154–161. Finally, I interviewed over a dozen Makin veterans who corroborated the incident.

9. According to the accounts, Captain Ralph Coyte, accompanied by Private William McCall, was ordered to contact the Japanese commander on the island and deliver the following note:

> *Dear Sir:*
>
> *I am a member of the American forces on Makin. We have suffered severe casualties and wish to make an end of the bloodshed and bombings.*
>
> *We wish to surrender according to the rules of military law and be treated as prisoners of war. We would also like to bury our dead and care for our wounded.*
>
> *There are approximately 60 of us left. We have all voted to surrender.*

> *I would like to see you personally as soon as possible to prevent future bloodshed and bombing.*

Several versions exist on what happened after Coyte and McCall delivered the note to a Japanese soldier hiding in a village hut. Both versions end with the soldier accidentally being killed shortly after he left the hut to deliver the note. Coyte claims he heard a shot fired and remembers two Raiders coming up the road shortly after he gave the soldier the note who claimed they killed a Japanese soldier. Coyte assumed it was the messenger. McCall believes he killed the soldier. After staying in the village, when Coyte returned to inform Carlson the note was delivered, he heard movement in the nearby bushes and shot two Japanese soldiers—one who was carrying a first aid kit, and the other he believes was carrying the surrender note.

10. The reader should not draw the conclusion that Carlson was a timid commander. In fact, most Raiders I interviewed believed he was the most courageous individual they had ever met. He was the holder of two Distinguished Service Crosses and other decorations for valor. As a leader, Carlson always put his men first.

CHAPTER TWO: STARVATION ISLAND: GUADALCANAL

1. "Report on Tasimboko: Raid by Raider Battalion and 1st Parachute Battalion" (Sept. 8, 1942).

2. Primary sources for the Battle for Bloody Ridge include "Operations for the 1st Parachute Battalion, 13–14 September" (Oct. 15, 1942), and "Report of Operations of the 1st Raider Battalion, 12–14 September 1942" (Sept. 21, 1942).

3. The Japanese shore bombardment began around 9:30 P.M. and lasted for about an hour. Faced with an impossible situation, C Company's Lieutenant Salmon's platoon fell back toward the ridge. The right flank platoon was also forced to retire. Oscar Peatross, *Bless 'Em All: The Raider Marines in World War II* (Irvine, Calif.: Review Publications, 1995), p. 103.

4. John Hoffman, *Once a Legend: Red Mike Edson of the Marine Raiders* (Novato, Calif: Presidio Press, 1994). Hoffman places Raider losses on September 12–14 at 34 killed and 129 wounded, for a total of 163. Losses in the 1st Parachute Battalion totaled 55 percent.

5. It is worth noting that the Raiders refer to the "Second Battle of Matanikau" as the "First Battle of Matanikau" since this was their first action in the area. Accordingly, they refer to the "Third Battle of the Matanikau" as the "Second Matanikau." I use the official designations in the text.

6. "Report of Operations, 2nd Raider Battalion" (Dec. 20, 1942).

7. The first Raider regiment activated was the 1st Provisional Raider Regiment. Later the 2nd and 3rd Raider Battalions were formed into the 2nd Provisional Raider Regiment, which sailed for Bougainville in November 1943 with the 3rd Marine Division.

8. Dean Winters' account of the incident at the aid station was independently verified by several other 2nd Raider Battalion veterans.

9. Ray Bauml's account was verified by other members of his platoon. The official muster rolls record Lt. Miller died of his wounds on December 4, 1942.

CHAPTER THREE: UP THE SOLOMONS: STRANGLING RABAUL

1. A prelude to the New Georgia operation involved seizing the Russell Islands. Located about thirty miles northwest of Guadalcanal, the Russells were a staging area for the Japanese reinforcement of and withdrawal from Guadalcanal. The 43rd Infantry Division stormed ashore at Banika, while the 3rd Raider Battalion landed at nearby Pavuvu Island, which the Japanese had abandoned.

2. The 4th Raiders' actions in the capture of Viru Harbor are documented in "4th Raider Battalion Operations Report" (June–July 1943).

3. Most of the details surrounding Raider operation on New Georgia came from "1st Raider Battalion, Operations Report" (July 4–Aug. 29, 1942); "1st Marine Regiment Journal, New Georgia Campaign" (July–Aug. 1943).

4. Both battalions were spent after the battle for Bairoko. Casualties are based on effective strength. Oscar Peatross, *Bless 'Em All: The Raider Marines in World War II* (Irvine, Calif.: Review Publications, 1995), p. 232.

5. The effect of the Choiseul raid is referenced in Jon Hoffman's *Silk Chutes and Hard Fighting: Marine Parachute Units in WWII* (Washington, D.C.: Marine Corps Historical Division, 1999), p. 28.

6. Raider actions on Bougainville can be found in several sources, including "3rd Marine Division Unit Journal" (Nov. 1943), "2nd Raider Regiment SAR" (Jan. 8, 1944), and Henry Shaw and Douglas Kane, *Isolation of Rabaul* (Washington, D.C.: Historical Branch USMC, 1963), pp. 198–210.

7. George French's account is confirmed by several Raiders. One veteran even remarked, "I carried some of the wounded back but George French was outstanding in this regard. He, like so many guys, should have received all kinds of medals but didn't."

8. I interviewed Sergeant Tom Siefke, who confirmed Corporal Mike Vinich's account. Out of the nine-man squad, nearly all of them would be killed or wounded on Iwo Jima.

CHAPTER FOUR: BURMA

The chapter-opening epigraph is from James Hopkins, *Spearhead* (Baltimore: Johns Hopkins University Press, 2000), p. 406.

1. Robert Dallek, *Franklin D. Roosevelt and American Policy, 1932–1945* (New York: Oxford University Press, 1963), pp. 426–429.

2. With the Burma Road in Japanese hands, supplies had to be airlifted into China. Pilots had to fly a 900-mile semicircular flight over the Himalayas known as the "Hump," to avoid Japanese fighters operating out of northern Burma's Myitkyina airfield. Eliminating the airfield to shorten the route became another reason to clear northern Burma. Moreover, the Allies were interested in building airbases in China to mount a strategic bombing campaign against Japan, and the road could potentially supply those needs.

3. The Burma Road stretched from Lashio in northern Burma to the Chinese capital of Chungking. Before the fall of Burma in 1942, supplies were brought into the southern Burmese port of Rangoon and transported to Lashio by rail. To reopen the road, another road would have to be built from Ledo, India, down toward Myitkyina. This road was known as the Ledo Road. A road from Myitkyina to Lashio existed before the war and did not require much work to connect to the Burma Road.

4. The ultimate goal of the road was delivery of sixty-five thousand tons of supplies to China. The road was not meant to supply all three hundred divisions of the Chinese army. It was hoped that the supplies could fill gaps in Chinese divisions, permit them to train, and bring them to full strength for offensive operations. It was also hoped that additional supplies could be brought through the road to help sustain Allied B-29 bombers based in China. Charles F. Romanus and Riley Sunderland, *Stilwell's Command Problems* (Washington, D.C.: Office of the Chief of Military History, 1987), p. 10.

5. "Minutes of 26 August 1943; CCS, 107th Meeting," Quadrant Conference.

6. The operation at Walawbum was a success. While the 18th Division escaped Stilwell's trap, it nevertheless yielded most of the Hukawng Valley to the Allies.

7. Stilwell's promise is documented in Romanus and Sutherland, *Stilwell's Command Problems*, pp. 223–225.

8. Glider reinforcement is referenced in "Stilwell's Diary" (May 17, 1944), and "G-3 per Rpt, HQ Chich HQ Chih Hui Pu" (May 24, 1944).

9. Losses are documented in "The Marauders and the Microbes," *Infantry Journal*, no. 64 (1949).

10. Calls for an investigation started in August 1944 with the Senate Military Affairs Committee.

11. Charles F. Romanus and Riley Sunderland, *Time Runs Out in CBI* (Washington, D.C.: Office of the Chief of Military History, 1958), pp. 120–128; John Randolf, *Marsmen in Burma* (Houston, Tex.: Gulf Publishing, 1946), p. 56.

CHAPTER FIVE: NEW GUINEA

1. To retain control of American troops, MacArthur labeled the Sixth Army "Alamo Force." The force was commanded by General Krueger, effectively keeping most American troops engaged in tactical operations with the Australians under his command.

2. "SWPA G-3 7/43–9/43"; "Report of Operations: 503rd Parachute Infantry Regiment" (Sept. 1943). Elements of B Company were also involved in a brief firefight.

3. The 41st Division's 162nd Regiment was pushed back on Biak.

4. Samuel Eliot Morison, *History of United States Naval Operations in World War II* (Boston: Little, Brown, 1958), 8:138.

5. The revised estimate of Japanese strength on Noemfoor was based on a single prisoner who claimed there were as many as seven thousand defenders. Later in the day, Patrick, the 158th commander, had second thoughts on the accuracy of the report but nevertheless still wanted the 503rd.

6. Krueger, "Report of Tabletennis Operation" (July 1944), p. 335.

7. Reports of cannibalism are corroborated in the 503rd's S-2 Unit Journal, July 1944. Several veterans I interviewed corroborated the account.

8. A few months after the Noemfoor operation, the 503rd was designated a Parachute Regimental Combat Team; an artillery battalion (462nd Parachute Artillery Battalion) and an Engineer (161st Parachute Engineer Company) were attached to the regiment.

CHAPTER SIX: INTO THE MARIANAS

1. The 4th Marines' first mission was an unopposed landing at Emirau Island, helping complete the final encirclement of Rabaul (refer to the New Guinea map for the location of Emirau).

2. Prior to Guam, U.S. forces recaptured Kiska and Attu in the Aleutian Islands.

3. "Operations and Special Action Report, 1st Marine Provisional Brigade," July–August 1944, pp. 1–11.

4. The number of Japanese killed around the base of Hill 40 varies; however, every veteran I interviewed recalls the body count to be at least five hundred. Official documentation on the Japanese losses is sparse.

5. "Operations and Special Action Report," p. 12, and "1st Provisional Marine Brigade SAR" (Aug. 15, 1944).

6. Henry Shaw, Bernard Nalty, and Edwin Turnbladh, *History of U.S. Marine Corps Operations in World War II*, Vol. 3: *Central Pacific Drive* (Washington, D.C.: Historical Branch, HQ USMC, 1966), p. 567.

7. Tetsuro Morimoto, *Twenty-Eight Years in the Guam Jungle* (Tokyo and San Francisco: Japan Publications, 1972).

8. I interviewed half a dozen veterans who corroborated Luther Fleming's account regarding the aftermath of the battle for Hill 40.

9. Mel Heckt's wartime diary was used to underpin his oral history.

10. Dan Gallagher's account was verified by other veterans that witnessed the event.

CHAPTER SEVEN: LEYTE: THE RETURN TO THE PHILIPPINES

1. M. Hamlin Cannon, *Leyte: The Return to the Philippines* (Washington, D.C.: Center for Military History, United States Army, 1954), pp. 2–7, provides a detailed discussion of the strategic plan for the return to the Philippines.

2. Minutes for the JCS 171st Meeting, Sept. 1, 1944.

3. The decision to invade Luzon came on October 3, 1944: "Memo JCS to CINCSSWPA" (Oct. 3, 1944).

4. "6th Ranger Battalion, Operations Report Leyte" (Oct. 1944). One Ranger was killed and another wounded.

5. "Operations Report 127th Airborne Engineers" (Dec. 1944); "11th Airborne Division to XXIV Corps" (Dec. 1944).

6. "Unit Journal, 11th Airborne Division Operations" (Dec. 16–22, 1944), "11th Airborne Division Operations Report Leyte," pp. 1–12.

7. E. M. Flanagan, *The Angels* (Novato, Calif.: Presidio Press, 1989), pp. 169–171.

8. It is worth noting that to combat the nearly impassable terrain, small elements of the 11th Airborne Division were parachuted into the mountains of Leyte.

9. The 511th led the breakthrough on the southern portion of the ridge called West Ridge and later named "Hacksaw Ridge" after 2nd Battalion commander Colonel "Hacksaw" Holcomb.

10. After the 11th's linkup with other American forces on Leyte's west coast, near Ormoc, most of the 11th's units were withdrawn to Bito Beach base camp on the east coast of the island. All of the division's units were finally off the mountains by January 15.

11. A series of heavily defended ridges and mountains guarded the main Japanese supply trail to Ormoc. Critical mountains were named by the 11th, such as Rock Hill, Purple Heart Hill, and Maloney Hill. Holzem's story centers around heavily contested Maloney Hill.

CHAPTER EIGHT: LUZON

1. Williamson Murray and Allan Millett, *A War to Be Won: Fighting the Second World War* (Boston: Harvard University Press, 2000), p. 497.
2. Robert Smith, *Triumph in the Philippines* (Washington, D.C.: Department of the Army, 1961), pp. 94–98. The Manila defense force was sixteen thousand strong, within the Shimbu Group consisting mainly of Japanese naval forces.
3. "Narrative of the 6th Ranger Battalion, January–July 1945," pp. 4–8; Henry Mucci, "Rescue at Cabanatuan," *Infantry Journal*, no. 56 (Apr. 1945).
4. "11th Airborne Division Operations Report Luzon," pp. 14–18 (Jan.–Feb. 1945).
5. "188th Glider Infantry Report Luzon," pp. 1–5 (Jan.–Feb. 1945).
6. The 457th Parachute Artillery Battalion would not jump until the morning of February 4. The ridge is the dominant terrain feature behind Nichols Field and McKinley, a distance of about thirty-seven miles.
7. "511th S-2 Journal, Luzon" (Feb. 1945); "511th S-3 Journal, Luzon" (Feb. 1945).
8. The 11th took most of Nichols Field on February 12, but some strong points were cleared the following day.
9. The ammunition in Fort McKinley was detonated on the afternoon of February 16.
10. Smith, *Triumph in the Philippines*, p. 307, provides an estimate for civilians killed in the battle.

CHAPTER NINE: CLEARING THE PHILIPPINES: CORREGIDOR, LUZON, AND NEGROS

1. Sixth Army estimate on enemy strength on Corregidor: "Sixth Army G-3 Journal, Luzon" (Feb. 1945). Most modern estimates place enemy strength on Corregidor at more than six thousand.
2. "503rd Parachute Regimental Combat Team Report, Corregidor" (Feb. 1945), pp. 1–8; "503rd Parachute Regimental Combat Team S-2 Report, Corregidor" (Feb. 1945); "503rd Parachute Regimental Combat Team S-3 Report, Corregidor" (Feb.–Mar. 1945).
3. "Sixth Army Report Luzon" (Apr. 1945); "11th Airborne Division Report Luzon" (Apr. 1945).
4. "11th Airborne Division: Gypsy Operation" (June 1945). The force numbered about thirteen hundred men.
5. "503rd Parachute Regimental Combat Team Reports" (Apr.–Aug. 1945).
6. Robert Smith, *Triumph in the Philippines* (Washington, D.C.: Department of the Army, 1961), p. 607, provides the number of Japanese who surrendered to the 503rd on Negros.

CHAPTER TEN: INTO THE JAWS OF HELL: IWO JIMA

1. George Garand and Truman Strobridge, *Western Pacific Operations: History of U.S. Marine Corps Operations* (Washington, D.C.: Historical Division, 1971), pp. 455–461. No oral history account of Kuribayashi's actions exists, but one can logically assume he read this crucial report signaling the beginning of the invasion. Details of the report are on page 461 of Garand and Strobridge, *Western Pacific Operation*

2. Ibid., pp. 508–511; "5th Marine Division G-1 Journal" (Mar. 1945).

3. Most historians agree that if Kuribayashi had opened up with his artillery and mortars earlier, the results could have been even deadlier.

4. "5th Marine Division Journal" and "28th Marine R-2 Journal" (Feb. 19–Mar. 16, 1945).

5. "28th Marines After Action Report" (Feb. 1945).

6. "5th Marine Division Casualty Report" (June 25, 1945).

7. Final casualty figures for the battle vary. I used the most recent official Marine source, written by Colonel Joseph Alexander, *Closing In: Marines in the Seizure of Iwo Jima* (Washington, D.C.: Marine Corps Historical Center, 1994), for killed and wounded Marines. The numbers do not include combat fatigue casualties, which were several thousand in number.

8. I reviewed Mr. Vinich's Purple Heart citation and the official muster roll to confirm his account.

9. I confirmed all of Mr. Maiden's accounts with his fellow platoon members and Colonel Tom Fields.

10. At the end of the battle, F Company commander Frank Caldwell reported a loss of 221 Marines. "26th Marine Regiment, 2nd Battalion Unit Journal" (Feb.–Mar. 1945).

11. Maiden paraphrased parts of Rabbi Gittelsohn's speech. I filled in the exact words.

CHAPTER ELEVEN: THE LAST BATTLE: OKINAWA

1. Soldier's quote from George Feifer, *Tennozan: The Battle of Okinawa and the Atomic Bomb* (San Francisco: Ticknor & Fields, 1992), p. 1.

2. "6th Marine Division Unit Journal, Phase I and II" (Apr. 1945).

3. Bevan Cass, *History of the Sixth Marine Division* (Nashville, Tenn.: Battery Press, 1987), p. 51.

4. *Kamikazes and the Okinawa Campaign* (Annapolis, Md.: U.S. Naval Institute, 1954), p. 506.

5. "4th Marines Operations Report" (Apr. 1945); "6th Marine Division Journal, Phase I and II" (Apr. 1945).

6. Roy Appleman, James Burns, and John Stevens, *Okinawa: The Last Battle* (Washington, D.C.: Center for Military History, 1991), pp. 299–301.

7. "6th Marine Division SAR, Phase III," pp. 5–8 (May 1945); "29th Mar Regt, R-2 and R-3 Journal"; "4th Mar Regt, R-2 and R-3 Journal"; Benis Frank and Henry Shaw, *Victory and Occupation: History of U.S. Marine Corps Operations in World War II* (Washington, D.C.: U.S. Marine Corps Historical Branch, 1967), pp. 244–270.

8. Frank and Shaw, *Victory and Occupation*, p. 321.

9. Okinawa's casualties are reported in the official U.S. Army history: Appleman, Burns, and Stevens, *Okinawa*, p. 473.

10. Gallagher's account corresponds with those of other veterans interviewed and the official records.

11. Robert Powers' account matches his Navy Cross citation and the accounts of other veterans in his platoon I interviewed.

12. James Wood's account was verified with other veterans in his squad, including Charles Kundert.

13. Kundert's account was corroborated by other veterans who witnessed the events he described. His wartime diary was also consulted.

Acknowledgments

THE HEART OF THIS BOOK is the deeply personal and moving experiences that these great men shared with me. Hundreds of veterans that I was not able to include within its pages shared their time, research, suggestions on whom to interview, and photos. But first, I'd like to thank the following veterans as they appear in *Into the Rising Sun:* Robert Moore, Frank Guidone, Brian Quirk, Dean Winters, Ray Bauml, Stephen Stigler, John Sweeney, Robert Youngdeer, Dave Taber, Ira Gilliand, John Mielke, Tom Lyons, James Smith, Harry Clark, David Van Fleet, Jesse Bradley, Olin Gray, George French, Mike Vinich, Joseph McNamara, Frank Fitz, Charles Meacham, Ken O'Donnell, Edward McLogan, William Duncan, Grant Hirabayashi, Edward McLogan, Roy Matsumoto, Melvin Clinton, Jim Sampson, Ray Mitchell, Marvin Chester, R. E. Broadwell, Andrew Amaty, David Elwood, Chester Nycum, John Bartlett, Emmitt Hays, Allen Shively, Luther Fleming, Mel Heckt, Ken Champlin, Fred Butcher, Dan Gallagher, James Holzem, William Hayes, Calvin Lincoln, John "Muggs" McGinnis, Jack Burn, Edwin Sorenson, William Walter, Jack Herzig, Miles Gale, Robert Prince, Bernard Coon, Jack McGrath, Merritt Hinkel, Deane Marks, Harry Akune, John Lindgren, Charles Sass, John Reynolds, Robert "Moose" Maiden, David Severance, Charles Lindberg, Luther "Juke" Crabtree, Frank Caldwell, Dean Voight, Howard Baxter, Elmer Mapes, Patrick Almond, Jerry Beau, Robert Powers, Jim Wood, Charles Kundert, and Jerome Mandel.

Special thanks need to go to Jack Herzig, Harry Akune, Frank Guidone, Howard Baxter, and Bob Maiden, who aided me throughout this process.

Nearly every veteran association has an individual designated as the unit historian or officer; I relied on them heavily. They provided me invaluable references and often furnished me rare nuggets of information that are not found in the official documents. I'd like to thank John Sweeney of the 1st Raider Battalion and Brian Quirk of the 2nd Raider Battalion. Raider historian Jerry Beau has dedicated a large part of his life to recording the Raiders' history and painstakingly gathering Raider casualty lists and acts of valor. He never asked "What do you want?" but always "How can I help?" Dave Richardson from Merrill's Marauders provided several key references. I am also grateful for the assistance provided by Colonel and Mrs. David Severance and Al Garbarino from the Association of the Survivors. From the 6th Ranger Battalion, Leo Strasbough provided several important references. John Cook, a Cabanatuan survivor, also helped in this capacity. Bob Flynn, from the 503rd, provided some important details. I'm also indebted to Leo Kocher, who has tirelessly served the 511th, and Dr. James Lorio, who has been the rock of the association and chronicler of his regiment's history. Don Lassen, "Mr. Airborne" and the editor of the *Static Line* airborne newspaper, www.staticline.net, has done so much for the airborne community and also supported the Drop Zone, www.thedropzone.org, over the years. Mark Christianson of www.paratrooper.net was also a big help. I'd like to acknowledge Gordon Sumner, National Director of the 82nd Airborne Division, a true leader and supporter of the Drop Zone. Peter Sheingold always generously gave me his time and ideas. I'd also like to thank Clark Archer, unit historian for the 517th, Dutch Schultz, and John Burke.

I'm indebted to my close friend Carl Fornaris, who was incredibly helpful throughout the entire process of putting this book together. Major Mike Horn and Brian Fitzpatrick also provided important historical insight and key comments to the text. I'm indebted to my editors Bruce Nichols and Dan Freedberg for their vision and editorial excellence.

While the heart of this book is its oral histories, a significant amount of time was spent reviewing the official documents and other primary source material. Therefore, I would like to extend my thanks to the archivists at the National Archives, in particular Wil Mahoney. The staff at the U.S. Army Military History Institute also went above and beyond the call of duty. I'd specifically like to thank David Keogh. Finally, I would like to thank Historian Lieutenant Colonel Jon Hoffman of the Marine Corps Historical Center for providing his time and references.

Several veterans also graciously furnished their time and personal photos for this book: Marine Raider and Photographer Frank Cannistraci, Miles Gale, Jack Herzig, Robert Maiden, and Dean Winters. Staffs at the Marine Corps Historical Center and the National Archives were also very helpful.

I'd also like to acknowledge the folks that over the years provided their time and assistance to the Drop Zone or helped this book along in various other important capacities: Gant Asbury, Eric Minkoff, Chris Robinson, and Jeff Baron. I am grateful to my agent, Andy Zack, at the Zack Company, Inc.

Finally, I'm indebted to my loving wife Robyn, who was extremely helpful and supportive throughout this entire process, as was my beautiful daughter Lily.

Index

Page numbers in *italics* refer to illustrations.

About the Author

Patrick K. O'Donnell is the author of *Beyond Valor: World War II's Ranger and Airborne Veterans Reveal the Heart of Combat*, and creator of The Drop Zone (www.thedropzone.org), the first virtual community for both World War II veterans and the interested public, dedicated to collecting and sharing stories of the war. The site has won praise from newspapers such as *The Wall Street Journal*, which said, "The Drop Zone presents the remarkable and often terrifying war stories of U.S. Army Airborne and Ranger troops. Browse through a few of these tales and you will probably gain new respect for the older men in the Veterans Day parade."

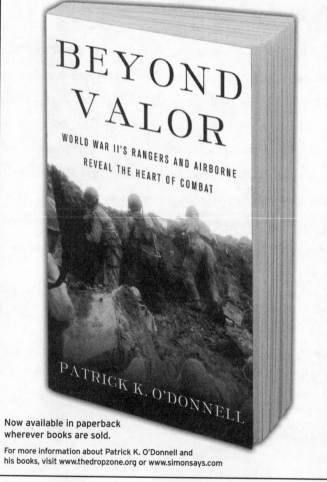